LANDLORD AND TENANT IN PRACTICE

LANDLORD AND TENANT IN PRACTICE

Inns of Court School of Law

Institute of Law, City University, London

OXFORD
UNIVERSITY PRESS

OXFORD
UNIVERSITY PRESS

Great Clarendon Street, Oxford OX2 6DP

Oxford University Press is a department of the University of Oxford.
It furthers the University's objective of excellence in research, scholarship,
and education by publishing worldwide in

Oxford New York

Athens Auckland Bangkok Bogotá Buenos Aires Cape Town
Chennai Dar es Salaam Delhi Florence Hong Kong Istanbul Karachi
Kolkata Kuala Lumpur Madrid Melbourne Mexico City Mumbai Nairobi
Paris São Paulo Shanghai Singapore Taipei Tokyo Toronto Warsaw

with associated companies in Berlin Ibadan

Oxford is a registered trade mark of Oxford University Press
in the UK and certain other countries

Published in the United States
by Oxford University Press Inc., New York

A Blackstone Press Book

ᴄ Inns of Court School of Law, 2002

British Library Cataloguing in Publication Data

Data available

Library of Congress Cataloging in Publication Data

Data available

ISBN 1-84174-314-3

1 3 5 7 9 10 8 6 4 2

Typeset by Style Photosetting Limited, Mayfield, East Sussex
Printed in Great Britain
on acid-free paper by
Selwood Printing Ltd, Burgess Hill, West Sussex

FOREWORD

These manuals are designed primarily to support training on the Bar Vocational Course, though they are also intended to provide a useful resource for legal practitioners and for anyone undertaking training in legal skills.

The Bar Vocational Course was designed by staff at the Inns of Court School of Law, where it was introduced in 1989. This course is intended to equip students with the practical skills and the procedural and evidential knowledge that they will need to start their legal professional careers. These manuals are written by staff at the Inns of Court School of Law who have helped to develop the course, and by a range of legal practitioners and others involved in legal skills training. The authors of the manuals are very well aware of the practical and professional approach that is central to the Bar Vocational Course.

The range and coverage of the manuals have grown steadily. All the practice manuals are updated every two years, and regular reviews and revisions of the manuals are carried out to ensure that developments in legal skills training and the experience of our staff are fully reflected in them.

This updating and revision is a constant process, and we very much value the comments of practitioners, staff and students. Legal vocational training is advancing rapidly, and it is important that all those concerned work together to achieve and maintain high standards. Please address any comments to the Bar Vocational Course Director at the Inns of Court School of Law.

With the validation of other providers for the Bar Vocational Course it is very much our intention that these manuals will be of equal value to all students wherever they take the course, and we would value comments from tutors and students at other validated institutions.

The enthusiasm of the publishers and their efficiency in arranging the production and publication of these manuals is much appreciated.

The Hon. Mr Justice Elias
Chairman of the Advisory Board of the Institute of Law
City University, London
December 2001

CONTENTS

CONTENTS

CONTENTS

PREFACE

Barristers in most general common law and general chancery chambers, as well as in some criminal chambers, are likely in their early years of practice to receive instructions in possession proceedings acting for or against a tenant or licensee whose landlord or licensor seeks a court order for possession of the premises concerned. This Manual is intended to be a helpful initial guide to them and to others undertaking this work. It may also prove useful to readers in determining the nature of their rights of occupation in their own accommodation!

The areas of law which barristers and others are most likely to encounter at the start of their practice are covered in some depth. The Manual gives only a brief outline of two important and complex areas of practice often met later on, that is the business tenancy legislation under part II of the Landlord and Tenant Act 1954 and the agricultural holdings legislation, and also provides a brief outline of some other more specialised areas of practice.

The Civil Procedure Rules came into effect in April 1999. Under the Rules, the majority of residential landlord and tenant proceedings will continue to be in the County Court and will be assigned to the 'fast track' in that court. Where the financial value of the claim does not exceed £5,000 (£1,000 in the case of claims against landlords for failure to repair), it will normally be assigned to the 'small claims' track in the County Court. Where a non-residential landlord and tenant case is either particularly complex or has a high financial value it may be assigned to the 'multi-track' and heard in the High Court. Some matters are dealt with by private arbitrators appointed under arbitration clauses in leases.

This Manual states the law as at November 2001.

TABLE OF CASES

TABLE OF CASES

TABLE OF STATUTES

TABLE OF STATUTORY INSTRUMENTS

ONE

INTRODUCTION

1.1 General

This Manual covers the following topics:

(a) the distinction between a lease and a licence;

(b) in outline only, the determination of tenancies and licences at common law, in particular by notice to quit and by forfeiture, and the distinction between an assignment and a sub-lease;

(c) protection from eviction: statutory restrictions on the owner's common law rights to gain possession from residential occupiers;

(d) the security of tenure provisions in the main statutory residential codes, i.e. assured tenancies and assured shorthold tenancies (Housing Act 1988), protected and statutory tenancies (Rent Act 1977) and secure tenancies (Housing Act 1985);

(e) possession claims and statements of case, particularly in relation to the statutory codes in (d);

(f) repairing covenants, express and implied, and remedies for their breach.

The Manual also covers, in outline only, some other areas which, it is hoped, will be of use later in practice although the Bar Vocational Course is too short for them to be included.

Many chapters end with a check list or practical guide to conducting possession claims in that area of law. There is also a guide to completing particulars of claim in CCR Form N119, and guides to conducting possession claims against trespassers, to conducting emergency applications for injunctions against landlords or licensors for reinstatement and on the implications when one of the parties is publicly funded.

There are many statutory provisions which alter or restrict the contractual rights and obligations of the parties to a tenancy or to a licence to occupy land. Of particular importance to the practitioner in early years are those provisions which restrict the landlord's or licensor's right, first, to recover the rent reserved under the tenancy or licence and, secondly, by bestowing statutory security of tenure, restrict his or her right to determine the tenancy or licence and recover possession. The table at **1.5** at the end of this chapter is intended to give the reader a chance of identifying quickly which statutory provisions are relevant to the tenancy or licence he or she is considering. He or she can then find an outline account of the nature of restriction imposed on the rent or of the security of tenure given in the appropriate paragraph of the text following the table.

1.2   Background Knowledge

A basic knowledge of the rules relating to the following fundamental concepts in the law of landlord and tenant is necessary and the following passages are suggested as a source for reading:

Megarry and Wade, *The Law of Real Property* (6th edn.), Sweet & Maxwell Ltd.
Cheshire and Burn, *Modern Law of Real Property* (16th edn.), Butterworth & Co.

(a)   The creation of tenancies: *Megarry and Wade*, pp. 758–779; *Cheshire and Burn*, pp. 399–408.

(b)   The different types of tenancies — fixed term and periodic: *Megarry and Wade*, pp. 779–796.

(c)   The distinction between a tenancy and a licence (also considered briefly in **Chapter 2** below): *Megarry and Wade*, pp. 758–769; *Cheshire and Burn*, pp. 388–396.

(d)   The determination of tenancies by:

(i)   expiry of time;

(ii)   surrender;

(iii) notice;

(iv)   forfeiture: *Megarry and Wade*, pp. 810–850.

1.3   Definitions

The following definitions of terms used are included only to help you to follow the text, not as a substitute for the suggested reading!

Tenancy for a fixed term: a tenancy granted for a fixed period of time, e.g., for five years, which will determine automatically without service of any notice, on the expiry of the fixed period.

Periodic tenancy: a tenancy granted by reference to a period of time but having no fixed expiry date, e.g., a weekly or monthly tenancy or tenancy from year to year. Such a tenancy will continue indefinitely until determined by service of a valid notice to quit.

Assignment of a lease: the transfer by the tenant of his or her entire interest in the demised land to another (not being the landlord). An assignment creates privity of estate (the relationship of landlord and tenant) between the landlord and the assignee. After the assignment, the assignor (the former tenant) retains no interest in the land and it is, in general, only the assignee who can sue and be sued on the covenants in the lease although in most cases the assignor will remain liable for payment of the rent and performance of the other tenant's covenants in the lease until there has been a further assignment of the lease: see Landlord and Tenant (Covenants) Act 1995.

Sub-lease: the creation of a new interest in land carved out of the grantor's own lease. It must be for a term shorter than that of the head lease if only by one day, otherwise it will take effect as an assignment. It creates no privity of estate between the sub-tenant and the head landlord and has no effect on the head tenant's liability to the head landlord to pay rent and perform the covenants in the lease.

Notice to quit: a formal written notice to determine a periodic tenancy which must comply with strict rules. To be valid it must be of at least the same length as the period of the tenancy (except in the case of a yearly tenancy where one half year's notice is required) and in all cases it must expire on the last day of the period: see further **3.2**.

Break clause: a contractual term in a tenancy for a fixed term entitling the landlord or, less usually, the tenant to determine the tenancy before its expiry date on giving notice at a stated time in stated circumstances, e.g., a right for the landlord to determine a 21-year term after the first seven years if he requires the land for redevelopment.

Tied accommodation: residential accommodation that 'goes with the job', i.e. the reason for the grant of the tenancy or licence is the owner's employment of the tenant or licensee.

Exclusive possession: the grantee has the right to exclude everyone from the land, including the grantor, i.e. to treat them as trespassers during the period of the grant. This is, in most cases, consistent only with the grant of a tenancy rather than a licence: see further **2.3**.

Exclusive occupation: the right to sole occupation of premises without having to share them with anyone else. The existence of such a right raises a presumption that a tenancy has been granted but is not necessarily inconsistent with the existence of a licence.

Premium (or 'fine'): a sum of money charged as the price of granting a tenancy or licence or of doing some other act such as giving consent to, e.g., an assignment of a lease, where the price is unrelated to any damage, loss or expense suffered or incurred by the landlord, i.e. is pure profit.

1.4   Abbreviations

1.4.1   STATUTES AND REGULATIONS

AHA 1986 — Agricultural Holdings Act 1986
ATA 1995 — Agricultural Tenancies Act 1995
CCA 1984 — County Courts Act 1984
CLPA 1852 — Common Law Procedure Act 1852
CPR — Civil Procedure Rules
HA 1980, 1985, 1988, 1996 — Housing Act 1980, Housing Act 1985, Housing Act 1988, Housing Act 1996
LGHA 1989 — Local Government and Housing Act 1989
LPA 1925 — Law of Property Act 1925
LPRA 1938 — Leasehold Property (Repairs) Act 1938
LRA 1967 — Leasehold Reform Act 1967
LRHUDA 1993 — Leasehold Reform, Housing and Urban Development Act 1993
LTA 1927, 1987, 1988 — Landlord and Tenant Act 1927, Landlord and Tenant Act 1987, Landlord and Tenant Act 1988
LTA 1954, part I — Landlord and Tenant Act 1954, part I
LTA 1954, part II — Landlord and Tenant Act 1954, part II
LTCA 1995 — Landlord and Tenant (Covenants) Act 1995
PEA 1977 — Protection from Eviction Act 1977
RA 1977 — Rent Act 1977
R (Ag) Act 1976 — Rent (Agriculture) Act 1976
RR(H)R — References to Rating (Housing) Regulations 1990.

1.4.2   TEXTBOOKS

Megarry & Wade	*The Law of Real Property*, 6th edn., Sweet & Maxwell
Megarry	*The Rent Acts*, 11th edn., Sweet & Maxwell
Woodfall	*Law of Landlord and Tenant*, Looseleaf edn., Sweet & Maxwell
	Encyclopedia of Housing Law, Looseleaf edn., Sweet & Maxwell
Garner	*A Practical Approach to Landlord and Tenant*, 2nd edn., Blackstone Press
Evans & Smith	*The Law of Landlord and Tenant*, 5th edn., Butterworths.

1.5   The Statutory Codes

(Numbers refer to the relevant paragraph in the text.)

	Act	Scope	Effect on Rent/ Price	Security of Tenure
1.	Housing Act 1988: Assured tenancies.	Most residential lettings on or after 15 January 1989: private sector.	None, except: (1) in the case of assured shorthold tenancy; (2) where landlord seeks rent increase for periodic tenancy.	Statutory periodic tenancy: grounds for possession.
	5.1	**5.5**	**5.7, 5.8**
2.	Housing Act 1988: Assured shorthold tenancies.	Most residential tenancies granted after 28 February 1997 and some fixed-term tenancies before that date.	Rent Assessment Committee may determine rent.	No possession order before expiry of fixed term or earlier than six months from start of tenancy.
	6.2, 6.3	**5.5**	**6.4**
3.	Rent Act 1977: Protected tenancies.	Most residential tenancies (not licences) granted or agreed before 15 January 1989: private sector.	Fair rent determined by Rent Officer: premium unlawful.	Statutory tenancy: grounds for possession.
	7.1	**7.4**	**7.7, 7.8**
4.	Housing Act 1985: A. Secure tenancies.	Local authority residential tenancies and some licences.	None.	Statutory periodic tenancy: grounds for possession.
	8.1	**8.3**	**8.7, 8.8**
	B. Introductory tenancies	As above, where local authority elects to operate introductory tenancy regime.	None.	Tenant can seek review of landlord's decision to seek possession: court possession order necessary.
	8.11	**8.3**	**8.11.4**

	Act	Scope	Effect on Rent/ Price	Security of Tenure
	C. Right to buy freehold or extended lease.	Same as in **8.1** provided occupation has lasted two years: some exceptions. **14.1**	Discounts on purchase price according to length of occupation: right to acquire on rent to mortgage terms. **14.2**	N/A
5.	Rent Act 1977: Restricted contract.	Residential tenancies and some licences granted or agreed before 15 January 1989 where owner lives in same house or supplies food or substantial attendance: private sector. **9.1**	Rent Tribunal can register rent: premium unlawful. **9.3**	If granted before 28 November 1980 Rent Tribunal can suspend notice to quit. If granted on or after that date, County Court power to suspend possession order for up to three months. **9.4**
6.	Landlord and Tenant Act 1954, part I: Long residential tenancies.	Long tenancies (21 years or more) at a low rent granted or agreed before 15 January 1989: private sector. **10.1**	None unless, after termination, statutory tenancy under RA 1977 follows (then see **7.4**), or assured tenancy under HA 1988 follows (see **5.5**). **10.2, 10.4**	Continuation tenancy if tenant is resident at end of term. If termination was before 15 January 1989, statutory tenancy under RA 1977 may follow (see **7.7**). If termination was after, then assured tenancy under HA 1988 may follow (see **5.7**). **10.3, 10.4**
7.	Local Government and Housing Act 1989, s. 186 and sch. 10: long residential tenancies.	Long tenancies (21 years or more) at a low rent granted on or after 1 April 1990: private sector. **11.1**	Possible interim rent after expiry of fixed term. Rent Assessment Committee may determine rent if assured periodic tenancy follows. **11.2**	Continuation tenancy if tenant is resident after termination: assured periodic tenancy under HA 1988 may follow (see **5.7**). **11.3**

	Act	Scope	Effect on Rent/ Price	Security of Tenure
8.	Rent (Agriculture) Act 1976: Protected occupancies.	Residential tenancies and licences of tied agricultural accommodation granted or agreed before 15 January 1989: private sector.	None until statutory tenancy arises, then either registered rent or rent calculated by reference to rateable value.	Statutory tenancy: grounds for possession: right to local authority rehousing.
		12.1	**12.2**	**12.3**
9.	Housing Act 1988: Assured agricultural occupancies (AAO).	Same as in **12.1** where licence or tenancy was granted on or after 15 January 1989: private sector.	Same as in **5.5** for assured tenancies but no shortholds.	Same as in **5.7**, **5.8** but statutory periodic tenancy may be AAO: right to local authority rehousing.
		13.1	**13.2**	**13.3**
10.	Leasehold Reform Act 1967: leasehold enfranchisement — right to buy freehold or extended lease.	Long residential leases (not licences) of houses (not flats): private sector.	Price based on market value of land making specified assumptions.	N/A
		15.1	**15.2**	
11.	Leasehold Reform, Housing and Urban Development Act 1993: collective enfranchisement of flats, individual rights to extended lease.	Long residential leases of flats.	Price based on market value making specified assumptions and 'marriage value'.	N/A
		16.1	**16.4**	
12.	Landlord and Tenant Act 1954, part II: business tenancies.	Business tenancies not licences.	None until tenant applies for new lease when court determines market rent subject to assumptions and disregards.	Continuation tenancy: right of tenant to apply to court for new tenancy.
		17.1	**17.2**	**17.3**

	Act	Scope	Effect on Rent/ Price	Security of Tenure
13.	Agricultural Holdings Act 1986: agricultural tenancies.	Tenancies and some licences of agricultural land granted to tenant farmers who are not employees of the landlord/ licensor.	Fixed by arbitrator every three years.	Conversion to tenancy from year to year and continuation as such: restrictions on notices to quit: grounds for possession.
		18.1	**18.2**	**18.3**
14.	Agricultural Tenancies Act 1995: farm business tenancies.	Agricultural tenancies of land farmed for trade or business purposes.	None except for right of landlord or tenant to initiate rent review procedure roughly every three years unless tenancy otherwise provides.	Continuation tenancy normally arises after expiry of fixed term. Notices to quit must be of between 12 and 24 months length.
		19.1	**19.2**	**19.3**

This table is derived from one originally devised by His Honour Judge Colyer QC who has very kindly permitted its use.

TWO

DISTINCTION BETWEEN A LEASE AND A LICENCE

2.1 The Distinction

A tenancy bestows an interest or estate in the land itself so that any person including the grantor commits trespass if he or she enters during the period of the grant without the grantee's consent.

A licence to occupy land creates only personal rights between the grantor and the grantee so that the grantor may be guilty of breach of contract but not of trespass if he or she enters without the grantee's consent.

2.2 Importance of Distinction

The chief reason in practice for the importance of the distinction is the valuable statutory protection given by certain statutes to tenants but not to licensees. The LTA 1954, part II applies to tenants occupying premises for business purposes but not to licensees. The RA 1977 and the HA 1988 give substantial protection — security of tenure in particular — to residential tenants but not to licensees, although note that this security has been considerably reduced by HA 1996 in respect of residential tenancies granted after 28 February 1997 which, subject to important exceptions, will all be assured shorthold tenancies: see **6.3**.

It is therefore generally in the owner's interests in such cases to grant a licence rather than a lease and there is an incentive for an owner, by the use of appropriate drafting techniques, to disguise the true nature of an agreement in an attempt to persuade the court that it creates a mere licence in order to avoid the impact of the relevant statute. The court then has to determine whether a document before the court which is expressed to be a licence, is in fact a tenancy either mis-labelled or disguised as a licence. In construing such a document the court will look at the substance rather than the form.

2.3 Exclusive Possession

In deciding whether a lease has been granted, the court will start by determining whether 'exclusive possession' of the premises has been granted.

2.3.1 MEANING

This expression is, unfortunately, used in two distinct senses by the courts: see *Heslop v Burns* [1974] 1 WLR 1241 at 1247, CA for a discussion of this. The senses are:

    (a) Exclusive or legal possession of the premises, entitling the grantee to exclude everyone else including the grantor, i.e. to treat them as trespassers during the currency of the grant. Exclusive possession in this sense amounts to an interest in the land itself and is inconsistent with occupation under a mere licence. If, therefore, the court finds that such exclusive possession has been granted, it will almost certainly hold that a tenancy has been created.

(b) Exclusive possession meaning no more than exclusive occupation, i.e. the right to sole occupation with no obligation to share with anyone else. Used in this sense exclusive possession (referred to as 'exclusive occupation' after this) will raise a presumption of a tenancy, but is not necessarily inconsistent with occupation under a mere licence.

The fact that the grantor retains a key to the premises does not necessarily preclude the grant of exclusive occupation. The purpose for which the key was retained must be considered: see *Family Housing Association* v *Jones* [1990] 1 WLR 779 at 789, 792, CA, and *Vandersteen* v *Agius* (1993) 65 P & CR 266, CA.

2.3.2 PRESUMPTION IN *STREET* v *MOUNTFORD*

If exclusive occupation in sense (b) is found to have been granted for a stated term whether fixed or periodic and for a money rent, the court will presume the existence of a tenancy *(Street* v *Mountford* [1985] AC 809, HL), unless the circumstances fall within one of the exceptions discussed by Lord Templeman in *Street*, see **2.3.3**. It is still, however, possible for a grant of exclusive occupation at a rent and for a term to amount only to a licence even in the absence of any of these circumstances: *Westminster CC* v *Clarke* [1992] 1 All ER 695, HL.

2.3.3 EXCEPTIONS TO THE PRESUMPTION IN *STREET* v *MOUNTFORD*

Even where the three elements mentioned in **2.3.2** are present, these are not decisive in determining whether a tenancy exists in circumstances where other factors of equal importance fall to be considered: *Mehta* v *Royal Bank of Scotland plc and Others*, *The Times*, 25 January 1999, QBD, and no tenancy will be created where:

(a) The occupier is a lodger, i.e. where the grantor provides attendance or services which require the grantor or his or her employees to exercise unrestricted access to and use of the premises: see *Street* v *Mountford*. A lodger is a mere licensee.

(b) The occupier is a service occupier, i.e. an employee occupying accommodation provided by his or her employer where either the terms of the contract of employment or the nature of the duties of the employment make it either necessary or overwhelmingly convenient that the employee should occupy the accommodation for the better performance of his or her duties: see *Glasgow Corporation* v *Johnstone* [1965] AC 609 and *Hughes* v *London Borough of Greenwich* [1994] 1 AC 170, HL. In such a case the employee's occupation is treated as being for the benefit of the employer not the employee and only a licence is created.

(c) The arrangement is attributable to an act of generosity or friendship or other circumstances are present which would negate any intention to create legal relations: see *Street* v *Mountford*.

The fact that the grant is intended to provide temporary accommodation for a homeless person does not of itself bring the grant within one of the exceptions discussed in *Street's* case: *Eastleigh BC* v *Walsh* [1985] 1 WLR 525, HL; *Family Housing Association* v *Jones* (above) at 794.

There can certainly be no tenancy without exclusive occupation: *AG Securities* v *Vaughan* [1990] AC 417, HL. Under a licence, on the other hand, the grantee may enjoy exclusive occupation or may only have a right to share the premises with others.

2.4   Sharing Premises

It is common for rights to occupy residential premises to be granted to several people to share together. Such rights may be of the following two types:

(a) A right to exclusive occupation of one room together with the right to use, in common with others, other rooms such as a kitchen or bathroom. Such a right will in most cases create a tenancy of the one room, except in the exceptional circumstances mentioned in *Street* v *Mountford* (above).

(b) A right jointly with others to share the whole of the premises. Whether such a right creates a joint tenancy or only a number of individual licences is often a difficult question for the court to determine. For a joint tenancy to exist the four unities must be present: *AG Securities* v *Vaughan* (above); *Mikeover* v *Brady* [1989] 3 All ER 618. Thus, if persons now sharing entered the premises under agreements granted at different times, it is unlikely that they can be joint tenants. Where the agreements were granted simultaneously, the circumstances may still give rise to a licence only (see *Stribling* v *Wickham* [1989] 2 EGLR 35, CA), and the presence of a term entitling the owner to introduce another person to share with the existing occupiers or, indeed, to enter and share himself or herself, may, if held genuine rather than a pretence (see **2.5**), destroy the argument that together they enjoy exclusive occupation and render them mere licensees: *Antoniades* v *Villiers* [1990] AC 417, HL. If, however, the true bargain is that the occupiers are entitled to exclusive occupation unless and until the owner requires them to share, they will be tenants, and a later requirement that they should share their occupation will not change their status unilaterally: *Duke* v *Wynne* [1990] 1 WLR 766, CA.

2.5   The Court's Approach

Where the agreement is a written one, the court should construe it in the normal way, ignoring the statutory consequences, e.g. that construing the agreement as a licence will deprive the grantee of statutory protection: *Shell-Mex & BP* v *Manchester Garages* [1971] 1 WLR 612, 619, CA.

However, for the reasons mentioned at **2.2**, the court must be quick to detect terms which are not genuine but pretences, intended to deceive or mislead: *Street* v *Mountford* (above) at 825; *Antoniades* v *Villiers* (above) at 1216. In such cases the court, rather than treating the whole agreement as a 'sham', will ignore the 'sham' term in construing the agreement: see *Aslan* v *Murphy (No. 1)* [1990] 1 WLR 766 at 770–771, CA; and for a definition of the word 'sham', see *Snook* v *London and West Riding Investments Ltd* [1967] 1 All ER 518.

Further, the court should look at the substance of the document rather than accepting the words used in it at their face value. If, whatever label is attached to it, the document in fact confers on the grantee in substance the rights and obligations of a tenant, then it must be treated as a tenancy: *Addiscombe Garden Estates* v *Crabbe* [1958] 1 QB 513, CA. If however the rights and powers reserved in the document to the grantor looked at cumulatively are inconsistent with exclusive possession of the premises being granted to the grantee, although they confer on the grantee the exclusive right to use the premises for a particular purpose, then the document will be construed as a licence only: *Shell-Mex & BP* v *Manchester Garages* (above) and *Esso Petroleum Co. Ltd* v *Fumegrange Ltd*, [1994] 2 EGLR 90, CA. An express agreement that exclusive possession was not granted may be disregarded as merely a false label: *Family Housing Association* v *Jones* [1990] 1 WLR 779 at 788, CA, as may a clause that 'possession and control' is to be retained by the grantor: *Skipton BS v Clayton* (1993) 66 P & CR 223, CA.

2.6 Relevance of External Circumstances

External circumstances, too, may show that one of the terms in the agreement is not genuine, i.e. not intended to take effect. For instance, the grantor may, before the agreement is signed, state that he or she will never act upon a term entitling him or her to introduce another person to share with the grantee and that the term is only included for 'legal reasons': *Walsh* v *Griffith-Jones* [1978] 2 All ER 1002 and see *Aslan* v *Murphy (No. 1)* (above). Or the physical state of the premises may show that the grantor could never have genuinely intended to exercise a power under the terms of the agreement to introduce others to share: *Antoniades* v *Villiers* (above), and *Aslan* v *Murphy* (above) where the premises consisted of one room 12′ × 4′.

2.7 Further Reading

This section has concentrated on the areas where the law is currently developing through the cases. Before attempting any of the exercises on this topic you are advised to read a more general account of the distinction between lease and licence, e.g. *Megarry*, vol. 1, pp. 67–76, or *Woodfall*, vol. 1, pp. 1/9–1/27.

2.8 Methods of Creation and Termination of Leases and Licences

The fundamental difference between a lease and a licence is clearly illustrated by contrasting the methods by which the two interests may be created and terminated.

2.8.1 CREATION OF LEASES

The general rule is that in order to create a legal estate in land a lease must be granted by deed: LPA 1925, s. 52(1). This requirement does not apply to the creation of a lease taking immediate effect for a term not exceeding three years at the best rent reasonably obtainable without taking a fine (premium): ibid. s. 54(2). Thus a periodic tenancy or a tenancy for a term of less than three years may be created by an informal written agreement or even orally.

2.8.2 CREATION OF LICENCES

Since in general a licence creates no interest or estate in land, the rules described in **2.8.1** do not apply and a licence may be granted either orally or by an informal written agreement.

2.8.3 TERMINATION OF LEASES

A lease may be terminated in the following ways:

(a) effluxion of time;

(b) notice to quit (see **3.2**);

(c) exercise of a contractual right to determine the lease at an agreed point of time — a 'break clause' (see **1.3** for a brief definition);

(d) forfeiture (see **3.3**);

(e) surrender;

(f) merger;

(g)   frustration;

(h)   disclaimer.

Since a lease is an interest in land, many of these methods of termination are subject to strict common law rules (see *Megarry and Wade*, pp. 788–92, 810–60), which, if disregarded, leave the lease still in existence. A landlord entering the land during the currency of a lease, except in the exercise of a right to do so under the lease, will be a trespasser and the tenant can bring possession proceedings against him or her: see **20.3**.

2.8.4   **TERMINATION OF LICENCES**

A revocable licence may be revoked by:

(a)   effluxion of time;

(b)   giving notice of the length required by the contract;

(c)   where the contract is silent as to its termination, then by giving reasonable notice;

(d)   by the death of the licensor or the licensee or the alienation of the land over which the licence was granted;

(e)   by a simple demand for possession even though this is in breach of contract.

After a licence has been revoked in any of these ways the former licensee will become a trespasser even if the revocation is a breach of contract. In the case of residential licences, however, the owner first must, if the licence is periodic, serve a notice to quit complying with PEA 1977, s. 5 (see **3.2.2**) and secondly, irrespective of the nature of the licence, cannot, in most cases, evict the former licensee without obtaining a court order: PEA 1977 as amended by HA 1988, considered in **3.4.1.2**. Note that if the licence is not periodic then no notice to quit is required: *Norris* v *Checksfield* [1991] 1 WLR 1241. Note also that a residential licence may qualify for statutory protection as a restricted contract under RA 1977, if granted before 15 January 1989 (see **9.1**) or as a secure tenancy under HA 1985 (see **8.1.2**).

For revocation of licences and for licences which are irrevocable, see *Megarry and Wade*, pp. 1046–58, and *Woodfall*, vol. 1, pp. 1/26–1/27.

2.9   Alienation of Leases and Licences

Another fundamental difference between the two is in the grantee's power to alienate his or her rights. A licensee having no interest in the land concerned but merely personal rights against the licensor, has nothing to transfer to any other person and any purported assignment or other disposition of the licence will be ineffectual. A tenant, however, may effectively either assign or sublet his or her interest in the land subject to the tenancy. The difference between an assignment and a sublease is fundamental: see **1.3**.

THREE

DETERMINATION OF TENANCIES AND PROTECTION FROM EVICTION

3.1 Determination of Tenancies

It is sufficient for the purposes of this course if you have read and thoroughly digested the passage in *Megarry and Wade* (pp. 810–60) on the common law rules for the determination of tenancies. In practice, however, you may encounter difficult problems, particularly on the subject of forfeiture, and you should expect to carry out further research in this area. The brief outline of the common law rules relating to notices to quit and to forfeiture in **3.2** and **3.3** is given as an aid to users of this Manual. For a full treatment of this subject see *Woodfall*, vol. 1, paras 17.057–17.195. See also **3.7** for a practical guide to bringing possession actions based on forfeiture.

There are also statutory restrictions, in the PEA 1977, on a licensor or landlord's power to exercise his or her common law rights to determine a licence or a tenancy and to regain possession. Many of these statutory restrictions do not apply to excluded licences or tenancies as defined in the PEA 1977: see **3.5**.

3.2 Notice to Quit

A notice to quit is the appropriate method of determining a periodic tenancy, e.g. a weekly, monthly or yearly tenancy.

3.2.1 COMMON LAW RULES

To be valid at common law a notice to quit must satisfy two conditions:

(a) It must be of the correct length. Subject to any contrary agreement between the parties this will, in most cases, correspond with the period of the tenancy. Thus at least a week's notice is necessary to determine a weekly tenancy and at least one month's notice to determine a monthly tenancy. An important exception to this rule is a yearly tenancy which must be determined by at least half a year's notice expiring at the end of a complete year of the tenancy.

(b) It must be expressed to expire on the correct day. The rule is that a notice to quit must expire on the anniversary of the commencement of the tenancy. Thus in the case of a weekly tenancy commencing on a Monday, the notice to quit must be of at least one week's length and expressed to expire either on a Sunday or a Monday: in either case this will be taken to refer to the midnight between the two days being the last moment of the Sunday or the first moment of the Monday. The same rule applies to monthly, quarterly, half yearly and yearly tenancies; e.g. a monthly tenancy commencing on the 25th of a month may be determined by a notice on the 24th or 25th of a month.

Where, as sometimes happens, either party is not sure of the exact date of commencement, a notice to quit may be expressed to expire on the date thought to be the anniversary or 'on whatever day one week (or month or quarter, etc.) after the service of this notice, a complete period of the tenancy comes to an end', or some other similar phrase. For an example, see **29.9**, paragraph 4. The notice must be served on or before the date from which time starts to run. In the case of joint tenancies, service by one joint tenant upon the landlord, or vice versa, is effective to determine the interests of all the joint tenants: *Hammersmith and Fulham LBC* v *Monk* [1992] 1 AC 478.

3.2.2   STATUTORY RULE

Any notice to quit served by a landlord or by a tenant in respect of premises let as a dwelling, or notice served by a licensor or by a licensee to determine a periodic licence to occupy premises as a dwelling, will be invalid unless it is written and contains certain prescribed information (as to the occupier's legal rights and where the occupier can obtain further legal advice as to his or her rights) and expires no earlier than four weeks from the date of its service: PEA 1977, s. 5(1) and (1A). A notice to quit which fails to comply with this provision may, nevertheless, be treated as valid by agreement between landlord and tenant, provided that, in the case of joint tenants, all agree: *Hounslow LBC* v *Pilling* [1994] 1 All ER 432, CA. Section 5 does not apply to excluded tenancies if granted on or after 15 January 1989, nor to excluded licences: PEA 1977, s. 5(1B). For excluded licences and tenancies, see **3.5**.

3.3   Forfeiture

3.3.1   PRELIMINARY

A landlord may determine a tenancy by forfeiture only if, first, the lease expressly reserves a right of forfeiture or re-entry — none will be implied — and, secondly, the tenant's act or omission falls within the scope of that forfeiture clause.

It is important to understand that it is not the court but the landlord who effects the forfeiture. The usual role of the court is to order possession when satisfied that the landlord has made a valid forfeiture. For it is the forfeiture that will have determined the tenancy and, hence, the tenant's right to occupy the premises demised, thus entitling the landlord to a possession order.

The procedure the landlord should then follow varies according to whether the cause of forfeiture is non-payment of rent or some other cause.

3.3.2   FORFEITURE FOR NON-PAYMENT OF RENT

3.3.2.1   General
These rules apply also to the non-payment of service charges where these are expressed to be payable as extra rent. Note that there are special rules which apply where a landlord seeks to forfeit a residential lease for non-payment of service charges: see **20.5**. No preliminary notice is generally necessary in the case of non-payment of rent, though a quick check should be made to investigate both the need to make a formal demand (**3.3.2.2**) and the need to notify the tenant of the landlord's address: see **20.4**.

3.3.2.2   Formal demand
A formal demand for rent (which is a time-consuming procedure) must be made as a necessary precondition to a valid forfeiture for non-payment of rent unless either:

(a)   the lease expressly dispenses with the need for a formal demand (every well-drafted lease will do this by including words such as 'whether formally/legally demanded or not'); or

(b) the amount of at least six months' rent is in arrears and there is insufficient distress to be found on the premises to satisfy the arrears: see CCA 1984, s. 139 (County Court), CLPA 1852, s. 210 (High Court).

3.3.2.3 Actual re-entry
If the premises are unoccupied, i.e. the tenant has vacated them, then the landlord may exercise his or her right to forfeit and thus bring the lease to an end by making a physical entry on to the land without any court proceedings.

3.3.2.4 Notional re-entry
If, however, the premises are still occupied, a physical entry may well be illegal (see **3.3.6**). In this case the landlord's entry must be a notional one and the normal method is by the service of proceedings claiming possession based on a valid forfeiture, the lease being determined at the moment of service: see *Canas Property Co. Ltd* v *K.L. Television Services Ltd* [1970] 2 QB 433.

3.3.3 FORFEITURE FOR OTHER CAUSES

3.3.3.1 Notice under LPA 1925, s. 146
It is a necessary pre-condition to a valid forfeiture for most causes other than non-payment of rent that the landlord has served a notice under LPA 1925, s. 146 which must:

(a) specify the breach complained of;

(b) require the tenant to remedy the breach if capable of remedy. Apart from a breach of the covenant against assignment or subletting without consent, which cannot be remedied (*Scala House* v *Forbes* [1974] QB 575), any breach where the mischief resulting from it can be cured is capable of remedy: *Savva* v *Houssein* [1996] 2 EGLR 65. A s. 146 notice which fails to call on the tenant to remedy such a breach will be invalid;

(c) require the tenant to pay financial compensation if the landlord requires this.

Note that the s. 146 notice must be served on the person or body who is the tenant at the time of service. This is so even where the cause of forfeiture is an action by a previous tenant, e.g. where the previous tenant assigned the lease to the present tenant in breach of covenant: see *Old Grovebury Manor Farm* v *Seymour Plant Sales & Hire (No. 2)* [1979] 1 WLR 1397.

3.3.3.2 Re-entry
If the tenant fails within a reasonable time to remedy the breach complained of (if capable of remedy: see (b) above) or to pay any required compensation, the landlord may then enforce his or her right to re-enter (by one of the methods considered in **3.3.2.3, 3.3.2.4**).

3.3.3.3 Special cases
In a few cases the s. 146 procedure does not apply: see LPA 1925, s. 146(8), (9), (10). There are special rules governing a s. 146 notice served in respect of:

(a) a breach of a repairing covenant in a lease granted for a term of seven years or more with at least three years left to run: see **23.6.1**; and

(b) a breach of a covenant in a residential lease to pay service charges: see **20.5**.

3.3.4 WAIVER OF THE RIGHT TO FORFEIT

The consequences of forfeiture are plainly harsh to the tenant and, consequently, it has been said that the law leans against a forfeiture. This is illustrated by the doctrine of waiver — the rule that a landlord will lose his or her right to forfeit if, with knowledge of the existence of a cause of forfeiture, he or she does some act which unequivocally recognises the continued existence of the lease.

The most common example of an act of waiver is the acceptance of rent due for a period after the cause of forfeiture was known to the landlord. Note that the acceptance will equally waive his or her right to forfeit even if expressed to be 'without prejudice' to that right. However, this rule does not apply to a statutory tenancy: *Trustees of Henry Smith's Charity* v *Willson and Others* [1983] QB 316, CA.

Note that where the cause of forfeiture is a continuing breach of covenant, e.g. breach of a repairing covenant or of a user covenant (rather than a once for all breach, e.g. failure to pay rent or an assignment in breach of covenant), a fresh breach arises each day when the lack of repair or forbidden use continues. Thus waiver of a right to forfeit up to a certain date will not bar the right to forfeit in respect of the continued failure to repair or continued use after that date.

3.3.5 RELIEF AGAINST FORFEITURE

3.3.5.1 General

Another doctrine which mitigates the harshness of forfeiture is the court's jurisdiction to grant relief against forfeiture. Where such relief is granted, the tenant gets his or her lease back as if it had never been forfeited. The rules here, again, vary according to whether the forfeiture was for non-payment of rent or for some other cause.

3.3.5.2 Relief against forfeiture for non-payment of rent

Relief is readily granted against forfeiture for non-payment of rent, provided that all arrears and the landlord's costs are paid.

(a) *Relief where re-entry was by court proceedings.* Where, as is usually the case, the landlord brings court proceedings for possession, relief is automatically granted in the County Court on payment of the arrears and costs either before the court hearing of the possession proceedings or within the time limited for their payment at the hearing: see County Courts Act 1984, s. 138(1)–(5). Note that 'arrears' will include mesne profits payable for the tenant's continued occupation of the land after the lease has been determined: see *Maryland Estates Ltd* v *Joseph, The Times,* 6 May 1998, CA.

If the tenant does not obtain relief under these provisions and the landlord re-enters under the possession order, the court still has a discretion to grant relief if the tenant applies at any time within six months of the date of the landlord's re-entry: see ibid. s. 138(9A)–(9C). Relief will only be granted on payment of all arrears and costs and the exercise of the court's discretion will depend on factors such as whether the landlord has re-let the premises. Section 138 does not apply or provide relief to an assured tenant against whom an order for possession has been made under the HA 1988: *Artesian Residential Investments* v *Beck* [2000] 2 WLR 357.

An application for relief may be made not only by the tenant but also by any sub-tenant, including a mortgagee. Where the order for possession was made in the High Court, the rules regarding relief are slightly different: see CLPA 1852, ss. 210–212, Supreme Court Act 1981, s. 38.

(b) *Relief where physical re-entry made.* In the more unusual case where the premises are vacant and the landlord makes a physical re-entry on the land, the provisions mentioned in (a) above do not apply but the County Court has a discretion to grant relief if the tenant applies to the court for this within six months of the landlord's actual re-entry: see CCA 1984, s. 139(2).

Again application may be made by a sub-tenant including a mortgagee and again payment of arrears and costs will be a condition of relief being granted. The High Court has a similar discretionary power to grant relief in these circumstances: see *Thatcher* v *Pearce* [1968] 1 WLR 748.

3.3.5.3   **Relief against forfeiture for causes other than non-payment of rent**

This is harder to obtain and there is no automatic right to relief. The same statutory provisions (in LPA 1925, s. 146) apply whether relief is sought in the High Court or the County Court and whether the landlord brings court proceedings or makes a physical re-entry without court action.

An application for relief may be made by the tenant or a sub-tenant, including a mortgagee, at any time before the landlord has re-entered the premises.

Once the landlord has re-entered pursuant to a possession order, the court no longer has jurisdiction to grant relief. Where, however, the landlord has made a physical re-entry on the premises without a court order, the tenant or sub-tenant may well not discover the landlord's intention to re-enter before it is carried out. In such a case, the right to apply for relief is not lost provided that the tenant or sub-tenant acts promptly on discovering the landlord's re-entry and applies for relief within a short time: *Billson v Residential Apartments* [1992] 1 All ER 141.

In deciding whether to grant relief the court will take into account factors such as the gravity of the breach, the conduct of the parties, the damage caused by the breach to the landlord as compared with the loss to the tenant if relief were not granted.

The court may, as a condition of granting relief under s. 146, impose terms as to the payment of damages, costs, expenses, etc.

3.3.6   **FORFEITURE BY COURT PROCEEDINGS: STATUTORY REQUIREMENT**

Any right of forfeiture or re-entry in a lease of premises let as a dwelling can only be lawfully exercised by court proceedings while any person is lawfully residing in the premises or any part of them: PEA 1977, s. 2. No physical re-entry on the premises may lawfully therefore be made in such a case. This provision is one of the few in the PEA 1977 that extends to excluded tenancies as well. For excluded tenancies, see **3.1.1**.

3.4   Court Order for Possession

3.4.1   **TENANCIES AND LICENCES PROTECTED**

Tenancies which are protected under the main statutory codes, e.g. Housing Act 1988 (assured tenancies), the Rent Act 1977 (protected and statutory tenancies) and the Housing Act 1985 (secure tenancies), which extends to some licences too, can be validly determined only by a court order for possession. There is thus no question of lawfully evicting such occupiers without a court order.

A court possession order is also required in respect of other residential occupiers after their licence or tenancy has ended: PEA 1977, s. 3.

See **20.3** and also **3.9** for a practical guide to conducting proceedings on behalf of a residential occupier evicted in breach of these rules.

3.4.1.1   **The rule**

Where a tenancy has come to an end but a person is then lawfully residing in the premises, it is unlawful for the owner to enforce against the occupier other than by court proceedings his or her right to recover possession of the premises: PEA 1977, s. 3. This provision applies where premises have been let as a dwelling under a tenancy other than:

(a)   an excluded one granted after 15 January 1989 (see **3.5**); or

(b)   a statutorily protected one, i.e. one protected under one of the three acts mentioned in **3.4.1**, or under any of the other statutory provisions specified (in PEA 1977, s. 8(1): see s. 3(1)).

'Occupier' for the purposes of s. 3 means any person lawfully residing in the premises at the termination of the tenancy: s. 3(2).

3.4.1.2 Licences protected
Section 3 applies not only to tenancies but also to:

(a) a licence created by a restricted contract entered into after 28 November 1980: s. 3(2A);

(b) a licence granted to an employee giving exclusive possession of premises under the terms of his or her employment: s. 8(2);

(c) generally, licences, other than excluded licences, to occupy premises as a dwelling: s. 3(2B). This does not include a licence to occupy a hotel room: *Brillouet* v *Landless* (1996) 28 HLR 836;

(d) residential occupiers in occupation after the death of a statutory tenant under the RA 1977 or the R(Ag)A 1976 where the owner is entitled to possession, e.g. where there is no statutory successor: PEA 1977, s. 3(3).

3.4.1.3 Regaining possession
After a possession order has been made the landlord must regain possession by procuring the execution of the order by the bailiff in the normal way and may not re-enter himself or herself: PEA 1977, s. 2; *Haniff* v *Robertson* [1993] 1 All ER 185, CA.

3.4.1.4 Excluded tenancies and licences
Note that although PEA 1977, s. 3 does not apply to excluded tenancies and licences (see **3.5**), court possession proceedings are still advisable where the premises are still occupied, in order to avoid committing the criminal offence of using or threatening violence in order to secure entry to premises, under Criminal Law Act 1977, s. 6 as amended by Criminal Justice and Public Order Act 1994, s. 72: see **3.6.3**.

3.4.2 EFFECT OF BREACH

A landlord or licensor who evicts a residential occupier in breach of PEA 1977, s. 3 may well be guilty of a criminal offence (see **3.6**). PEA 1977, s. 3 also creates a statutory tort for which damages and, in some circumstances a mandatory injunction for reinstatement or, where the eviction is only threatened, a prohibitory injunction, may be awarded against the landlord or licensor: *Warder* v *Cooper* [1970] 1 Ch 495. See also *Megarry*, vol. 1, Chapter 20, section 2, vol. 3, Chapter 15, section 4.

3.5 Excluded Tenancies and Licences

The following tenancies and licences are excluded for the purposes of the PEA 1977 (see PEA 1977, s. 3A):

(a) A tenancy or licence where:

(i) under the terms of the grant the occupier shares accommodation with the landlord or licensor, and

(ii) both at the time of the grant and at the time when the tenancy or licence ends, the landlord or licensor occupies as his or her only or principal home premises which include the whole or part of the shared accommodation.

(b) A licence or tenancy where:

(i) under the terms of the grant the occupier shares accommodation with a member of the family of the landlord or licensor and that member fulfils condition (ii) in (a) above, and,

(ii) both at the time of grant and at the end of the tenancy or licence, the landlord or licensor occupied as his or her only or principal home premises in the same building as the shared premises and the building is not a purpose-built block of flats.

'Accommodation' for the purposes of (a) and (b) excludes storage areas, staircases, passages, corridors and other means of access: PEA 1977, s. 3A(5).

(c) A tenancy or licence granted as a temporary expedient to a person who entered either these premises or any other premises as a trespasser (a squatter).

(d) A tenancy or licence which:

(i) confers on the tenant or licensee the right to occupy the premises for a holiday only, or

(ii) is granted otherwise than for money or money's worth.

(e) A licence which confers rights of occupation in a hostel provided by a local authority or by various other specified bodies: s. 3A(8).

3.6 Criminal Offences

3.6.1 UNLAWFUL EVICTION: PEA 1977, s. 1(2)

Any person who unlawfully deprives the residential occupier of any premises of his or her occupation of the premises is guilty of an offence unless he or she proves that he or she believed, and had reasonable cause to believe, that the occupier had ceased to reside in the premises: PEA 1977, s. 1(2).

'Any person' clearly includes persons other than the landlord and his or her agents.

'Residential occupier' means any person occupying the premises as a residence whether under a contract or under a rule of law which gives that person the right to remain in occupation or restricts the rights of the owner to recover possession.

'Rule of law' here would include the rule giving security of tenure under RA 1977 after the contract of tenancy ended and those rules preventing a landlord from forfeiting or otherwise obtaining possession of residential premises without a court order: PEA 1977, ss. 2, 3; see **3.3.6**, **3.4**.

3.6.2 HARASSMENT: PEA 1977, s. 1(3)

Any person who, with intent to cause the residential occupier of premises either:

(a) to give up occupation of the premises, or

(b) to refrain from exercising any right or pursuing any remedy in respect of the premises,

does acts likely to interfere with the peace and comfort of the residential occupier or members of his or her household, or persistently withdraws or withholds services reasonably required for residential occupation, is guilty of an offence: PEA 1977, s. 1(3).

Here, too, the offence may be committed by any person and is not restricted to landlords.

The rights referred to in (b) would include the right of a tenant protected under RA 1977 to apply to have a lower rent registered for the premises.

The phrase 'acts likely to interfere' replaces the former 'acts calculated to interfere' and shows that here it is unnecessary to prove any intention to interfere — the test is an objective one.

3.6.3   HARASSMENT BY LANDLORD OR HIS OR HER AGENT: PEA 1977 s. 1(3A)

The landlord of a residential occupier or an agent of the landlord, but no other person, will be guilty of an offence if:

(a)   he or she does acts likely to interfere with the peace or comfort of the occupier or members of his or her household; or

(b)   he or she persistently withdraws or withholds services reasonably required for residential occupation of the premises; and,

(c)   in either case, he or she knows or has reasonable cause to believe that this conduct is likely to cause the occupier to leave the premises or to refrain from exercising any right or pursuing any remedy in respect of the premises: PEA 1977, s. 1(3A).

Here no intent to cause the occupier to leave or refrain from exercising rights, etc. need be proved: the element of *mens rea is* wholly absent. It will be a good defence, however, if the landlord (or his or her agent) can prove that he or she had reasonable grounds for doing the act or withdrawing or withholding the relevant services, e.g. where the tenant's removal of coins from the gas meter leads to the landlord's refusal to pay the gas bill and the gas supply is then disconnected: s. 1(3B).

Penalties are imposed for those found guilty of any of these offences (s. 1(4)). The provisions, however, create no civil liability: see s. 1(5) and *McCall* v *Abelesz* [1976] QB 585, although those guilty of any of the offences may have committed the tort of unlawful eviction. See **3.7**.

See *R* v *Burke* [1991] AC 135, HL for a helpful discussion of PEA 1977, s. 1, and see *Megarry*, vol. 1, pp. 381–3, vol. 3, Chapter 15, sections 1 and 2.

3.6.4   CRIMINAL LAW ACT 1977

Note also the broader offence of threatening or using violence for the purpose of securing entry to premises under Criminal Law Act 1977, s. 6, as amended by the Criminal Justice and Public Order Act 1994, s. 72, which is not restricted to landlords, licensors or residential occupiers.

3.7   Civil Liability

3.7.1   POSITION AT COMMON LAW

In most cases a landlord who harasses or unlawfully evicts a tenant will, in addition to criminal liability, incur civil liability as such conduct will amount to a breach of the covenant for quiet enjoyment or the tort of trespass or both. In addition to the tenant's right to seek an injunction for reinstatement, the landlord may be liable for damages which, where the claim is tortious and the case a bad one, may include aggravated and exemplary damages: see *Branchett* v *Beaney* [1992] 3 All ER 910, CA, for a helpful contrast of the damages available in contract and tort, and *Ramdath* v *Oswald Daley (Auto Spares)* [1993] 1 EGLR 82, CA for a useful contrast of exemplary and aggravated damages. For a helpful precedent of a claim for damages for breach of covenant and trespass, including exemplary and aggravated damages and damages for the statutory tort under HA 1988, ss. 27, 28 (see **3.7.2**), see *Butterworths Civil Court Precedents*, vol. 1, division O, para. 207, pp. 813–5.

3.7.2   HOUSING ACT 1988, ss. 27, 28: THE STATUTORY TORT

For a practical guide to conducting a claim for damages for commission of this tort, see **3.9**. Claims for damages for harassment or unlawful eviction based on either this tort or the common law actions in **3.7.1** will, under the Civil Procedure Rules 1998, normally be assigned to the 'fast track' rather than the 'small claims track' irrespective of the financial value of the claim.

3.7.2.1   The tort
The tort is committed if, at any time after 9 June 1988, a landlord or a person acting on behalf of the landlord:

   (a)   unlawfully deprives the residential occupier of premises of his or her occupation; or

   (b)(i)   attempts unlawfully to deprive the residential occupier of premises of his or her occupation, or

       (ii)   knowing or having reasonable cause to believe that the conduct is likely to cause the residential occupier to give up occupation or to refrain from exercising any of his or her rights or pursuing any of his or her remedies, does acts likely to interfere with the peace or comfort of the occupier or members of his or her household or persistently withdraws or withholds services reasonably required for residential occupation, and, in either case, the residential occupier gives up occupation of the premises as a result: HA 1988, s. 27(1), (2).

The wording in (b) is very similar to that used in the criminal offence set out in PEA 1977, s. 1(3A): see **3.6.3** and 'residential occupier' has the same meaning as in s. 1: see **3.6.1**.

3.7.2.2   Nature of liability
The liability created by HA 1988, s. 27 is expressed to be tortious and to be additional to any other common law liability in contract or tort. Further, it is not to affect the residential occupier's right to enforce any common law liability in respect of the loss of his or her right to occupy premises as his or her residence, though the occupier is barred from recovering both common law damages and statutory damages on account of the same loss of right to occupy.

Thus if there has been an unlawful eviction and the former occupier sues for damages for breach of the covenant for quiet enjoyment based on the eviction and also for trespass, claiming aggravated damages in respect of the particularly distressing method of eviction, both of these claims will be for damages for loss of the right to occupy and must be set off against any statutory damages under HA 1988, s. 27: see *Mason* v *Nwokorie* [1994] 26 HLR 60.

Where, however, the breach of the covenant for quiet enjoyment is based not on an eviction but on acts of harassment, then damages awarded for the breach of covenant need not be set off against any statutory damages recovered for wrongful eviction: see *Kaur* v *Gill, The Times*, 15 June 1995.

3.7.2.3   Defences
There will be no liability for this tort if the residential occupier is reinstated either before the proceedings in respect of it are finally disposed of, or as a result of an order for reinstatement made in the court proceedings.

Further, it will be a defence to liability if the defendant proves that he or she reasonably believed either that the residential occupier had ceased to reside in the premises at the time when he or she was deprived of occupation or when any of the other unlawful acts occurred or, where the unlawful act was the withdrawing of services, if the landlord had reasonable grounds for doing so: HA 1988, s. 27(8).

3.7.2.4   Reduction of damages

The court is given the power to reduce the statutory damages to such amount as it thinks appropriate where the court considers that:

(a) prior to the unlawful eviction, the tenant's conduct had been such that it would be reasonable to mitigate the damages the landlord should otherwise pay; or

(b) the tenant has unreasonably refused an offer of reinstatement made before the tenant's proceedings were begun, or, in a case where the tenant has already found alternative accommodation before such an offer was made, that it would have been unreasonable for the tenant to have refused the offer: HA 1988, s. 27(7).

'Conduct' in (a) means 'behaviour' and is not restricted to serious acts of misfeasance but will include failure to carry out an obligation such as paying the rent: see *Regalgrand Ltd* v *Dickerson & Wade* (1997) 29 HLR 620 (which has a useful general discussion of factors governing the exercise of the court's power to reduce the statutory damages).

3.7.3   THE MEASURE OF DAMAGES

A landlord who commits this statutory tort will be liable to pay damages assessed on the basis set out in HA 1988, s. 28. Where the tort has been committed by a person acting on the landlord's behalf, it is the landlord and not the agent who is liable to pay the damages: *Sampson* v *Wilson* [1995] 3 WLR 455, CA.

Damages for breach are based not on the actual loss to the evicted occupier, but on the owner's potential profit from the unlawful eviction.

The basis for calculation of the damages is the difference between:

(a) the value, as at the date when the residential occupier gave up occupation, of the landlord's interest subject to the rights of the occupier, and

(b) its value on the same date free of those rights: HA 1988, s. 28(1).

For the purposes of this valuation, certain statutory assumptions are to be made: see s. 28(3), (5), (6).

This measure is, presumably, aimed at depriving the landlord of the profit he or she had hoped to make by unlawfully evicting the occupier. The damages may, accordingly, be substantial: see e.g. £31,000 in *Tagro* v *Cafane* [1991] 2 All ER 235, which contains a helpful discussion of the tort. It is important to note that in cases where the occupier had little security of tenure (e.g. an assured shorthold tenancy) or where the building is in multiple occupation, there is unlikely to be any difference in value: *Melville* v *Bruton* (1997) 29 HLR 319. Where damages are awarded under the 1988 Act there should be no additional award for exemplary damages: *Francis* v *Brown* (1998) 30 HLR 143.

For a practical guide to conducting proceedings on behalf of an unlawfully evicted residential occupier, see **3.9**.

3.8   Possession Claim Based Upon Forfeiture

3.8.1   INTRODUCTION

We are here concerned with a claim for possession by a landlord who alleges he or she has the right to forfeit a lease on the ground of the tenant's breach of covenant. Reference should be had to **20.8** for an overview of possession claims, and to **3.3** for the substantive law.

The substantive law relating to forfeiture is complex, unnecessarily so in many respects, but it is important to get to grips with the basic principles and the nomenclature. The following elementary points should be remembered:

(a) A landlord does not make 'a claim for forfeiture'. Forfeiture is a means by which a tenancy may be determined. The landlord claims possession of the premises on the ground that the lease has been forfeited.

(b) The terms 'forfeiture' and 're-entry' are interchangeable, as are the terms 'forfeiture clause' and 'proviso for re-entry'.

(c) In this context, forfeiture is a remedy available only to landlords, who may elect to rely upon the remedy or not. The tenant cannot rely upon his or her own breach to bring the lease to an end.

(d) A lease cannot be forfeited on the ground of the tenant's breach of covenant unless the lease or tenancy agreement contains a forfeiture clause; a forfeiture clause will not be implied.

3.8.2   **WHETHER TO FORFEIT**

As stated, if a tenant is in breach of a covenant which permits the landlord to forfeit the lease, the landlord has a choice: he or she can elect to forfeit or not. Where premises are over-rented, that is the rent reserved is higher than the market rent (a common phenomena not so long ago), it may be in the landlord's financial interests not to forfeit the lease. Rather the landlord may simply rely upon other remedies available to him or her: for example suing for sums due under the lease, or seeking an injunction to ensure performance of the tenant's covenants.

Thus, if instructed on behalf of a landlord whose tenant is in breach of covenant, the first question is whether forfeiting the lease and obtaining possession is the best remedy for your lay client; it may not be.

3.8.3   **WAIVING THE RIGHT TO FORFEIT**

If a landlord has knowledge of the breach of covenant which gives rise to his or her right to forfeit the lease, and does some act which is consistent with the continuation of the lease (accepting future rent most obviously), the right to forfeit will be lost by waiver. It is very common for tenants to allege the right to forfeit has been waived; this is a real battle ground in such cases.

This is a particularly complex area, and reference should be made to the substantive law. As a rule of thumb landlords must proceed with caution once they have knowledge of the breach of covenant. Doing nothing, for the time being, is often the best course.

The effect of waiver varies with whether the breach of covenant is a 'once and for all' breach or a continuing breach. Where the breach of covenant is continuing, for example a breach of repairing covenant, waiver of the right to forfeit up to a given date does not prevent the landlord forfeiting after that date, for a fresh cause of action accrues on every day the breach is continuing. Once the right to forfeit for a 'once and for all' breach, for example breach of a covenant against sub-letting, has been waived, that is the end of the matter, and the right to forfeit is lost.

Three general points to have in mind: first, if the right to forfeit is waived, this does not mean the breach of covenant is waived. In other words the landlord's other remedies remain available to him or her. Secondly, acceptance of rent which accrued due before the cause of action arose will not waive the right to forfeit the lease even if accepted after the landlord has knowledge of the breach. Thirdly, once the landlord has forfeited the lease, by serving possession proceedings for example, there can be no waiver of the right to forfeit.

3.8.4   SECTION 146 OF THE LPA 1925

3.8.4.1   The s. 146 notice

Essentially LPA 1925, s. 146 provides for the service of a statutory letter before action before a landlord can forfeit a lease on certain grounds. If instructed on behalf of the landlord to settle the s. 146 notice, make sure it clearly indicates to the tenant what it is alleged he or she has done wrong. Where it is alleged the tenant is in breach of a repairing obligation, check to see if the LPRA 1938 applies. If it does, the s. 146 notice must contain additional information and leave to issue forfeiture proceedings will be required. It is not now possible to forfeit a lease of a dwelling on the ground of non-payment of service charges unless the arrears are agreed or admitted, or have been determined by the court or leasehold valuation tribunal (LVT). However, this restriction does not prevent a landlord serving a s. 146 notice in respect of a breach of covenant to pay service charges, but in such a case, the s. 146 notice must contain additional information.

The s. 146 notice must also require the tenant to remedy the breach or breaches. Although s. 146 seems to require that the s. 146 notice contain a demand for compensation for the breach, this is not a mandatory requirement. Having said that, if a landlord fails to make such a demand, he or she may be prevented from claiming damages for the breach.

Care must also be had with service of the s. 146 notice. At trial, it will be necessary to prove the notice was served.

3.8.4.2   Whether notice is valid

If instructed on behalf of the tenant, look at the s. 146 notice closely. If it is confused and confusing, this may invalidate it, although a s. 146 notice may contain bits that are wrong and still be effective. As counsel for the tenant you should also consider whether the time given to remedy the breach is reasonable. Sensible landlords do not specify a particular period, they just say a reasonable time, but if a particular time is specified, ensure it is sufficient to allow the tenant to make good the breaches. This may involve taking advice from a surveyor.

If the tenant makes it clear he or she will not comply with the s. 146 notice, the landlord need not wait until the end of a reasonable period before forfeiting the lease. If the breach is incapable of remedy, the landlord need only give the tenant a very short period in order to consider his or her position. Seven days is sufficient, but make sure the breach is one that is incapable of remedy.

3.8.4.3   Non-payment of rent and assignment without consent

A s. 146 notice is not needed if the breach of covenant is non-payment of rent, and if the breach of covenant is assigning the lease without consent, the s. 146 notice should be served on the unlawful assignee.

3.8.4.4   Tenant's action for relief

A tenant can apply for relief at once upon service of a s. 146 notice. Thus, a tenant can commence his or her own proceedings seeking relief. Such proceedings are now, since 15 October 2001, dealt with by CPR, Part 55. This is useful in the case of commercial premises, where the landlord may seek to re-enter the premises. If this is a risk, the tenant should make his or her application for relief at once.

3.8.5   FORFEITING THE LEASE

If the landlord elects to forfeit the lease, he or she must take some unequivocal step to so forfeit: he or she must issue and serve possession proceedings, or physically re-enter the premises.

3.8.5.1   Issue and service of possession proceedings

There is rarely a difficulty with the first means of forfeiting a lease provided the claim is properly formulated. It should be noted that a right to forfeit can be waived by a statement of case; a claim for an injunction restraining a breach of covenant is inconsistent with a claim for possession based upon a forfeiture as a result of the breach. Thus care must be taken when settling a claim. The forfeiture takes place once the proceedings are served, although the lease continues to have an existence for certain purposes.

3.8.5.2 Physical re-entry of premises

As to physical re-entry, this is not available in cases where there is someone lawfully residing in the demised premises; that someone need not be the tenant: see **3.3.6**. It follows that for the most part landlords may only re-enter commercial premises.

On a physical re-entry, the locks should be changed and a suitable notice placed at the premises stating that the lease has been forfeited.

Not all entries by the landlord will constitute forfeiture by re-entry. Tenants of over-rented premises are often very happy for their landlords to bring their leases to an end by forfeiture, and often rely upon any entry as a ground for contending their burdensome lease has come to an end. If a landlord enters vacant premises to secure them, for example, there will be no forfeiture. There must be an intention to forfeit on the part of the landlord.

If instructed by a landlord and asked to advise on how he or she should forfeit, do not be frightened to suggest peaceful re-entry if that means of forfeiture can be lawfully used. It is cheap, quick and certainly brings home to the tenant in a dramatic fashion the fact that his or her landlord means business.

3.8.6 EFFECT OF THE FORFEITURE

3.8.6.1 Re-entry of premises

If the landlord re-enters the premises and forfeits in that fashion, the lease comes to an end on re-entry, subject to the tenant's right to apply for relief. A tenant who claims, for whatever reason, that the forfeiture was unlawful, should apply to the court for an order allowing him or her back into the premises pending the determination of that issue. If there is a real issue, it is more likely than not that the court will allow the tenant back into the premises until the issue has been determined.

A sensible landlord, who perhaps has some doubts as to whether he or she had a ground upon which to forfeit the lease, or some doubts as to whether or not the right has been waived, will agree to allow the tenant back in until the issue is decided. The landlord will receive payment during the period of occupation, and the tenant's claim for damages, in the event that the forfeiture was unlawful, will be much reduced if he or she was in the premises whilst the issue was determined.

3.8.6.2 Service of possession proceedings

The position is not so simple when the landlord forfeits by the service of possession proceedings. Until an order for possession is obtained, the lease continues to have an existence for some purposes. Essentially a tenant can seek to rely upon the landlord's covenants in the lease, but the landlord may not rely upon the tenant's. Thus, a tenant can seek an injunction after forfeiture proceedings have been served seeking the performance of the landlord's covenants, for example repairing covenants.

Once an order for possession has been made, the forfeiture relates back to the date proceedings were issued.

If the rent reserved by the lease was payable in advance, and forfeiture proceedings are issued during the middle of a rent period, all the rent due for that period should be claimed in the proceedings, and mesne profits thereafter. Rent payable in arrear is apportionable, and therefore only rent down to the date of the forfeiture should be claimed, and mesne profits thereafter.

3.8.7 THE HEARING

The forensic course of the hearing of such a claim is much the same as any other civil action, although claims for possession of residential premises based upon non-payment of rent are now heard in private. Further, unless the claim has been allocated to the fast or the multi-track, witness statements alone can be relied upon to prove the claim or defence as the case may be. It will be necessary for the landlord to prove his or her case, which may simply involve establishing that some rent is in arrear, or proving, by means of expert evidence, that there has been a breach of repairing covenant or whatever the case may be.

As counsel for the landlord you should take the judge to the relevant parts of the lease, namely the covenants which it is alleged have been broken and the proviso for re-entry. If a s. 146 notice was served, that must be proved.

3.8.8 RELIEF AGAINST FORFEITURE

3.8.8.1 Application of the law

Another complex area and another battle ground. The law varies between cases where the forfeiture was on the ground of non-payment of rent and forfeiture on other grounds, whether proceedings are taken in the High Court or County Court, and whether the landlord has forfeited by re-entry or by the service of possession proceedings.

3.8.8.2 Non-payment of rent

Where the landlord forfeits by County Court proceedings on the ground of non-payment of rent, there is a statutory code (see **3.3.5.2**) which provides for relief against forfeiture. At its simplest, if the tenant pays the rent in arrears at the date proceedings were issued and any other rents which would have accrued due down to the date of the hearing, and pays the costs, he or she will be relieved from the forfeiture, as of right, provided the payments are made within the times specified. If the code is not complied with, the County Court has no other jurisdiction to grant relief against forfeiture for non-payment of rent.

A tenant has six months within which to apply for relief in the County Court if the landlord has re-entered the premises and forfeited the lease on the ground of non-payment of rent. It is always important for the tenant to move quickly.

3.8.8.3 Other breaches

Relief against forfeiture in the County Court on the ground of other breaches of covenant is governed by the LPA 1925, s. 146: see **3.3.5.3**. The courts lean against forfeitures and therefore provided the tenant makes good that complained of, and pays the costs, relief will usually be granted, although if the breach has been deliberate, or has in some way 'tainted' the premises, relief may not be so forthcoming. If acting for a landlord, explain this to your lay client who may be surprised that he or she is forced to keep a bad tenant. Warn your lay client that if an application for relief is unreasonably opposed, there may be a costs penalty.

3.8.8.4 Relief from forfeiture

If acting for a tenant, always claim relief from forfeiture in your statement of case, even if you are convinced the forfeiture was unlawful and ineffective. If relief is given on terms, the tenant is not obliged to comply with those terms. He or she can simply leave the premises if that is the best course. For example, it may be too expensive to comply with terms that the tenant repair the premises, but remember the tenant will still be liable in damages.

3.8.8.5 Effect of grant of relief

If relief is granted, the tenant holds without a new lease. That means the forfeited lease is resurrected.

3.8.8.6   Sub-tenants

If there is a sub-tenant, he or she is entitled to apply to the court for relief under the LPA 1925, s. 146(4). It is not, strictly speaking, an application for relief against forfeiture, because the forfeited lease is not resurrected, rather an order vesting a new term in the sub-tenant is made. This jurisdiction is used sparingly and with caution, and therefore there is no certainty that the sub-tenant will obtain such an order.

The sub-tenant will usually be required to remedy the breaches of covenant by the tenant. If the sub-tenant is sub-tenant of part of the premises, it is unlikely he or she will be required to make good all breaches, but only some of them. This often is hard for the sub-tenant to accept, as he or she may have performed his or her covenants perfectly, but is now expected to do more, pay more money usually, just to keep the premises sub-demised.

3.8.8.7   Re-letting

Landlords are often a little uncertain as to the future because of the tenant's right to apply for relief against forfeiture. It is not advisable for a landlord to try and frustrate a tenant's application for relief by, for example, re-letting the premises to a third party. If the tenant is entitled to relief as of right, he or she will be granted relief, and that may place the landlord in some difficulty with his or her new tenant.

Even when the court has a discretion whether or not to grant relief, under the LPA 1925, s. 146 for example, the fact a new tenant has been installed in the premises will not be fatal to the tenant's application. If the court takes the view the landlord has acted precipitously by granting the new tenancy, it will carry little weight with the court when it comes to the exercise of its discretion.

If a landlord wishes to re-let, he or she should inform his or her former tenant, who has the right to apply for relief, what he or she intends to do. In that way, if the tenant fails to make an application for relief before the new letting, the landlord will be in a stronger position when it comes to whether relief should be granted or not.

3.8.9   ENFORCING THE ORDER

Where a landlord successfully proves a lease has been forfeited, an order for possession will be made and that is enforced in the same way as any other order for possession in the County Court, for which see **20.8.11**.

3.9   Unlawful Eviction of a Residential Occupier

3.9.1   INTRODUCTION

We are here concerned with a situation where a residential occupier has been unlawfully evicted from his or her home. These are inevitably very distressing cases and by definition have a high degree of urgency about them.

Chapter IV of the HA 1988 provides a residential occupier with a cause of action in damages against a person who has unlawfully deprived the occupier of any premises which he or she occupied: see **3.7.2**. It should be noted that it is not only tenants who are residential occupiers for the purpose of these provisions: see **3.6.1**, **3.7.2.1**.

3.9.2   GETTING BACK IN

3.9.2.1   Application without notice

Damages are of course important, but as counsel for the occupier your first goal is to get your lay client back into possession. This will mean making an application without notice to the appropriate County Court. In cases of extreme urgency, you need only turn up at court, explain the situation to the judge, and give undertakings to issue proceedings, make a witness statement, serve the other side, etc. Having said that, some judges are reluctant to proceed on this basis, and so if at all possible you should to go to court with all the necessary material.

3.9.2.2   The necessary material

Preparation of the material should not take too long as it is all pretty straightforward, and provided your lay client is available to give instructions, it should not take longer than an hour or so to prepare.

What is needed is draft claim form with particulars of the claim, an application notice, witness statement, on behalf of the occupier, a draft order and money to issue the proceedings. Several copies of these documents must also be available.

3.9.2.3   At court

Once you and your solicitor arrive at court, you should approach the usher and/or court clerk and tell them that you wish to make an application without notice. They will want to know how long the application will take and what it is about. Unless there are complications, the application should not take longer than 20 minutes or so. They will want to know what the application is about because applications without notice concerning domestic violence and/or children always get priority whereas a landlord and tenant application is not treated so favourably.

Whilst you are informing the court staff of the application you wish to make, your solicitor should be issuing the proceedings in the court office. It is better to have a live claim before the court, but, as stated, this is not essential: an undertaking can be given to issue proceedings forthwith.

In most courts applications without notice will be heard before the cases listed in the daily cause list, although it is ultimately a matter for the judge. The general rule now is that the hearing will take place in public, in which case wig and gown are required, but it is ultimately a matter for the judge who may hear the application in private.

The judge will want to know about the circumstances in which your lay client came to occupy the premises, and the circumstances in which he or she was unlawfully evicted. Make sure you know your lay client's status in the premises; for example, if a tenant, the nature of the tenancy. A good witness statement will essentially do all this for you. The judge will usually not require submissions on the substantive law, it is self-evident that one cannot dump tenants and their belongings on the street, but be prepared just in case.

3.9.2.4   The order

The form of the substantive order is that the owner, who will be the defendant, allow your lay client to re-enter the premises forthwith. There may be other substantive parts of the order: provision of a key to a new lock, and an injunction restraining any interference with services are common. Ask for whatever you think is necessary to ensure your lay client can get back in the premises as soon as possible, will be safe in the premises, and can enjoy them in accordance with his or her rights in respect of the same.

It will be a very rare case indeed that an order allowing the residential occupier to return to his or her home will not be made. When made, the order must be served on the other side in accordance with the order of the court. The judge will inevitably order that the application come back before the court on a hearing on notice within a couple of days or so.

It may be that the owner of the premises cannot be found in order to effect service. Or he or she may simply refuse to allow the occupier back. In the former case, there is not much one can do, save to prepare a witness statement for use on the return day giving details of the efforts made to effect service. If the latter is the case, an application to commit must be made.

3.9.3   THE HEARING ON NOTICE

At the hearing on notice, it is likely the order will be continued even if the owner advances an arguable case. Clearly the balance of convenience requires that the occupier remain in his or her home. As the issues are fairly straightforward in such cases, it is unusual for there to be lengthy interim skirmishing. It is more common for the judge to order that there be a speedy trial of the claim. If this is the course taken by the judge, directions, with a tight timetable, will be given at the hearing on notice. You should encourage the judge to do this.

Do not be concerned about making fresh interim applications. Frequently owners do not learn, and will continue to harass the occupier during the pendency of the claim. Get an injunction restraining the owner attending at the premises if that is practical, and apply to commit if there is a breach. The court takes a dim view of those who unlawfully interfere with a residential occupier.

3.9.4   THE HEARING

3.9.4.1   The course of the trial
The forensic course of the trial of a claim by a residential occupier against the owner of the premises is the same as in any civil claim.

3.9.4.2   Re-entry of premises
If, by the date of the hearing, the owner has allowed the occupier to re-enter the premises, damages under the HA 1988 (see **3.7.2**) will not be recoverable; however general damages at common law are still recoverable and therefore the proceedings will not come to an end merely because the occupier is allowed back in.

3.9.4.3   Evidence
The court will want to know how long your lay client was out of the premises, where he or she was staying during that period, and the circumstances in which he or she was residing elsewhere. Evidence of extra expense to which your lay client was put will be needed. Often it is alleged by occupiers that whilst they were away from the premises the owner removed some or all of their belongings. Of course advance such a case, but be careful for occupiers often use the opportunity to exaggerate the extent and/or value of their belongings.

3.9.4.4   Re-entry prevented
If the owner fails or refuses to allow your lay client to re-enter the premises damages under the HA 1988 (see **3.7.2**) are recoverable. The measure of damages is the difference in value between the value of the owner's interest in the premises on the assumption that the occupier continues to have a right to occupy the premises, and the value of the owner's interest determined on the assumption that the occupier has ceased to have that right. Thus, it will be necessary to have expert evidence.

3.9.4.5   Defences
There are defences (see **3.7.2.3**, **3.7.2.4**) to such a claim based upon the owner's reasonable belief that the occupier had ceased to reside, and that there were reasonable grounds for withdrawing services. These defences are easily raised, but often difficult to substantiate. As counsel for the occupier, use your cross-examination to test these defences.

3.9.4.6   Effect of HA 1988
An order that the occupier be permitted to return to the premises and an award for damages, perhaps with an injunction to restrain the future behaviour of the owner, is a victory. Often however the occupier is too frightened to return. Before the HA 1988 that was often victory for the owner. Now substantial damages may be awarded, and thus whilst the owner gets vacant possession, he or she has to pay a price.

FOUR

POSSESSION CLAIMS: INTRODUCTION TO THE STATUTORY CODES

4.1 General

A possession claim by a landlord against his or her tenant, or, less frequently, by a tenant against his or her landlord, is the most common landlord and tenant action in which a practitioner in his or her early years in either specialist landlord and tenant chambers or in general chancery or common law chambers may expect to be instructed.

4.2 Identifying the Statutory Code

When you are instructed to advise with a view to possession proceedings, your first task will be to determine which, if any, of the various statutory codes applies to the tenancy.

For this purpose you should look first at the chart of statutory codes at **1.5**, to attempt a quick identification of the appropriate statutory code. Then check in the text paragraph referred to under the heading 'scope' in the chart that your identification is correct and that the tenancy does not fall within any of the exceptions mentioned there. Having ascertained the appropriate code, you will then be able to advise your client as to his or her rights and chances of success in possession proceedings.

4.3 Common Statutory Codes

It is probable that possession actions you are likely to encounter early on will relate to tenancies falling within one of the statutory codes discussed in the following four chapters: assured and assured shorthold tenancies (HA 1988) **Chapters 5** and **6**, protected and statutory tenancies (RA 1977) **Chapter 7**, secure tenancies (HA 1985) **Chapter 8**.

4.4 Historical Introduction

A brief historical note may help explain the origin of the codes.

4.4.1 PRIVATE SECTOR: ORIGINS OF RENT ACT TENANCIES

Statutory protection has been given to the tenants of private rented unfurnished accommodation since 1915 — a time when war-time building restrictions resulted in a shortage of such accommodation and allowed landlords to demand high rents and to evict those who were unable or unwilling to pay these rents.

A series of Acts first limited the rent that the landlord could lawfully charge in respect of unfurnished residential premises below a certain value, and, secondly, barred the landlord from evicting the tenant from such premises unless the landlord could prove the existence of one or more statutory grounds for possession.

These grounds were based in the beginning on some misconduct of the tenant, though later Acts added further grounds which were based on the landlord's needs for the premises, provided that those needs had been notified to the tenant at the start of the tenancy.

The Rent Act 1974 applied these Acts to furnished premises too.

These early Acts have now, for the most part, been repealed and their provisions consolidated in the Rent Act 1977 which still applies to most existing tenancies created before 15 January 1989 and to some tenancies created after that date, see **5.2**.

4.4.2 PRIVATE SECTOR: ASSURED TENANCIES

Most tenancies created on or after 15 January 1989 will qualify for protection as assured tenancies under the Housing Act 1988. This Act was intended to increase the supply of private residential accommodation for letting, by removing most of the restrictions on the rent that a landlord could charge for premises. The tenant's security of tenure was preserved by the requirement that the landlord must prove grounds for possession as a condition for obtaining a possession order.

The HA 1988 also continued a concept introduced by the HA 1980 into the RA 1977 of shorthold tenancies — tenancies (called 'protected shorthold tenancies' in that Act) granted for a fixed period which bestowed no security of tenure and could be terminated, once the fixed term had expired, by notice of the requisite length without proof of any of the statutory grounds for possession. The court had a discretion to dispense with the normal requirement of a protected shorthold tenancy that the tenant should be notified at the start of the tenancy that it was to be shorthold.

The HA 1988, however, contains no such discretion and unless the tenant was notified at or before the start of the tenancy that the tenancy was to be shorthold, the tenancy would not be an assured shorthold tenancy (as they are called in HA 1988) but would be a full assured tenancy.

4.4.3 ASSURED SHORTHOLD TENANCIES AFTER FEBRUARY 1997

Under the provisions of the HA 1996 all tenancies granted after 28 February 1997 (unless they fall within one of the stated exceptions) are to be assured shorthold tenancies whether the tenancy is periodic or for a fixed term and no warning notice need be served before the start. Thus, in the case of most new tenancies, the landlord will not have to prove the existence of grounds for possession.

4.4.4 PUBLIC SECTOR: SECURE TENANCIES

The provisions mentioned above apply only to the tenants of private landlords. Security of tenure was given to local authority residential tenants for the first time by the HA 1980. This Act designated existing tenants, as well as tenants under leases granted after 1980, 'secure tenants' and required a local authority seeking possession against a secure tenant to prove the existence of one of the statutory grounds for possession.

There are no statutory restrictions in either that Act or its successor, the current HA 1985, on the rent that secure tenants may be charged.

FIVE

ASSURED TENANCIES

5.1 Scope

5.1.1 TENANCIES PROTECTED

As a general rule a tenancy granted on or after 15 January 1989 (the date when the HA 1988 came into force) will be an assured tenancy:

(a) where the dwelling house is let as a separate dwelling;

(b) if and so long as the tenant is an individual and occupies the dwelling house as his or her only or principal home: HA 1988, s. 1.

Some tenancies granted after that date, however, will be protected under the RA 1977: see **5.2** (transitional tenancies) and there are some tenancies granted before that date which, although originally protected tenancies under the RA 1977, have, after the death of the original tenant, become assured tenancies under statutory transmission provisions: see **7.6**. Note that condition (b) prevents a company from being an assured tenant. Contrast the position under the Rent Act 1977. See **7.1.1**.

5.1.2 'LET AS A DWELLING'

It is clear from condition (a) that the Act only applies to tenancies not to licences and that the purpose of the letting must be residential rather than, e.g. business or mixed business and residential. Thus where premises were let as an artist's residential studio they were not let 'as a dwelling' and condition (a) was not satisfied: see *Wagle* v *Henry Smith's Charity Trustees* [1989] 2 WLR 669, a decision on the same wording in RA 1977, s. 1.

5.1.3 'SEPARATE'

5.1.3.1 Sharing with the landlord
A dwelling house will not be let as a separate dwelling within condition (a) and the tenancy will not be assured where, under the terms of the tenancy, the tenant is required to share living accommodation with the landlord. 'Living accommodation' includes rooms such as sitting rooms, bedrooms and also kitchens if these are large enough to sit down and eat in but excludes bathrooms, lavatories and possibly kitchens too, if large enough only to cook and wash up in: see *Marsh* v *Cooper* [1969] 1 WLR 803.

In such a case the tenancy will not be assured under the HA 1988 even in respect of the part of the premises that the tenant is not required to share.

5.1.3.2 Sharing with others
If the terms of the tenancy require the tenant to share living accommodation with persons other than the landlord, then the tenant will be deemed to have an assured tenancy of the part of which he or she has exclusive occupation and is not required to

share (the separate part) and the landlord is restricted in the exercise of his or her contractual rights in respect of the shared part in two ways: see HA 1988, ss. 3, 10.

First, the landlord is barred from enforcing any contractual right to terminate or modify the tenant's rights to use any of the shared accommodation which is living accommodation except in so far as the modification is only in the number or identity of persons with whom the tenant has to share. The court, however, on the landlord's application, may either terminate the tenant's rights to use any part of the shared accommodation other than living accommodation or may modify the tenant's rights to use any part of the shared accommodation provided that, in both cases, this is within the terms of the contract.

Secondly, the court may not make a possession order in respect of the shared accommodation unless it is also making or has already made a possession order in respect of the separate accommodation.

5.1.4 OCCUPATION AS ONLY OR PRINCIPAL HOME

Condition (b) in **5.1.1** requires the tenant to occupy the dwelling house at all times as his or her only or principal home and if this ceases to be the case then the tenancy will cease to be assured; cf. the position under the RA 1977: see **7.1**. See *Crawley BC* v *Sawyer* (1988) 20 HLR 98 and **8.1.2**. (Note the different wording in HA 1988 'if and so long as' and the HA 1985 'at any time when': see **8.1.2**.)

5.1.5 MATRIMONIAL HOME: CONSTRUCTIVE OCCUPATION

Where the dwelling house is the matrimonial home, occupation by the non-tenant spouse is treated, for the purposes of HA 1988, as occupation by the tenant spouse, thus maintaining the occupation condition. Further, payment of the rent and performance of the other obligations of the tenancy by the non-tenant spouse is treated as if done by the tenant spouse: Family Law Act 1996, s. 30.

These provisions first prevent the tenant spouse from causing the tenancy to cease to be an assured one by giving up occupation and, secondly, rebut any presumption that the landlord intended to grant a new contractual tenancy to the non-tenant spouse that might otherwise arise from the landlord's acceptance of rent from the non-tenant spouse.

This doctrine of constructive occupation will, in most cases, cease to apply once the marriage has been terminated by decree absolute, and the non-tenant occupying spouse should, before decree absolute, seek an order under the Family Law Act 1996, for a transfer to himself or herself of the assured tenancy.

5.1.6 ASSURED SHORTHOLD TENANCIES

An assured shorthold tenancy (AST) is a type of assured tenancy and must, therefore, satisfy the conditions in **5.1**. It bestows less security of tenure than an ordinary assured tenancy as it is subject to an easily satisfied mandatory ground for possession. ASTs are considered in **Chapter 6**. Note that most assured tenancies granted after 28 February 1997 will be ASTs. See **6.3.1**.

5.2 Transitional Provisions

Some tenancies which satisfy the conditions in **5.1** and are granted on or after 15 January 1989, will nevertheless be protected tenancies under the RA 1977 rather than assured tenancies under the HA 1988, s. 34. The most important cases are:

(a) where the tenancy was entered into pursuant to a contract made before 15 January 1989;

(b) where the grant is of premises found by the court in earlier possession proceedings to be suitable alternative accommodation pursuant to a possession order made against a Rent Act tenant on that ground, and the court, considering that an assured tenancy would not provide the tenant with adequate security of tenure, directed that the new tenancy should be a protected one (under RA 1977). In the absence of such a direction, the new tenancy will be an assured one under HA 1988: *Laimond Properties Ltd v Al-Shakhani, The Times*, 23 February 1998;

(c) where the grant of the new tenancy is to a tenant who was, immediately prior to the grant, a tenant of the same landlord under a protected tenancy (under RA 1977). But if that earlier protected tenancy was a protected shorthold tenancy (PST), then the new tenancy will be an assured shorthold tenancy (AST), unless before its grant the landlord notified the tenant that the new tenancy was not to be shorthold (when the new tenancy will, presumably, be a full assured tenancy): see HA 1988, s. 34(2), (3).

5.3   Exceptions

There are certain tenancies which satisfy conditions (a) and (b) in **5.1.1** but cannot be assured. These excluded tenancies are set out in the HA 1988, sch. 1 and the following are the most important of them:

(a) *Tenancies where the landlord is exempt*, e.g., the Crown, a local authority, certain housing associations and resident landlords (see (b)): see sch. 1, paras 10–12. Tenants of local authorities and of housing associations may enjoy a different statutory protection: see **Chapter 7**.

(b) *The resident landlord exception* (in sch. 1, para. 10 and part III) is easy to miss and needs explanation. Its purpose is to ensure that a landlord who lets part of his or her own home can easily obtain possession against the tenant if living in close proximity proves unsatisfactory. The exception only applies if and so long as three conditions are satisfied:

(i) The dwelling house let forms part of a larger building which is not a purpose-built block of flats (defined as a building containing two or more flats horizontally separated, as originally constructed).

The reason for this condition is, presumably, that the landlord will be little affected by the tenant's behaviour in another flat in a purpose-built block and so does not need this exception. The condition is, however, satisfied in the case of a purpose-built block where the dwelling house let forms part of one of the individual flats.

(ii) At the date of grant of the tenancy, the landlord occupied as his or her only or principal home another dwelling house in the same building (or, where the letting is of part of a flat in a purpose-built block, another dwelling house in the same flat).

(iii) At all times after the date of grant of the tenancy the landlord's interest has belonged to someone who fulfils the occupation condition in (ii).

'Occupation as his only or principal home' has the same meaning as in HA 1988, s. 1: see **5.1.4**.

If, at any time, this third condition ceases to be satisfied, the exception is lost and the tenancy will immediately become assured. In cases where the landlord sells his or her interest or dies and where, therefore there is an inevitable risk of the exception being lost, part III of sch. 1 provides first, for periods of disregard during which, without loss of the exception, the new owner can decide whether or not to move into occupation and, secondly, for periods when the occupation condition is deemed to be fulfilled after the landlord's death. During periods of disregard no possession order can be made on the basis that the resident landlord exception applies and the landlord will have to prove grounds for possession under the HA 1988. During periods when the occupation condition is deemed to be fulfilled, however, a possession order can be obtained on the basis that the resident landlord exception applies and no ground for possession need be proved.

There is one important qualification to the rules above, enacted in order to prevent a landlord from abusing this exception and depriving an existing tenant of his or her security of tenure by granting him or her a fresh tenancy after the landlord has moved into occupation of another dwelling house in the same building. The qualification is that a landlord who grants a tenancy to someone who was, immediately previously, an assured tenant from the same landlord of either the same dwelling house or of any other dwelling house in the same building, cannot claim the resident landlord exception: HA 1988, sch. 1, para. 10.

(c)   *Lettings by specified educational institutions to students pursuing or intending to pursue a course of study,* and it should be stressed that lettings to students by private landlords do not fall within this exception.

(d)   *Tenancies of dwelling houses with high value.* Tenants of very valuable properties are not thought to be in need of statutory security of tenure and, therefore, a tenancy will be excluded where:

(i)   if the tenancy was granted or contracted for before 1 April 1990, the dwelling house had on 31 March 1990 a rateable value exceeding £1,500 (if the dwelling house is in Greater London) or £750 (if it is elsewhere); or

(ii)   if the tenancy was granted on or after 1 April 1990 (when domestic rateable values ceased to exist), the annual rent exceeds £25,000: see HA 1988, sch. 1, paras 2, 2A. 'Rent', here, is a net rent and excludes sums payable in respect of rates, repairs, services, etc.: para. 2(2).

(e)   *A tenancy which gives the tenant the right to occupy the dwelling house for a holiday.* This exception has given rise to much abuse and, although the court will follow the normal rules of construction in construing a document purporting to grant a holiday tenancy, the court will be astute to detect 'shams', i.e. agreements where the stated purpose is not the true purpose. Thus in *R v Rent Officer for Camden LB, ex parte Plant* (1980) 7 HLR 15 where the landlord granted a second tenancy to some students, to his knowledge, in the middle of a three-year course of study, a recital in the agreement that the students were to have the right to occupy and use the premises 'for a holiday' was a sham and the tenancy did not fall within this exception.

(f)   *Tenancies to which the Landlord and Tenant Act 1954 applies,* i.e. tenancies where the premises or some part of them are occupied for the purposes of a business carried on by the tenant.

As already considered (see **5.1.1**), if the premises are not let 'as a dwelling' the tenancy will not satisfy the definition in HA 1988, s. 1 and cannot be an assured one. Where, however, premises are let as a dwelling and the terms of the tenancy do not prohibit business use, a tenant who makes substantial business use of the premises will have protection under the LTA 1954, but will not have an assured tenancy: contrast *Royal Life Saving Society* v *Page* [1978] 1 WLR 1329, where the business use was too minimal to bring the tenancy within the LTA 1954, with *Cheryl Investments* v *Saldanha* [1978] 1 WLR 1329 where substantial business use produced a tenancy within the 1954 Act: for a brief consideration of business tenancies and for a practical guide to simple possession proceedings against 'business tenants', see **Chapter 17.**

(g) *Tenancies of licensed premises, tenancies of agricultural holdings and tenancies of agricultural land.* For agricultural holdings, see **Chapter 18**.

(h) *Dwelling house let with other land.* This is, in effect, another exception although it is not in sch. 1. Where the dwelling house is let together with other land, then the tenancy will not be an assured tenancy unless the main purpose of the letting is to provide a home for the tenant. Where the provision of a home is the main purpose of the letting, then the other land is to be treated as part of the dwelling house: HA 1988, s. 2.

(i) *Tenancies at a low rent.* This exception applies to rent-free tenancies and, for this purpose, a tenancy granted in return for services rather than a money rent is rent free unless, at the start of the tenancy, the parties put a value on the services, a value on the dwelling house and set off one against the other: see *Montague* v *Browning* [1954] 1 WLR 1039 and cf. *Barnes* v *Barratt* [1970] 2 QB 657.

The exception also applies to a tenancy at a low rent, i.e. a tenancy where:

(i) if the tenancy was granted or contracted for before 1 April 1990, the rent is less than two-thirds of the rateable value of the dwelling house on 31 March 1990; or

(ii) if it was granted on or after 1 April 1990 the rent is £1,000 or less (if the dwelling house is in Greater London) or £250 or less (if it is elsewhere): see HA 1988, sch. 1, paras 3, 3A, 3B.

5.4   Implied Terms

5.4.1   ASSIGNMENT AND SUBLETTING

5.4.1.1   The prohibition
Periodic but not fixed-term assured tenancies are subject to an implied term that, except with the landlord's consent, the tenant shall neither assign the tenancy nor sub-let or part with possession of the dwelling house or any part of it: HA 1988, s. 15. Moreover this implied term is expressly excluded from the operation of LTA 1927, s. 19 (which normally imports a proviso into terms prohibiting assignment or sub-letting without the landlord's consent, that such consent shall not be unreasonably withheld): HA 1988, s. 15(2). Thus, in the case of periodic assured tenancies, the tenant has no remedy, however unreasonable the landlord's refusal.

5.4.1.2   Effect of prohibition
If the tenant makes an assignment or sub-lease in breach of this implied term, it will be effective to vest the tenancy in the assignee or create a valid sub-lease but the landlord will be able to seek possession against the assignee or the tenant (in the case of a sub-lease) under Ground 12 (breach of term of the tenancy, see **5.9.5.4**).

5.4.1.3   Prohibition not implied
This term will not be implied where the tenancy is either:

(a) a periodic tenancy other than a statutory periodic tenancy, e.g. a periodic tenancy by grant; or

(b) arises after the expiry of a long tenancy at a low rent under LGHA 1989, sch. 10 (for the LGHA 1989, see **Chapter 11**);

where either:

(i) the tenancy contains express provisions prohibiting, restricting or permitting assignment, sub-letting or parting with possession of the dwelling house: these will prevail over the statutory implied term; or

(ii)   a premium was required to be paid on the grant or renewal of the tenancy. 'Premium' here includes any fine or other pecuniary consideration in addition to rent and any deposit exceeding one-sixth of the annual rent: see s. 15(3), (4).

5.4.2   ACCESS FOR REPAIRS

It is an implied term of every assured tenancy that the tenant shall allow the landlord access and reasonable facilities for carrying out any repairs that the landlord is entitled to carry out: HA 1988, s. 16.

5.5   Rent

The HA 1988 imposes no limit on the contractual rent a landlord may charge in respect of an assured tenancy, nor does it give any general right to apply to the Rent Assessment Committee to register a fair rent. An assured tenant may refer his or her rent to the Rent Assessment Committee in two situations only:

(a)   Where the landlord proposes a rent increase in respect of an assured periodic tenancy, then the tenant may, if he or she does not agree with the increase, ask the Rent Assessment Committee to determine the rent: HA 1988, s. 13. In doing this the Rent Assessment Committee is directed to make certain assumptions and to disregard certain factors, though, here, not the 'scarcity' factor: HA 1988, s. 14. Contrast the position for protected tenancies under RA 1977: see **7.4**.

(b)   Where the landlord grants an assured shorthold tenancy, i.e. a fixed-term tenancy or, in the case of post-Housing Act 1996 tenancies, a periodic or fixed-term tenancy, subject to a special mandatory ground for possession, the tenant may seek a determination by the Rent Assessment Committee of the rent that the landlord could reasonably expect to obtain: HA 1988, s. 22, as amended by HA 1996, s. 100. The Committee will only make such a determination if satisfied that the rent proposed by the landlord is significantly higher than that being charged for similar dwelling houses in the locality let on assured tenancies: s. 22(3).

The HA 1988 does not forbid a landlord to require a premium as a condition of the grant of an assured tenancy.

5.6   Statutory Succession by Spouse

5.6.1   PERIODIC TENANCY

On the death of an assured periodic (but not fixed-term) tenant, whether the periodic tenancy is statutory or not, the assured tenancy will, instead of devolving under the deceased tenant's will or intestacy, vest in his or her spouse, if that spouse fulfils certain residence requirements: HA 1988, s. 17. 'Spouse' here includes a person living with the tenant as his or her wife or husband. Note that these words apply only to heterosexual and not to homosexual relationships: *Fitzpatrick* v *Sterling HA*, *The Times*, 2 November 1999, HL. In a case where more than one person claims to have been so living and the contenders cannot agree amongst themselves, the County Court is given the delicate task of deciding which of the contenders is to be treated as the spouse for this purpose. Only one such statutory succession is allowed and, if that has already occurred or if there is no-one qualified to succeed to the assured tenancy, it will then devolve under the deceased tenant's will or intestacy: see s. 17(1)(c). A tenant will be treated as a successor for this purpose not only where he or she has succeeded to the tenancy under s. 17 but also where:

(a)   he or she inherited it under the will or intestacy of a former tenant; or

(b)   he or she was one of joint tenants and became sole tenant by survivorship; or

(c) in the case of a former Rent Act 1977 tenancy, the tenant became an assured tenant under the succession provisions in that Act (see RA 1977, sch. 1, part 1 at **7.6** and HA 1988, s. 39(5)): HA 1988, s. 17(2), (3).

Where the tenancy is periodic and has devolved under the former tenant's will or intestacy rather than under a statutory succession, the landlord will have a mandatory ground for possession available to him or her if he or she brings proceedings within 12 months of learning of the former tenant's death: see HA 1988, sch. 2, Ground 7 (see **5.9.4.7**).

5.6.2   DEVOLUTION OF FIXED TERM

Where the tenant under an assured tenancy for a fixed term dies, there are no statutory succession provisions under the HA 1988 and the tenancy will vest in the course of the administration of the deceased tenant's estate. It will continue to be an assured tenancy if the new tenant satisfies the conditions in HA 1988, s. 1: see **5.1**.

5.7   Security

5.7.1   GENERAL RESTRICTION ON TERMINATION

The HA 1988 does not affect the tenant's common law rights to terminate an assured tenancy whether by notice to quit, surrender or exercise of a contractual power to determine. The landlord, however, can determine an assured tenancy whether periodic, statutory periodic or for a fixed term (unless subject to a contractual power to determine — a 'break clause'), only by obtaining a court order for possession on establishing one or more of the statutory grounds for possession (HA 1988, s. 5(1) and see **5.9**). Consequently service of a notice to quit by a landlord in respect of a periodic assured tenancy, whether statutory or not, is of no effect (ibid.). For a practical guide to bringing possession claims against assured tenants, see **5.13**.

5.7.2   FIXED-TERM TENANCIES: THE STATUTORY PERIODIC TENANCY

Where an assured tenancy for a fixed term determines by effluxion of time or by the landlord's exercise of a contractual power to determine the tenancy in certain circumstances (a 'break clause'), then a statutory periodic tenancy will arise: HA 1988, s. 5(2).

Note that a right of re-entry or forfeiture is not such a contractual power (HA 1988, s. 45(4)), and it therefore seems that since the landlord cannot determine an assured tenancy in this way, the landlord cannot effectively exercise any contractual right to forfeit the lease. Instead, if a cause of forfeiture under the lease arises, the landlord must seek a court order for possession: HA 1988, ss. 5(1), 45(4), see **5.8.2**.

This statutory periodic tenancy is an interest in land and can be determined only by a court order for possession. The periods of this tenancy are to be the same as those for which rent was last payable under the terms of the fixed-term tenancy. The terms of the tenancy are to be generally the same as those in the previous fixed-term tenancy, except that any term providing for the tenancy's determination by the landlord or by the tenant is rendered ineffective so long as the tenancy remains assured.

5.8   Possession Order

5.8.1   NOTICE

To obtain a possession order the landlord must first serve notice in the prescribed form (see Assured Tenancies and Agricultural Occupancies (Forms) Regulations 1997 (SI 1997 No. 194)) on the tenant, specifying the statutory grounds on which he or she seeks possession and particulars of these grounds and must then, within certain time limits, commence proceedings on those grounds: HA 1988, s. 8 (as amended by HA 1996, s. 151), and s. 8A (inserted by HA 1996, s. 150).

Although it is not obligatory for the s. 8 notice to set out verbatim the wording of any ground relied on, the substance of each ground must be fully set out to enable the tenant to discover whether and, if so, how, he or she can avoid a possession order being made: *Mountain v Hastings* [1993] 2 EGLR 53, CA.

The court may, where any of the grounds except one is relied on, dispense with the requirement of service of this notice where it considers it just and equitable to do so. For the circumstances where this requirement may be dispensed with, see *Kelsey HA v King* (1996) 28 HLR 270.

If, however, the landlord relies on Ground 8 (a mandatory ground where the tenant is in two months' arrears of rent both at the date of service of the s. 8 notice and at the date of the hearing), there is no power to dispense with the s. 8 notice: see HA 1988, s. 8(5).

5.8.2   FIXED-TERM TENANCIES

If the tenancy is one for a fixed term which has not yet expired, the landlord is further limited to seeking possession on certain of the grounds (mostly involving a breach of the terms of the tenancy or some other bad behaviour by the tenant) and then only if the ground is also a cause of forfeiture under the lease: HA 1988, s. 7(6). Here too, the landlord must comply with the statutory notice requirements in s. 8.

There is, however, no apparent need to comply with the common law requirements for effecting a valid forfeiture such as the service of a notice under LPA 1925, s. 146 (where the forfeiture is based on a cause other than non-payment of rent, see **3.3.3**), as under the HA 1988 the lease will be determined not by forfeiture but by court order.

In *Artesian Residential Investments Ltd v Beck* [1999] EGCS 46, CA, it was held that as HA 1988, s. 5(1) sets out the only route to bringing an assured tenancy to an end and s. 7(6) merely requires permission for forfeiture and does not set up forfeiture as an independent ground for terminating the tenancy, there is therefore no jurisdiction to grant relief under CCA 1984, s. 138. In a case where relief against forfeiture might have been granted, the tenant will, instead, have to rely on the court's discretion not to make an order for possession where this would be unreasonable. Where, however, the ground for possession relied on is one of the mandatory ones, no such discretion exists: see especially Ground 8 (non-payment of two months' rent).

5.9   Grounds for Possession

5.9.1   MANDATORY AND DISCRETIONARY GROUNDS

The grounds for possession in HA 1988, sch. 2 are divided into two categories: the mandatory grounds (in part I), where the court must make an order if the ground is made out, and the discretionary grounds (in part II) where, in addition to the landlord making out the ground, the court must be satisfied that it is reasonable to make a possession order.

There is no closed list of the factors relevant to the issue of reasonableness. It is clear that all the circumstances (financial, professional and social) of the landlord and the tenant affecting their interest in the dwelling house and the relative hardship they will suffer if a possession order is made or refused, are relevant factors, as well as the conduct of the parties and the public interest.

5.9.2   COMPENSATION FOR LANDLORD'S MISREPRESENTATION

Where the landlord obtains a possession order on any of the grounds in sch. 2 by means of any misrepresentation or concealment of material facts, the court, on being satisfied that this is the case, may order the landlord to compensate the tenant for damage or loss caused by the making of the possession order: HA 1988, s. 12.

5.9.3   ASSURED SHORTHOLD TENANCIES

These are subject to any of the grounds in sch. 2 and, in addition, are subject to an extra mandatory ground (in HA 1988, s. 21) considered at **6.4**.

5.9.4   MANDATORY GROUNDS

The grounds are reproduced as amended by HA 1996.

5.9.4.1   Ground 1: owner-occupier

Not later than the beginning of the tenancy the landlord gave notice in writing to the tenant that possession might be recovered on this ground or the court is of the opinion that it is just and equitable to dispense with the requirement of notice and (in either case)—

(a)   at some time before the beginning of the tenancy, the landlord who is seeking possession or, in the case of joint landlords seeking possession, at least one of them occupied the dwelling-house as his only or principal home; or

(b)   the landlord who is seeking possession or, in the case of joint landlords seeking possession, at least one of them requires the dwelling-house as his or his spouse's only or principal home and neither the landlord (or, in the case of joint landlords, any one of them) nor any other person who, as landlord, derived title under the landlord who gave the notice mentioned above acquired the reversion on the tenancy for money or money's worth.

Although this ground is commonly referred to as the 'owner-occupier' ground and although both conditions may frequently be satisfied, conditions (*a*) and (*b*) are alternatives and the landlord need establish only one of them. The occupation in (*a*) need not have been immediately before the grant of the tenancy but may have been at any time in the past.

The landlord's requirement in (*b*) must be genuine but need not be reasonable. In order to prevent a landlord who purchases the dwelling house subject to an existing tenancy from evicting the sitting tenant under this ground, it is provided that such a landlord cannot fulfil condition (*b*), but this will not apply to a landlord who inherits the reversionary interest in the dwelling house.

In deciding whether it is just and equitable to dispense with the required written notice the court should consider all the circumstances of the case and these need not be exceptional: see *Mustafa* v *Ruddock* (1998) 30 HLR 495, CA, on matters relevant to the exercise of the court's discretion and *Boyle* v *Verrall* [1996] EGCS 144, CA (applying the RA 1977 case of *Bradshaw* v *Baldwin-Wiseman* (1985) 49 P & CR 382) where the landlord intended to grant an assured shorthold tenancy but never completed the necessary notice under HA 1988, s. 20, a mistake of which the tenant was aware and deliberately did not draw to the landlord's attention, and the court dispensed with the Ground 1 notice. Relevant circumstances will, no doubt, be similar to those held to be relevant in decisions on the similar 'owner-occupier' ground in the RA 1977, sch. 15, Case 11: see, e.g. *Fernandes* v *Parvardin* (1982) 5 HLR 33 (dispensation granted where oral rather than written notice given), and *Minay* v *Sentongo* (1982) 45 P & CR 190 (dispensation granted where notice had been sent but never arrived).

5.9.4.2   Ground 2: mortgagee

The dwelling-house is subject to a mortgage granted before the beginning of the tenancy and—

(a)   the mortgagee is entitled to exercise a power of sale conferred on him by the mortgage or by section 101 of the Law of Property Act 1925; and

(b)   the mortgagee requires possession of the dwelling-house for the purpose of disposing of it with vacant possession in exercise of that power; and

(c)   either notice was given as mentioned in Ground 1 above or the court is satisfied that it is just and equitable to dispense with the requirement of notice; and

for the purposes of this ground 'mortgage' includes a charge and 'mortgagee' shall be construed accordingly.

The mortgagee will only need to rely on this ground if it has consented to the grant of the tenancy either by a general consent under the terms of the mortgage deed or by giving consent to the particular tenancy. If no consent was given, the tenancy will not be binding on the mortgagee who will, therefore, not need this case.

5.9.4.3 Ground 3: out of season holiday home

The tenancy is a fixed-term tenancy for a term not exceeding eight months and—
(a) not later than the beginning of the tenancy the landlord gave notice in writing to the tenant that possession might be recovered on this ground; and
(b) at some time within the period of twelve months ending with the beginning of the tenancy, the dwelling-house was occupied under a right to occupy it for a holiday.

This ground enables the landlords of accommodation normally let for holiday purposes during the holiday season (lettings excluded from being assured tenancies: see **5.3**(e)) to make out-of-season residential lettings of the accommodation, knowing that they will have a mandatory ground for possession available in order to recover possession in time for the next season's holiday lets. The ground applies only to fixed-term tenancies and the court here is given no power to dispense with the requisite written notice at the start of the tenancy. The 'right to occupy for a holiday' referred to in condition (b) is not restricted to tenancies but would also include licences.

5.9.4.4 Ground 4: vacation let of educational accommodation

The tenancy is a fixed term tenancy for a term not exceeding twelve months and—
(a) not later than the beginning of the tenancy the landlord gave notice in writing to the tenant that possession might be recovered on this ground; and
(b) at some time within the period of twelve months ending with the beginning of the tenancy, the dwelling-house was let on a tenancy falling within paragraph 8 of Schedule 1 to [HA 1988].

This ground fulfils a similar function to Ground 3 in that it enables vacation lettings to be made of accommodation let, during the academic year, to students by educational institutions (lettings excluded from being assured tenancies: see **5.3**(c)), without fears that the landlord will be unable to recover possession in time for the next academic year. These vacation lets will be subject to Ground 4 whether they are made by a private landlord or by a specified institution. Again, the court has no power to dispense with the requisite written notice at the start of the tenancy.

5.9.4.5 Ground 5: minister of religion

The dwelling-house is held for the purpose of being available for occupation by a minister of religion as a residence from which to perform the duties of his office and—
(a) not later than the beginning of the tenancy the landlord gave notice in writing to the tenant that possession might be recovered on this ground; and
(b) the court is satisfied that the dwelling-house is required for occupation by a minister of religion as such a residence.

The court has no power to dispense with the requisite written notice at the start of the tenancy where this ground is relied on.

5.9.4.6 Ground 6: demolition/reconstruction/substantial works

The landlord who is seeking possession or, if that landlord is a registered housing association or charitable housing trust, a superior landlord intends to demolish or reconstruct the whole or a substantial part of the dwelling-house or to carry out substantial works on the dwelling-house or any part thereof or any building of which it forms part and the following conditions are fulfilled—

> (a)   the intended work cannot reasonably be carried out without the tenant giving up possession of the dwelling-house because—
>
> (i)   the tenant is not willing to agree to such a variation of the terms of the tenancy as would give such access and other facilities as would permit the intended work to be carried out, or
>
> (ii)   the nature of the intended work is such that no such variation is practicable, or
>
> (iii)   the tenant is not willing to accept an assured tenancy of such part only of the dwelling-house (in this sub-paragraph referred to as 'the reduced part') as would leave in the possession of his landlord so much of the dwelling-house as would be reasonable to enable the intended work to be carried out and, where appropriate, as would give such access and other facilities over the reduced part as would permit the intended work to be carried out, or
>
> (iv)   the nature of the intended work is such that such a tenancy is not practicable; and
>
> (b)   either the landlord seeking possession acquired his interest in the dwelling-house before the grant of the tenancy or that interest was in existence at the time of that grant and neither that landlord (or, in the case of joint landlords, any of them) nor any other person who, alone or jointly with others, has acquired that interest since that time acquired it for money or money's worth; and
>
> (c)   the assured tenancy on which the dwelling-house is let did not come into being by virtue of any provision of Schedule 1 to the Rent Act 1977, as amended by Part I of Schedule 4 to this Act or, as the case may be, section 4 of the Rent (Agriculture) Act 1976, as amended by Part II of that Schedule.

The ground continues with definitions of 'registered housing association', 'charitable housing trust' and further circumstances where the landlord will be deemed to have acquired the dwelling house after the grant of the tenancy or where an acquisition of the landlord's interest will be deemed to be one for money or money's worth.

Here there is no requirement as to notice at the start of the tenancy. The substance of this ground is self-explanatory but it contains complex provisions to prevent a landlord purchasing property already let and exercising this ground against the sitting tenant. Nor is the landlord allowed to avoid these provisions by granting a fresh tenancy to a sitting assured tenant. A landlord cannot rely on this ground against a tenant whose tenancy was originally protected under the RA 1977 and became assured as a result of the statutory transmission provisions (see **7.8**). A landlord who gains possession under this ground must pay the tenant's reasonable removal costs: HA 1988, s. 11.

5.9.4.7   Ground 7: devolved tenancy

> The tenancy is a periodic tenancy (including a statutory periodic tenancy) which has devolved under the will or intestacy of the former tenant and the proceedings for the recovery of possession are begun not later than twelve months after the death of the former tenant or, if the court so directs, after the date on which, in the opinion of the court, the landlord or, in the case of joint landlords, any one of them became aware of the former tenant's death.
>
> For the purposes of this ground, the acceptance by the landlord of rent from a new tenant after the death of the former tenant shall not be regarded as creating a new periodic tenancy, unless the landlord agrees in writing to a change (as compared with the tenancy before the death) in the amount of the rent, the period of the tenancy, the premises which are let or any other term of the tenancy.

This ground applies only to periodic, not fixed-term, tenancies which have devolved under the will or intestacy of the former tenant, i.e. where the statutory transmission provisions have not operated on the death of the previous tenant, either because there was no-one qualified to succeed or because there had already been one statutory transmission (see **5.6.1**). The acceptance of rent from a new tenant by the landlord is not to be regarded as creating a new periodic tenancy but may be evidence that the landlord was aware of the death of the previous tenant so as to start the 12 months running. The requirement for written notice at the start of the tenancy has no application to this ground.

5.9.4.8   Ground 8: rent arrears

Both at the date of the service of the notice under section 8 of this Act relating to the proceedings for possession and at the date of the hearing—
(a)   if rent is payable weekly or fortnightly, at least eight weeks' rent is unpaid;
(b)   if rent is payable monthly, at least two months' rent is unpaid;
(c)   if rent is payable quarterly, at least one quarter's rent is more than three months in arrears; and
(d)   if rent is payable yearly, at least three months' rent is more than three months in arrears;
and for the purpose of this ground 'rent' means rent lawfully due from the tenant.

Again there is no requirement for written notice at the start of the tenancy. For this ground to be established, there must be two months' or eight weeks, etc., as appropriate, rent outstanding both at the date of service of the s. 8 notice and at the date of the hearing. The tenant can thus avoid this ground, which is the only mandatory ground based on non-payment of rent (but see discretionary Grounds 10 and 11), by paying the arrears or at least reducing them to less than two months, etc. worth, on the day before the hearing.

The rent must be 'lawfully due' for this ground to be made out and, in this context, see the requirement in LTA 1987, s. 48 (considered at **20.4**) that, before rent will be lawfully due, the landlord must notify the tenant of an address in England and Wales where notices (including notices in proceedings) can be served on him or her.

5.9.4.9   Assured shorthold tenancies
These are subject to all the grounds for possession available against all assured tenants and, in addition, are subject to an extra mandatory ground: see **6.4**.

5.9.5   DISCRETIONARY GROUNDS

The grounds are reproduced as amended by HA 1996.

5.9.5.1   Ground 9: suitable alternative accommodation

Suitable alternative accommodation is available for the tenant or will be available for him when the order for possession takes effect.

. . .
PART III
SUITABLE ALTERNATIVE ACCOMMODATION
1.   For the purposes of Ground 9 above, a certificate of the local housing authority for the district in which the dwelling-house in question is situated, certifying that the authority will provide suitable alternative accommodation for the tenant by a date specified in the certificate, shall be conclusive evidence that suitable alternative accommodation will be available for him by that date.
2.   Where no such certificate as is mentioned in paragraph 1 above is produced to the court, accommodation shall be deemed to be suitable for the purposes of Ground 9 above if it consists of either—
(a)   premises which are to be let as a separate dwelling such that they will then be let on an assured tenancy, other than [a tenancy where notice was given before the start that the landlord might recover possession under any of mandatory Grounds 1 to 5, or an assured shorthold tenancy], or
(b)   premises to be let as a separate dwelling on terms which will, in the opinion of the court, afford to the tenant security of tenure reasonably equivalent to [that given by the HA 1988 to an assured tenancy of a kind within] (a) above,
and, in the opinion of the court, the accommodation fulfils the [conditions in paragraph 3].
3.—(1)   For the purposes of paragraph 2 above, the relevant conditions are that the accommodation is reasonably suitable to the needs of the tenant and his family as regards proximity to place of work, and either—

(a)   similar as regards rental and extent to the accommodation afforded by dwell-ing-houses provided in the neighbourhood by any local housing authority for persons whose needs as regards extent are, in the opinion of the court, similar to those of the tenant and his family; [both the rent and extent of such accommodation may be proved by a certificate of the local authority, which is to be conclusive evidence of those matters] or

(b)   reasonably suitable to the means of the tenant and to the needs of the tenant and his family as regards extent and character; and

that if any furniture was provided for use under the assured tenancy in question, furniture is provided for use in the accommodation which is either similar to that so provided or is reasonably suitable to the needs of the tenant and his family.

Ground 9 must be read in conjunction with the provisions in part III of sch. 2 which deem certain accommodation to be suitable. They do not purport to be exhaustive: suitable alternative accommodation, for instance, is not restricted to accommodation provided by the landlord and an order might be made under this ground where the tenant already owned an empty flat.

In view of the shortage of local authority housing it is very rare for the landlord to be able to rely on a certificate of the sort mentioned in part III, para. 1.

Accommodation to be let on an assured shorthold tenancy or on an assured tenancy susceptible to a possession order under mandatory Grounds 1 to 5 will not be deemed suitable, as it bestows inadequate security of tenure.

The ground does not require that the proposed alternative accommodation should be equal to or as good as the tenant's present accommodation but merely that it should be reasonably suitable to specified needs of the tenant.

If an order is made under this ground, the landlord must, as with Ground 6, pay the tenant's reasonable removal costs: HA 1988, s. 11.

5.9.5.2   Ground 10: rent arrears

Some rent lawfully due from the tenant—

(a)   is unpaid on the date on which the proceedings for possession are begun; and

(b)   [except where the court has thought it just and equitable to dispense with service of notice under HA 1988, s. 8], was in arrears at the date of the service of the notice under that section relating to those proceedings.

This differs from Ground 8 in that:

(a)   it is discretionary rather than mandatory;

(b)   no particular amount of rent needs to be in arrears;

(c)   provided that rent is in arrears on the date that the possession proceedings are begun, this ground cannot be avoided by the payment of the arrears before the hearing date (and, consequently, a landlord will usually rely on this ground in addition to Ground 8);

(d)   in a case where the landlord does serve a s. 8 notice, the rent must be in arrears on the date of its service but this requirement is removed in a case where the court exercises its power to dispense with service of this notice (a power which does not exist if Ground 8 is relied on).

5.9.5.3   Ground 11: rent arrears

Whether or not any rent is in arrears on the date on which proceedings for possession are begun, the tenant has persistently delayed paying rent which has become lawfully due.

Although the availability of this ground does not depend on there being rent arrears in existence on any particular date, it is unlikely that the court would consider it reasonable to order possession if there were no arrears either at the date of service of the s. 8 notice or at the date of trial, unless the tenant had a bad history of paying up only when taken to court by the landlord.

5.9.5.4   Ground 12: breach

> *Any obligation of the tenancy (other than one related to the payment of rent) has been broken or not performed.*

This ground will cover breaches of implied as well as express terms of the tenancy (for implied terms see **5.4**). The fact that the breach has been remedied by the date of the hearing does not deprive the court of jurisdiction to make a possession order but will obviously be a relevant factor on the issue of whether it is reasonable to make an order.

5.9.5.5   Ground 13: condition of premises

> *The condition of the dwelling-house or any of the common parts has deteriorated owing to acts of waste by, or the neglect or default of, the tenant or any other person residing in the dwelling-house and, in the case of an act of waste by, or the neglect or default of, a person lodging with the tenant or a sub-tenant of his, the tenant has not taken such steps as he ought reasonably to have taken for the removal of the lodger or sub-tenant.*
>
> . . .

'Common parts' means any part of a building comprising the dwelling house and any other premises which the tenant is entitled under the terms of the tenancy to use in common with the occupiers of any other dwelling house in which the landlord has an estate or interest.

Where the acts of neglect or default are committed not by the tenant or by a member of the tenant's family, but by a sub-tenant or lodger, they will only come within this ground if the tenant has failed to take reasonable steps to remove the sub-tenant or lodger.

Acts of waste may also fall within Ground 12 as being in breach of the tenant's implied obligation of tenant-like user of the premises and so may the tenant's failure to comply with any express repairing obligations in so far as these are enforceable (see **23.2.2.2**).

5.9.5.6   Ground 14: nuisance etc.

> *The tenant or a person residing in or visiting the dwelling-house—*
> *(a)   has been guilty of conduct causing or likely to cause a nuisance or annoyance to a person residing, visiting or otherwise engaging in a lawful activity in the locality, or*
> *(b)   has been convicted of—*
> *(i)   using the dwelling-house or allowing it to be used for immoral or illegal purposes, or*
> *(ii)   an arrestable offence committed in, or in the locality of, the dwelling-house.*

This ground consists of two quite separate limbs and it is important to note that each must be strictly made out. Thus, for instance, using the dwelling house for illegal or immoral purposes is not, on its own, sufficient to establish this ground: there must have been a conviction (limb 1) or it may be that the illegal/immoral user has caused nuisance or annoyance (limb 2). Limb 1 has been extended by HA 1996 to cover conduct causing nuisance to visitors etc. to the locality rather than just to other residents. Limb 2, similarly, now includes convictions for offences committed in the locality rather than being confined to offences involving the use of the dwelling house. There is no requirement that, if the conduct complained of is committed by someone other than the tenant, the ground is made out only if the tenant has failed to take reasonable steps to remove that person.

5.9.5.7   Ground 14A: domestic violence

> *The dwelling-house was occupied (whether alone or with others) by a married couple or a couple living together as husband and wife and—*
> *(a)   one or both of the partners is a tenant of the dwelling house*
> *(b)   the landlord who is seeking possession is a registered social landlord or a charitable housing trust,*
> *(c)   one partner has left the dwelling-house because of violence or threats of violence by the other towards—*
> *(i)   that partner, or*
> *(ii)   a member of the family of that partner who was residing with that partner immediately before the partner left, and*
> *(d)   the court is satisfied that the partner who has left is unlikely to return.*

There are definitions of 'registered social landlord', 'charitable housing trust' and 'member of the family'.

This ground was added by HA 1996 and can be relied on only by registered social landlords and charitable housing trusts as defined in the ground. It may prove difficult for such landlords to prove condition (d) until a considerable time has elapsed after the departure of the relevant partner. Note that when this ground is relied on there are additional requirements (in HA 1988, s. 8A) to serve the s. 8 notice on the partner who has left.

5.9.5.8   Ground 15: condition of furniture

> *The condition of any furniture provided for use under the tenancy has, in the opinion of the court, deteriorated owing to ill-treatment by the tenant or any other person residing in the dwelling-house and, in the case of ill-treatment by a person lodging with the tenant or by a sub-tenant of his, the tenant has not taken such steps as he ought reasonably to have taken for the removal of the lodger or sub-tenant.*

This ground applies only to furniture provided by the landlord under the terms of the tenancy. There is the same qualification to the tenant's liability under this ground where the damage is caused by a lodger or sub-tenant as in Ground 13.

5.9.5.9   Ground 16: employment

> *The dwelling-house was let to the tenant in consequence of his employment by the landlord seeking possession or a previous landlord under the tenancy and the tenant has ceased to be in that employment.*

. . .

A letting will be 'in consequence of' the tenant's employment by the landlord if it is the case that the landlord would not have otherwise made the letting: see *Royal Crown Derby Porcelain Co. v Russell* [1949] 2 KB 417. It is not necessary that the landlord's motive was to improve the tenant's performance of the duties of the employment, nor need the tenant have been aware of the landlord's motive in granting the tenancy. Nor, unlike the position under the similar ground in RA 1977, Case 8, is it necessary for this ground to be made out that the landlord should require the dwelling house for another employee: it is enough that the tenant's employment by the landlord has ceased.

5.9.5.10   Ground 17: false statement

> *The tenant is the person, or one of the persons, to whom the tenancy was granted and the landlord was induced to grant the tenancy by a false statement made knowingly or recklessly by—*

(a) the tenant, or
(b) a person acting at the tenant's instigation.

This is a new ground added by HA 1996 and is self-explanatory.

5.10 Postponement or Suspension of Possession Order

5.10.1 ORDER ON MANDATORY GROUND

Where the court makes a possession order under any of the mandatory grounds for possession (in HA 1988, sch. 2, part 1) or under the shorthold tenancy ground (HA 1988, s. 21), the court has no jurisdiction to postpone the giving up of possession for more than 14 days or, in cases of exceptional hardship, for more than a maximum of six weeks from the date of the order: see HA 1980, s. 89 and **20.6**.

5.10.2 ORDER ON DISCRETIONARY GROUND

Where, however, the order is made under one of the discretionary grounds (in HA 1988, sch. 2, part 2), where the court must be satisfied that it is reasonable to make an order, the court may:

(a) adjourn the proceedings for such period or periods as the court thinks fit;

(b) on making a possession order or at any time before execution of that order, stay or suspend execution of the order or postpone the date of possession for such period or periods as the court thinks fit: HA 1988, s. 9.

If the court exercises any of these powers, then, unless this would cause exceptional hardship, it must impose conditions as to the payment of any rent arrears, and mesne profits after termination of the tenancy and may impose any other conditions it thinks fit: s. 9(3).

5.10.3 MATRIMONIAL HOME

In most cases the only person who may apply for an adjournment or stay under HA 1988, s. 9 is the tenant. Where, however, the dwelling house is the matrimonial home then so long as the tenant is entitled to remain in occupation, the tenant's spouse, who is given rights of occupation under provisions in the Family Law Act 1996, may apply for such an adjournment or stay. Once the tenancy has been terminated by a possession order, the tenant's right to remain in occupation ceases and, with it, the spouse's right to apply for a stay. The HA 1988 expressly provides, however, that the tenant's spouse, so long as he or she remains in occupation, should continue to have the same rights to apply for an adjournment or stay as if the tenant's right to remain in occupation had not terminated: HA 1988, s. 9(5).

5.11 Accelerated Possession Procedure

Where the landlord's claim for possession against an assured tenant does not include a money claim and the tenancy is an assured shorthold tenancy, then CPR, r. 55.11 provides for an accelerated possession procedure. This enables a landlord who fulfils certain conditions to avoid the delay and expense of a court hearing and obtain a possession order provided all the conditions in CPR, r. 55.12 are satisfied and the judge is satisfied that a properly completed claim form (N5B) has been served and the claimant has established that he is entitled to secure possession under HA 1988, s. 21, against the defendant.

5.12 Sub-tenants

The general common law rule is that, on the determination of a tenancy, any sub-tenancy carved out of that tenancy also comes automatically to an end although this is subject to exceptions where the tenant has voluntarily ended his or her own tenancy, e.g. in the case of a surrender: see LPA 1925, s. 139.

Under HA 1988 a sub-tenancy will, however, survive the determination of the head tenancy if:

(a) the sub-tenancy is itself an assured tenancy (note here that where the sub-letting is of part only of the dwelling house, the sub-tenancy will often be subject to the resident landlord exception and therefore not an assured tenancy), and

(b) the sub-tenancy is lawful, i.e. not granted in breach of any of the terms (whether express or implied, e.g. HA 1988, s. 15, see **5.4**) of the head tenancy: HA 1988, s. 18. Note here that a sub-tenancy initially unlawful may later become lawful if the landlord, with knowledge of the unlawful sub-letting, accepts without qualification rent from the head tenant.

If a sub-tenancy satisfies the conditions in HA 1988, s. 18 then, after the head tenancy has determined, the sub-tenancy will continue on the same terms as before and the head landlord 'steps down into the shoes of' the former head tenant and becomes the immediate landlord of the former sub-tenant: see s. 18(1).

In such a case the sub-tenant will be an assured tenant of the former head landlord and entitled as against him or her to the security of tenure given by HA 1988. If, however, the head landlord is the Crown or another exempted body (see HA 1988, sch. 1) then these provisions do not apply and the sub-tenancy will end on determination of the head tenancy in accordance with the normal common law rule: s. 18(2).

5.13 A Housing Act 1988 Possession Claim: General Guide

5.13.1 INTRODUCTION

We are here concerned with claims for possession by a landlord against a HA 1988 tenant. Reference should be had to **20.8** for a general guide to conducting possession claims, and to **5.1** to **5.12** for the substantive law.

The technical nature of many of the relevant statutory provisions, and the need for strict compliance with the same, means that claims under the HA 1988 contain rather more potential pitfalls than claims under the RA 1977. Having said that, the amendments made to the HA 1988 by the HA 1996 have eliminated some of the more dangerous pitfalls for landlords. However, care is still needed whether you are acting for the claimant or the defendant.

5.13.2 THE HEARING

The position is precisely the same as that under the RA 1977 and reference is made to **7.12.2** in this respect.

5.13.3 ASSURED SHORTHOLD TENANCIES

5.13.3.1 Notice provisions

Assured shorthold tenancies (AST) are very common, as they were intended to be, and it is more likely than not that this is the type of HA 1988 possession claim you will be briefed in. As counsel for either the claimant or the defendant you must ensure that the pre-tenancy notice provisions have been complied with, where required (for which see **5.13.3.2**). A pre-action notice by the landlord that possession is required is also necessary: see **6.4**. Ensure it was served at the correct time, as the relevant provisions in the HA 1988 are not entirely clear at first glance and errors are made by claimants.

Authority has established that the prescribed form of notices to be served under the HA 1988 must comply precisely with the statutory requirements. If there are any deviations from that required, or a precis of the statutory words, in any notice served under the HA 1988, counsel for the defendant may well be able to contend successfully that the notice is ineffective.

5.13.3.2 HA 1996 provisions

The failure to comply with pre-tenancy notice provisions (see **6.2.1**) often resulted in the inadvertent creation of assured tenancies. It was thought to be such a problem that since the day on which s. 98 of the HA 1996 came into force, namely 28 February 1997, the service of a pre-tenancy notice is not required to create an AST (see **6.3.1**), although the landlord is obliged to give the tenant a statement of the terms of the tenancy if the tenant makes a request.

5.13.3.3 Two types of AST

Now all new tenancies under the HA 1988 will automatically be ASTs unless the landlord chooses otherwise. Thus there are now two types of AST: those granted under the HA 1988 as originally enacted, and those granted since the HA 1988 was amended. There is a distinction between the two in respect of possession proceedings.

In the case of an AST granted under the HA 1988 as originally enacted a landlord cannot commence possession proceedings against a tenant before the end of six months from the date of the grant. In the case of a new AST, possession proceedings can be started before the end of six months, but if a possession order is made, it cannot take effect before the end of six months from the date of the grant. Thus whilst a new AST need not be for a minimum term of six months, tenants have a guaranteed minimum of six months' security of tenure.

5.13.4 POSSESSION ON THE GROUND OF RENT ARREARS

The HA 1996 also made a number of important changes to the grounds for possession available to a landlord who has let under a fully assured tenancy.

Perhaps the most important of these changes concerns claims for possession based upon rent arrears. Where there are serious rent arrears, the landlord is provided with a mandatory ground for possession provided he or she can prove there were arrears at the date the s. 8 notice was served and at the date of the hearing.

The change made by the HA 1996 is that the amount of arrears which must be proved has been reduced from thirteen weeks to eight where the rent is payable weekly or fortnightly, and from three months to two months where the rent is paid monthly. What is not made clear by the amendments is whether the change applies only to arrears which accrued after the date of the amendments. This would appear not to be the case. However, if instructed on behalf of the defendant and it is alleged the amendments apply to pre-amendment arrears, be prepared to take the point.

5.13.5 GENERALLY

Since the HA 1996 came into force, the security of tenure provisions of the HA 1988 have been much weakened. Provided the claimant's case is in order, there is little a defendant can do to avoid an order for possession being made. The best line of defence is to raise some technical objection to the claimant's case. The HA 1988 remains complicated, and the new provisions provide some additional material upon which the defendant can rely to take technical points.

5.13.6 ENFORCING THE ORDER

An order for possession against an assured or an assured shorthold tenant is enforced in the same way as in any other possession claim: see **20.8.11**.

SIX

ASSURED SHORTHOLD TENANCIES

6.1 General

An assured shorthold tenancy (AST) is a type of assured tenancy and it must, therefore, satisfy the conditions in **5.1.1**. It bestows less security of tenure than an ordinary assured tenancy, however, as it is subject to an easily satisfied mandatory ground for possession.

6.2 Pre-Housing Act 1996 Tenancies

6.2.1 CONDITIONS

Where the tenancy was granted or agreed on before 28 February 1997, it will be an AST only if it satisfies three conditions:

(a) it was granted for a fixed term of not less than six months; and

(b) the tenancy contained no power for the landlord to determine the tenancy at a time earlier than six months from its start; and

(c) the tenant was notified in writing using the prescribed form (see Assured Tenancies and Agricultural Occupancies (Forms) Regulations 1988 (SI 1988 No. 2203)) at or before the start of the tenancy that the tenancy was to be shorthold: HA 1988, s. 20.

Note that:

(a) Where the term is expressed to commence on a date earlier than the date of the grant of the lease, then in calculating its length, the term will be treated as one commencing on the date of its grant: see *Bradshaw* v *Pawley* [1980] 1 WLR 10.

(b) 'Power to determine' does not include a power of re-entry or forfeiture for breach of any term of the tenancy: HA 1988, s. 45(4). Thus a lease containing the usual proviso for forfeiture for non-payment of rent or breach of covenant, which may of course become exercisable within six months of the start of the tenancy, is not barred from being an AST.

(c) Unlike the position with protected shorthold tenancies (see **7.3.2**), the court has no power to dispense with service of the notice in condition (c) above. Mistakes or omissions in the notice may also make it invalid: *Clickex Ltd* v *Jonathan McCann, The Times*, 26 May 1999, CA.

(d) Unlike the position with protected shorthold tenancies (see **7.3.2**) the tenant has no statutory right to determine the tenancy before the expiry of the fixed term.

6.2.2 GRANTS TO ASSURED TENANTS

Even if it satisfies these three conditions, a tenancy will not be an AST but a full assured tenancy if it is granted by a landlord to someone who was, immediately prior to its grant, a non-shorthold assured tenant of his or hers: HA 1988, s. 20(3). This prevents a landlord depriving his or her existing assured tenants of their security of tenure.

6.2.3 SUBSEQUENT SHORTHOLD TENANCY

If the tenant remains in occupation after the fixed term expires, either under a new tenancy whether fixed term or periodic or under a statutory periodic tenancy (HA 1988, s. 5, see **5.7.2**), this subsequent tenancy will also be an AST unless before its start the landlord notifies the tenant that the new tenancy is not to be shorthold: HA 1988, s. 20(4), (5).

6 2.4 FORMER PROTECTED SHORTHOLD TENANTS

For the special situation where the tenant had, before 15 January 1989, held a protected shorthold tenancy under the RA 1977 from the same landlord, see HA 1988, s. 34 and **5.2**.

6.3 Post-Housing Act 1996 Tenancies

6.3.1 ALL NEW TENANCIES SHORTHOLD

Where the tenancy is granted on or after 28 February 1997 (other than pursuant to a contract made before that date), or arises under HA 1988, s. 5 (see **5.7.2**) on the expiry of a fixed-term tenancy granted on or after 28 February 1997, it will automatically be an AST whether it is for a fixed term or is periodic and no notice need be served to state that the tenancy is to be shorthold: HA 1988, s. 19A (added by HA 1996, s. 96).

6.3.2 EXCEPTIONS

There are exceptions to this rule (see HA 1988, sch. 2A) which include the case where:

(a) the terms of the tenancy state that it is not to be shorthold;

(b) the landlord notifies the tenant either before or after the start of the tenancy that the tenancy is not to be/is no longer an AST;

(c) the tenancy is granted to a former assured non-shorthold tenant by his or her former landlord (unless the tenant notifies the landlord before the grant of the tenancy that it is to be shorthold).

6.3.3 DUTY TO STATE TERMS

The landlord must, if so requested by the tenant, provide a statement of the terms of a post-HA 1996 tenancy: HA 1988, s. 20A, inserted by HA 1996, s. 97. Failure without reasonable excuse to comply with such a request is a criminal offence punishable with a level 4 fine: HA 1988, s. 20A(4).

6.4 Order for Possession

6.4.1 NOTICE

In addition to the grounds for possession available against all assured tenants (see **5.9**), the landlord has an extra mandatory ground against tenants under ASTs: HA 1988, s. 21. The requirements of this ground differ according to whether the AST is for a fixed term or is periodic.

6.4.1.1   Fixed-term tenancy

The landlord must, before or on the day when the fixed term expires, give to the tenant at least two months' written notice stating that he or she requires possession of the dwelling house.

6.4.1.2   Periodic tenancy

Where the tenancy is periodic, either because a statutory periodic tenancy has arisen after the fixed term expired or because the landlord then granted a new periodic tenancy, the written notice must satisfy two conditions:

(a)   it must be expressed to expire on the last day of a period of the tenancy;

(b)   it must be expressed to expire on a date at least two months after its service and that date must not be before the earliest date on which the tenancy could have been determined by a notice to quit at common law.

Thus, if the periodic tenancy is quarterly or six-monthly, the notice would have to be expressed to expire on a date at least three or six months ahead, respectively (see **3.2** for notices to quit).

6.4.2   POST-HOUSING ACT 1996 TENANCIES: EXTRA CONDITION

Most assured tenancies granted after 28 February 1997, whether fixed-term or periodic, will be ASTs (see **6.3.1**). The rule for pre-Housing Act 1996 tenancies that an AST had to be for a fixed term of at least six months has been replaced by a rule barring the court from making a possession order against an AST to take effect sooner than six months from the start of the tenancy. Where there has been more than one tenancy of the same premises made between the same parties, the order must not take effect sooner than six months from the start of the first tenancy: HA 1988, s. 21(5)–(7).

Thus even if the landlord's notice of determination fulfils the conditions in **6.4.1.1** or **6.4.1.2**, he or she cannot obtain a possession order to take effect sooner than six months after the start of the AST, whether the tenancy is for a fixed term or is periodic.

For a practical guide to bringing possession proceedings in respect of an AST, see **5.13.3**.

SEVEN

RENT ACT 1977: PROTECTED TENANCIES

7.1 Scope

7.1.1 TENANCIES PROTECTED

A tenancy of a dwelling house granted before 15 January 1989 will be a protected or statutory tenancy under the RA 1977 where the dwelling house is let as a separate dwelling: see RA 1977, s. 1. This condition also applies to assured tenancies and has been discussed at **5.1**.

An important difference is that an assured tenant must be an individual and must occupy the dwelling house as his or her only or principal home (see **5.1.1**, **5.1.4**), conditions which prevent companies from being assured tenants. There are no such conditions for Rent Act tenancies and companies may be protected, though not statutory, tenants under RA 1977.

7.1.2 TRANSITIONAL PROVISIONS

In general, residential tenancies are only capable of being protected under the RA 1977 if granted before 15 January 1989. Some tenancies granted after that date, however, may be protected under the RA 1977: for these transitional provisions see HA 1988, s. 34 considered at **5.2** and note in particular the case where, after 15 January 1989, a landlord grants a new tenancy to some one who was previously a protected tenant of his or hers under the RA 1977. There are also tenancies originally protected under the RA 1977, which may become assured tenancies under the HA 1988 after the death of the original tenant, as a result of the statutory transmission provisions: see **7.8**.

7.1.3 'SEPARATE'

7.1.3.1 Sharing with the landlord
Another difference between the RA 1977 and HA 1988 is in the protection given to tenants whose tenancies do not satisfy the condition (in RA 1977, s. 1) that the dwelling house should be let as a separate dwelling, only because the terms of the tenancy require the tenant to share living accommodation with the landlord (for the meaning of this, see **5.1.3.1**).

Such a tenancy will be a restricted contract under RA 1977, s. 21 and the tenant will be entitled to some security of tenure and protection as to the rent he or she may be charged: for restricted contracts, see **Chapter 9**. Under the HA 1988 such a tenancy will have no equivalent protection: see **5.1**.

7.1.3.2 Sharing with others
Where, under the terms of the tenancy, the tenant is required to share living accommodation with persons other than the landlord, the provisions (in RA 1977, s. 22) restricting both the landlord's rights to obtain a possession order in respect of the shared accommodation and also his or her contractual rights to terminate or modify

the tenant's rights to use the shared accommodation, are very similar to those already discussed in relation to assured tenancies under the HA 1988: see **5.1.3.2**.

7.2 Exceptions

Certain tenancies within the definition in RA 1977, s. 1 are excluded from protection under RA 1977. These exceptions are largely the same as the exceptions under HA 1988 in relation to assured tenancies (see **5.3**) but the following differences should be noted (**7.2.1** to **7.2.4**).

7.2.1 THE RESIDENT LANDLORD EXEMPTION

The residence test for a landlord claiming to be within the resident landlord exemption in RA 1977 (s. 12 and sch. 2) which is also the test imposed on one claiming to be a statutory tenant under RA 1977 (see **7.7.1**), is the easier one of whether the landlord occupies another dwelling house in the same building 'as his residence' rather than the stricter test in HA 1988 (sch. 1, para. 10 and part III, and see **5.3**(b)) of occupation 'as his only or principal home'.

Note also that a tenancy which, but for the resident landlord exemption, would have been protected under the RA 1977 is treated as a restricted contract: RA 1977, s. 20. This gives the tenant some security of tenure and restricts the amount of rent the landlord may charge: see **Chapter 9**.

7.2.2 BOARD OR ATTENDANCE

One exception in RA 1977 that has not been repeated in the HA 1988 is where the rent payable under the tenancy includes payments for board (food) or attendance (services performed in the dwelling house) provided that, in the case of attendance, the value of the attendance forms a substantial part of the whole rent: RA 1977, s. 7.

It was common for tenancies granted before 15 January 1989 to contain a term whereby the landlord agreed to provide a 'continental breakfast' for the tenant — the amount of the board did not have to be substantial — and this term kept the tenancy out of the Rent Act.

Note that if the attendance consists of services which involve the landlord retaining a key to the premises and exercising rights of unrestricted access to the premises to provide these services, the occupier may fulfil the definition of a lodger in *Street* v *Mountford* [1985] AC 809 and, lacking the necessary exclusive possession, be a licensee rather than a tenant.

7.2.3 HIGH VALUE DWELLING HOUSES

Where the tenancy was granted or contracted for before 1 April 1990, it may be necessary to look at the historic rateable values of the dwelling house as far back as March 1965 because of the principle that a dwelling house, once subject to the Rent Acts, remains within, even if a later change of rateable value limits would otherwise take it outside the Acts: see RA 1977, s. 4.

7.2.4 LOW RENT

Here too it may be necessary to look back at old rateable values: see RA 1977, s. 5. Also note that where the tenancy is a long one (over 21 years) the rent to be tested is the net rent, excluding sums payable for rates, repairs, services, etc. Otherwise it is the rent inclusive of these sums that is to be used: RA 1977, s. 5.

For the protection given by the LTA 1954, part I and the LGHA 1989 to tenancies granted before 15 January 1989 for a term of 21 years or more at a low rent, see **Chapter 10**.

7.3   Protected Shorthold Tenancies (PSTs)

7.3.1   HISTORY

Protected shorthold tenancies were introduced by the HA 1980 in an attempt to persuade landlords to grant tenancies for a fixed term of at least one year, giving tenants security for that fixed term. Provided that the landlord served an appropriate notice on the tenant at the correct time, the landlord would then have a mandatory ground for possession (under RA 1977, sch. 15, Case 19) against the tenant on expiry of that term. The complex provisions as to appropriate notices and the time for their service, however, led to the failure of many possession proceedings under Case 19 and this prevented the wide-spread use of PSTs. The HA 1988 contains much simpler provisions for terminating assured shorthold tenancies: see **6.4.1**.

In view of their maximum length (five years) and the fact that any grant after 15 January 1989 to the tenant under a PST will take effect as an AST (see HA 1988, s. 34(3) and **5.2**), few PSTs can still be in existence today.

7.3.2   CONDITIONS

A tenancy is a PST where:

(a)   it was granted for a term of between one and five years; and

(b)   it contains no right for the landlord to determine the tenancy before the expiry of the term except under a right to forfeit or re-enter for non-payment of rent or breach of obligation; and also

(c)   before the grant of the tenancy the landlord served a valid notice on the tenant stating that the tenancy was to be a PST: HA 1980, s. 52.

Note that the court is given a discretion to treat a tenancy as a PST for the purposes of making a possession order under RA 1977, sch. 15, Case 19 (see below), if satisfied that it is just and equitable to make a possession order despite failure to serve the notice within condition (c). Contrast the position with assured shorthold tenancies granted before 28 February 1997 (see **6.2.1**), where no such discretion exists. Note also the tenant's right (under HA 1980, s. 53) to terminate the PST at any time, on serving either one or two months' notice according to the length of the term. Tenants under assured shorthold tenancies have no such right: see **6.2.1**.

7.3.3   MANDATORY GROUND FOR POSSESSION

The effect of granting a PST is that after the expiry of the fixed term, the landlord may claim possession, not only in reliance on any of the grounds that apply to all Rent Act tenancies, but also under RA 1977, sch. 15, Case 19 which is a mandatory ground. The complex notice procedure provided in Case 19 needs careful compliance in order for a landlord to be successful in gaining possession under this case. Contrast the similar mandatory ground for possession in respect of assured shorthold tenancies: see **6.4.1**.

7.4   Rent

7.4.1   REGISTRATION OF A FAIR RENT

Either landlord or tenant may, at any time, apply to the Rent Officer and, on appeal, to the Rent Assessment Committee to have a fair rent registered for the dwelling house: RA 1977, s. 67. The rent so registered is the limit of what the landlord can lawfully demand even if the contractual rent is higher: RA 1977, ss. 44, 45.

The 'fair rent' is based on a notional market rent for the dwelling house but certain factors are to be regarded and other factors disregarded (in particular the 'scarcity element', which reflects the fact that demand exceeds the supply of residential accommodation, and which is often as much as 40 per cent of the market value in Greater London, is to be ignored): RA 1977, s. 70. It is also a criminal offence to require or receive any premium in connection with the grant of a protected tenancy: RA 1977, s. 119.

7.4.2 NO RENT REGISTERED

Where no rent is registered for the dwelling house, the landlord is still restricted in the extent to which he or she may either lawfully increase the rent of an existing tenancy or grant a new tenancy at a higher rent to an existing tenant. Such an increase or higher rent may only be made under the terms of a 'rent agreement with a tenant having security of tenure': see RA 1977, s. 51. Such an agreement will be valid only if it satisfies two conditions:

(a) it must be written and signed by both landlord and tenant;

(b) the agreement must state first that the tenant's security of tenure under RA 1977 will be unaffected if he or she refuses to enter into the agreement, and secondly, that entering into the agreement will not deprive either landlord or tenant of the right to apply to have a fair rent registered for the dwelling house: RA 1977, s. 51(4).

This statement must be no less conspicuous than the rest of the terms of the agreement and must be set out at the head of the document containing the agreement: s. 51(4). Any rent due under an agreement which does not comply with these conditions is irrecoverable from the tenant: s. 54.

7.5 Protected and Statutory Tenancies

The terms 'protected tenancy' and 'statutory tenancy' cause confusion and should be explained. A protected tenancy is a tenancy within RA 1977, s. 1 where the contract of tenancy is still in existence, e.g. in the case of a tenancy for a fixed term, where that term has not expired, or, in the case of a periodic tenancy, where no notice to quit has been served. A statutory tenancy is a former protected tenancy where the contract of tenancy has come to an end, e.g. on expiry of the fixed term by effluxion of time or on expiry of a notice to quit in respect of the periodic tenancy. A statutory tenancy will arise where, at the determination of the protected (contractual) tenancy, the tenant occupies the dwelling house as his or her residence: see **7.7.1**.

7.6 Implied Terms of a Protected Tenancy

7.6.1 ACCESS FOR REPAIRS

It is a condition of a protected tenancy that the tenant shall allow the landlord access and all reasonable facilities for carrying out any repairs he or she is entitled to execute: RA 1977, s. 148.

7.6.2 TENANT'S IMPROVEMENTS

It is a term of every protected or statutory tenancy that the tenant will not make any improvement to the dwelling house without the landlord's written consent. Such consent is not to be unreasonably withheld and, if it is unreasonably withheld, shall be treated as given: HA 1980, s. 81.

This term is not implied in tenancies where notice was given to the tenant at the start that the landlord might recover possession under one of the mandatory grounds for possession (including a notice that a tenancy was to be a PST).

There are further provisions defining 'improvements' and as to the required consents, see ss. 82, 83.

7.7 Statutory Tenancy

7.7.1 NATURE

On the determination of a protected tenancy a statutory tenancy will arise and the tenant will become a statutory tenant of the dwelling house if, at that time, he or she is occupying the dwelling house as his or her residence. The statutory tenancy will continue so long as the tenant's occupation as a residence continues: see RA 1977, s. 2(1)(a). There are several points to note here (**7.7.1.1** to **7.7.1.7**).

7.7.1.1 Determination of contract
Unlike the HA 1988, RA 1977 does not affect the common law rules for determining the contractual tenancy. Thus a tenancy for a fixed term will expire by effluxion of time and a landlord may effectively determine a protected tenancy by a valid notice to quit or by effecting a valid forfeiture. When the protected tenancy has ended in any of these ways a statutory tenancy will arise if the tenant fulfils the necessary residence test.

7.7.1.2 Companies
The residence condition prevents a company from being a statutory tenant though a company may be a protected tenant.

7.7.1.3 Status of statutory tenant
A statutory tenancy is not an interest in land but a mere personal right of occupation: compare the position of a statutory periodic tenancy under HA 1988, s. 5 (see **5.7.2**). Hence a statutory tenant cannot assign his or her tenancy (having no interest in land to assign) and it is dubious whether he or she can effectively sublet the whole of the premises: see *Smith's Trustees* v *Willson* [1983] QB 316.

7.7.1.4 Effect of acceptance of rent
Any acceptance of rent by a landlord after the protected tenancy has come to an end, will normally be attributed to the existence of a statutory tenancy rather than to an intention by the landlord to create a new contractual periodic tenancy. Thus the normal common law presumption of a new tenancy arising from the payment and acceptance of rent will not arise.

7.7.1.5 Two 'homes'
It has been held that a tenant may occupy more than one place as his or her residence, e.g. where he or she occupies one flat in London during his or her working week and has a cottage in the country where he or she spends weekends. Consequently it is possible for a tenant to claim a statutory tenancy under RA 1977 of two dwelling houses. This possibility does not exist in the case of assured tenancies, where the tenant must occupy the dwelling house as his or her only or principal home.

7.7.1.6 Absence
Occupation as a residence clearly does not cease when the tenant is absent for a short time, e.g. on holiday or for the purposes of his or her work. Longer absences may raise difficult questions as to whether residence has ceased and the statutory tenancy been lost.

7.7.1.7 Matrimonial home: constructive residence
Where the dwelling house is the matrimonial home, occupation by the non-tenant spouse is treated for the purposes of RA 1977 as occupation by the tenant spouse, thus maintaining the statutory tenancy. Further, payment of the rent and performance of the other obligations of the tenancy by the non-tenant spouse is treated as if done by the tenant spouse: Family Law Act 1996, s. 30.

These provisions first prevent the tenant spouse from ending the statutory tenancy by giving up occupation and, secondly, rebut any presumption that the landlord intended to grant a new contractual tenancy to the non-spouse that might otherwise arise from the landlord's acceptance of rent from the non-spouse.

This doctrine will, in most cases, cease to apply once the marriage has been terminated by decree absolute, and the non-tenant occupying spouse should, before decree absolute, seek an order under the Family Law Act 1996 transferring the statutory tenancy to the non-tenant spouse.

7.7.2 TERMS OF STATUTORY TENANCY

7.7.2.1 General rule

A statutory tenant is bound by and entitled to the benefit of all the terms in the original protected tenancy so far as these are consistent with the security of tenure provisions in the RA 1977: see s. 3(1). Thus a term in the protected tenancy against immoral use of the dwelling house will carry on into a statutory tenancy but not a term obliging the tenant to give up possession of the dwelling house at the end of the tenancy.

7.7.2.2 Access for repairs

As is the case for protected tenancies (see **7.6.1**), it is a condition of a statutory tenancy that the tenant shall allow the landlord access to the dwelling house and reasonable facilities for carrying out any repairs that the landlord is entitled to execute: RA 1977, s. 3(2).

7.7.2.3 Improvements

See **7.6.2** for the term implied by HA 1980, s. 81 into statutory and protected tenancies, prohibiting the tenant from carrying out improvements without the landlord's consent.

7.7.3 TERMINATION OF STATUTORY TENANCY

A statutory tenancy continues only so long as the tenant continues to occupy the dwelling house as his or her residence and, if the tenant ceases so to occupy the dwelling house, he or she will cease to be a statutory tenant and the landlord will be entitled to possession.

So long as the tenant's occupation continues, however, the landlord will be entitled to possession against a statutory tenant only if he or she can establish one or more of the statutory grounds for possession under RA 1977 against him or her.

Note that in a case where the contract creating the protected tenancy was rescinded on the ground that its grant was procured by the tenant's fraudulent misrepresentation which was discovered only after the protected tenancy had expired and a statutory tenancy arisen, the statutory tenancy too, ended on the rescission of the protected tenancy and the landlord recovered possession without needing to prove Rent Act grounds for possession: *Killick* v *Roberts* [1991] 4 All ER 289.

7.8 Succession to Protected and Statutory Tenancies

7.8.1 SURVIVING SPOUSE

On the death of a protected or statutory tenant, the tenant's surviving spouse who fulfils certain residence qualifications, may succeed to the tenancy and become a statutory tenant: see RA 1977, s. 2(1)(b), and sch. 1, part I. Any such statutory succession will prevail over the normal rules of inheritance under the tenant's will or intestacy. Spouse, here, includes a person living with the tenant as his or her wife or husband. These latter words apply only to heterosexual and not to homosexual relationships: *Fitzpatrick* v *Sterling HA*, *The Times*, 2 November 1999, HL.

7.8.2 NO QUALIFYING SURVIVING SPOUSE

Where there is no qualifying surviving spouse but there is a member of the deceased tenant's family who fulfils certain residence qualifications, then that person is entitled to an assured tenancy by succession: RA 1977, sch. 1, part I, para. 3. If more than one person is so qualified, the successor is to be decided by agreement or, in default of agreement, by the County Court. The deceased tenant's homosexual partner is a member of his family: *Fitzpatrick v Sterling HA*.

7.8.3   SECOND SUCCESSION

If, at his or her death, the first successor was still a statutory tenant and, at that time, there is a person who was a member of both the original tenant's family and the first successor's family immediately before their respective deaths, and that person fulfils certain residence qualifications, then that person is entitled to an assured tenancy under HA 1988 by succession: RA 1977, sch. 1, part I, paras 5, 6.

This would apply, for instance, where the original tenant was a woman at whose death her husband and daughter were living with her in the dwelling house. The husband would be entitled to succeed the tenant as a statutory tenant under the RA 1977 (the first succession) and, if the daughter was still living with her widowed father in the dwelling house at his death, she would be entitled, after his death, to an assured tenancy by succession (the second succession).

7.9   Seeking Possession of a Rent Act Tenancy

7.9.1   SERVICE OF NOTICE

There is no statutory requirement under the RA 1977 to serve a notice of intention to seek possession as there is under HA 1988 (see **5.8.1**) and the Housing Act 1985 (see **8.7.4.1**). However, any contractual tenancy still in existence must be terminated, for example, a notice to quit will have to be served to end a periodic protected tenancy.

For a practical guide to conducting possession actions against tenants protected under RA 1977, see **7.12**.

7.9.2   GROUNDS FOR POSSESSION

As in the case of assured tenancies under HA 1988, there are two types of grounds — discretionary and mandatory — in RA 1977: see s. 98 and sch. 15. If the landlord claims possession under one of the discretionary grounds, the court, in addition to being satisfied that the relevant ground is made out, must be satisfied that it is reasonable to make an order for possession. Where, however, the landlord establishes one of the mandatory grounds, the court has no discretion but must make the order.

The grounds, called 'Cases', are mostly set out in RA 1977, sch. 15. One of the discretionary grounds — that suitable alternative accommodation is available for the tenant — is set out in RA 1977, s. 98(1)(a). There is also, in effect, a further mandatory ground where the dwelling house is overcrowded in such circumstances as to constitute an offence under the HA 1985: see RA 1977, s. 101.

7.9.3   COMPENSATION FOR MISREPRESENTATION OR CONCEALMENT

Where the landlord obtains a possession order under either Case 8 or Case 9 in sch. 15, by misrepresentation or concealment of material facts, the court may order the landlord to compensate the tenant for loss or damage suffered as a result of the order: RA 1977, s. 102.

7.9.4   THE DISCRETIONARY GROUNDS

7.9.4.1   Suitable alternative accommodation (RA 1977)

> 98.—(1) . . .
> (a) *The court is satisfied that suitable alternative accommodation is available for the tenant or will be available for him when the order in question takes effect.*

This ground must be read in conjunction with the provisions in part IV of sch. 15 which deem certain accommodation to be suitable. They do not purport to be exhaustive: suitable alternative accommodation, for instance, is not restricted to accommodation provided by the landlord and an order might be made under this ground where the tenant already owned an empty flat.

SCHEDULE 15

PART IV
SUITABLE ALTERNATIVE ACCOMMODATION
3.   For the purposes of section 98(1)(a) of this Act, a certificate of the local housing authority for the district in which the dwelling-house in question is situated, certifying that the authority will provide suitable alternative accommodation for the tenant by a date specified in the certificate, shall be conclusive evidence that suitable alternative accommodation will be available for him by that date.

In view of the shortage of local authority housing it is very rare for the landlord to be able to rely on a certificate of the sort mentioned in para. 3 in part IV.

4.—(1)   Where no such certificate as is mentioned in paragraph 3 above is produced to the court, accommodation shall be deemed to be suitable for the purposes of section 98(1)(a) of this Act if it consists of either—
(a)   premises which are to be let as a separate dwelling such that they will then be let on a protected tenancy, other than [a tenancy under which the landlord might recover possession of the dwelling house under one of the mandatory grounds for possession in Part II of schedule 15], or
(b)   premises to be let as a separate dwelling on terms which will, in the opinion of the court, afford to the tenant security of tenure reasonably equivalent to [that given by the RA 1977 to a protected tenancy of a kind within] (a) above,
and, in the opinion of the court, the accommodation fulfils the [conditions in paragraph 5].

Accommodation to be let on a protected tenancy susceptible to a possession order under any of the mandatory grounds in part II of sch. 15 will not be deemed suitable, as such a tenancy bestows inadequate security of tenure.

The court will presumably direct that any assured tenancy granted after 28 February 1997 under para. 4(b) above as giving security of tenure reasonably equivalent to that given by RA 1977, should contain a provision that the tenancy is not to be an assured shorthold tenancy: see HA 1988, sch. 2A, para. 3 and **6.3.1**, **6.3.2**.

5.—(1)   For the purposes of paragraph 4 above, the relevant conditions are that the accommodation is reasonably suitable to the needs of the tenant and his family as regards proximity to place of work, and either—
(a)   similar as regards rental and extent to the accommodation afforded by dwelling-houses provided in the neighbourhood by any local housing authority for persons whose needs as regards extent are, in the opinion of the court, similar to those of the tenant and his family; [both the rent and extent of such accommodation may be proved by a certificate of the local authority, which is to be conclusive evidence of those matters] or
(b)   reasonably suitable to the means of the tenant and to the needs of the tenant and his family as regards extent and character; and
that if any furniture was provided for use under the protected or statutory tenancy in question, furniture is provided for use in the accommodation which is either similar to that so provided or is reasonably suitable to the needs of the tenant and his family.

The ground does not require that the proposed alternative accommodation should be equal to or as good as the tenant's present accommodation but merely that it should be reasonably suitable to specified needs of the tenant.

There is, here, no parallel to the landlord's obligation (in HA 1988, s. 11: see **5.9.5.1**, Ground 9) to pay an assured tenant's reasonable removal expenses where possession is ordered on this ground.

7.9.4.2   Case 1: rent arrears and breach

Where any rent lawfully due from the tenant has not been paid, or any obligation of the protected or statutory tenancy . . . has been broken or not performed.

'Obligation', here, includes a statutory obligation under the RA 1977 as well as contractual obligations and, in the case of statutory tenancies, includes obligations imposed by the former contractual tenancy in so far as these apply to the statutory tenancy: see **7.7.2.1**.

In contrast to the position under HA 1988 where there are three grounds, one of them mandatory, based on non-payment of rent, this is the only non-payment of rent ground available against a Rent Act tenant.

7.9.4.3   Case 2: nuisance etc.

Where the tenant or any person residing or lodging with him or any sub-tenant of his has been guilty of conduct which is a nuisance or annoyance to adjoining occupiers, or has been convicted of using the dwelling-house or allowing the dwelling-house to be used for immoral or illegal purposes.

This case is similar to Ground 14 relating to assured tenancies (see **5.9.5.6**) before that ground was expanded by HA 1996. The same comments as to there being two separate limbs, each needing to be strictly made out, apply here too.

7.9.4.4   Case 3: condition of premises

Where the condition of the dwelling house has, in the opinion of the court, deteriorated owing to acts of waste by, or the neglect or default of, the tenant or any person residing or lodging with him or any sub-tenant of his and, in the case of any act of waste by, or the neglect or default of, a person lodging with the tenant or a sub-tenant of his, where the court is satisfied that the tenant has not, before the making of the order in question, taken such steps as he ought reasonably to have taken for the removal of the lodger or sub-tenant, as the case may be.

This case is similar to Ground 13 in relation to assured tenancies (see **5.9.5.5**) and the same comments apply. Acts of waste or breach of express repairing obligation may constitute Case 1 above.

7.9.4.5   Case 4: condition of furniture

Where the condition of any furniture provided for use under the tenancy has, in the opinion of the court, deteriorated owing to ill-treatment by the tenant or any person residing or lodging with him or any sub-tenant of his and, in the case of any ill-treatment by a person lodging with the tenant or a sub-tenant of his, where the court is satisfied that the tenant has not, before the making of the order in question, taken such steps as he ought reasonably to have taken for the removal of the lodger or sub-tenant, as the case may be.

This case is very similar to Ground 15 in relation to assured tenancies (see **5.9.5.8**) and the same comments apply.

7.9.4.6   Case 5: tenant's notice to quit

Where the tenant has given notice to quit and, in consequence of that notice, the landlord has contracted to sell or let the dwelling-house or has taken any other steps as the result of which he would, in the opinion of the court, be seriously prejudiced if he could not obtain possession.

This case has no parallel in the assured tenancy grounds. There is nothing in HA 1988 to prevent a notice to quit by a tenant taking effect in the normal way: see HA 1988,

s. 5 which confines the landlord, but not the tenant, to terminating an assured tenancy by obtaining a court order. Under RA 1977, however, the tenant can resile from a notice to quit that he or she has served and claim a statutory tenancy after expiry of the notice, unless the landlord can prove serious prejudice.

7.9.4.7 Case 6: alienation without consent

Where, without the consent of the landlord, the tenant has . . . assigned or sublet the whole of the dwelling house or sublet part of the dwelling-house, the remainder being already sublet.

The full wording of the case refers to assignments, etc. after various dates which are no longer significant.

This case will apply even if the terms of the tenancy do not expressly prohibit or restrict the tenant's right to assign or sublet. If there is such an express term then Case 1 will apply as well. Case 6 contemplates assignment by a protected tenant — a statutory tenant has no estate in land to assign — and it is also dubious whether a statutory tenant has a sufficient interest to make an effective subletting of the whole of the dwelling house: see *Smith's Trustees* v *Willson* [1983] QB 317.

7.9.4.8 Case 7
Case 7 has been repealed

7.9.4.9 Case 8: employee

Where the dwelling-house is reasonably required by the landlord for occupation as a residence for some person engaged in his whole-time employment, or in the whole-time employment of some tenant from him or with whom, conditional on housing being provided, a contract for such employment has been entered into, and the tenant was in the employment of the landlord or a former landlord, and the dwelling house was let to him in consequence of that employment and he has ceased to be in that employment.

This case is similar to Ground 16 for assured tenancies (see **5.9.5.9**) and the same comments apply. Case 8 contains the extra condition, however, that the dwelling house must reasonably be required as a residence for another full-time employee. The landlord, accordingly, will have to have at least identified another employee before he or she can rely on this case. The meaning of 'reasonably required' is considered in Case 9 below.

For the court's power to order compensation where the order was obtained under this case by misrepresentation or concealment, see **7.8.2**.

7.9.4.10 Case 9: occupation by landlord/family

Where the dwelling-house is reasonably required by the landlord for occupation as a residence for—
  (a) himself, or
  (b) any son or daughter of his over 18 years of age, or
  (c) his father or mother, or
  (d) . . . the father or mother of his wife or husband,
and the landlord did not become landlord by purchasing the dwelling-house or any interest therein . . .

The dates referred to in the full wording of the case are not now relevant.

This case is also subject to the requirement (in part III of sch. 15) that the court is not to order possession under Case 9 if satisfied that, having regard to all the circumstances of the case, including that of whether other accommodation is available for the landlord or the tenant, greater hardship would be caused by granting the order than by refusing it.

In order for this case to be made out, the landlord must prove that he or she reasonably requires the dwelling house, i.e. that he or she has a genuine present need, not a dire necessity, for it. Once the landlord has proved this, the burden then shifts to the tenant who may defeat the landlord's claim if he or she can prove that greater hardship will be caused by the grant than by the refusal of the order. On this issue the court will weigh up matters such as the relative social and financial hardship suffered by the parties. A landlord by purchase — one who buys a house already let — will not be allowed to oust the sitting tenant under this case.

For the court's power to order compensation where the order was obtained under this case by misrepresentation or concealment, see **7.8.2**.

7.9.4.11 Case 10: excess rent on sublet

Where the court is satisfied that the rent charged by the tenant—
(a) for any sublet part of the dwelling-house which is a dwelling-house let on a protected tenancy or subject to a statutory tenancy is or was in excess of the maximum rent for the time being recoverable for that part, having regard to . . . Part III of this Act, or
(b) for any sublet part of the dwelling-house which is subject to a restricted contract is or was in excess of the maximum (if any) which it is lawful for the lessor . . . to require or receive having regard to the provisions of . . . [Part V of this Act].

This case only applies to sublettings which are either protected or statutory tenancies under the RA 1977 or restricted contracts under that Act. Further, the case will only be made out if a rent for the dwelling house has been registered under either part IV (protected and statutory tenancies) or part V (restricted contracts) of the RA 1977. Thus where there is no registered rent for the dwelling house, Case 10 cannot be relied on.

7.9.5 MANDATORY GROUNDS

7.9.5.1 Notice before start of tenancy
It is a requirement of all the mandatory grounds that, before the start of the tenancy, the landlord should have given written notice to the tenant that possession might be recovered under that ground. All the cases except Case 19 (the case applying to PSTs, which have their own notice requirement: see **7.2.2**) require this notice to be given 'not later than the relevant date', a phrase with a complex definition (see RA 1977, sch. 15, part III, para. 2) but, for all practical purposes, the 'relevant date' is now the date of the commencement of the tenancy. In some of the cases the court is given a discretion to dispense with this notice requirement: see Cases 11, 12, 20 and, in effect, Case 19.

7.9.5.2 Conditions for Cases 11, 12 and 20
In addition to the individual requirements of these cases, there are conditions relating to the purposes for which the dwelling house must be required, which apply to all three cases: see sch. 15, part V. The conditions are that:

(a) the dwelling house is required as a residence for the owner or for any member of his or her family who resided with the owner when he or she last occupied the dwelling house as a residence;

(b) the owner has retired from regular employment and requires the dwelling house as a residence;

(c) the owner has died and the dwelling house is required as a residence for a member of his or her family who was residing with him or her at the time of his or her death;

(d) the owner has died and the dwelling house is required by a successor in title as his or her residence or for the purpose of disposing of it with vacant possession;

(e)   the dwelling house is subject to a mortgage granted before the tenancy, and the mortgagee is entitled to sell the house and requires vacant possession for that purpose;

(f)   where the dwelling house is not located conveniently to the owner's place of work, the owner requires the house to sell it with vacant possession and use the proceeds to purchase as his or her residence a house which will be conveniently located for his or her place of work.

7.9.5.3   Case 11: owner occupier

This is known as the 'owner-occupier' ground and four conditions must be satisfied:

(a)   the owner must, at some time before the letting, have occupied the dwelling house as his or her residence; and

(b)   the owner must, not later than the relevant date (the start of the tenancy), have given written notice to the tenant that possession might be recovered under this case; and

(c)   the owner has not let the dwelling house on a tenancy in circumstances where condition (b) above was not satisfied; and

(d)   the court considers that one of the conditions set out in paras (a) and (c)–(f) in sch. 15, part V (see **7.9.5.2**) is satisfied.

The court is given power to dispense with the requirements of conditions (b) and (c) above where it considers that it is just and equitable to make a possession order despite non-compliance with either or both of these: see **5.9.4.1** for factors influencing the exercise of this discretion in relation to the similar discretion in HA 1988.

The occupation as a residence may have been at any time in the past, not necessarily just before the letting.

Of the conditions in part V, (see **7.9.5.2**), (a) is the one most commonly relied on in Case 11 proceedings. Unlike the position in relation to Case 9, condition (a) does not demand that the landlord's requirement for the dwelling house should be reasonable provided that the requirement is genuine. If the landlord satisfies the conditions within Case 11, the court must order possession, irrespective of any question of greater hardship or reasonability.

7.9.5.4   Case 12: landlord's retirement

This case applies where the landlord intends to occupy the dwelling house as his or her residence when he or she retires from regular employment and lets it before that retirement. Conditions (b) and (c) in Case 11 (see **7.9.5.3**) apply here too, as does the court's discretion to dispense with either or both of these conditions.

The court must also consider that of the conditions in sch. 15, part V (see **7.9.5.2**), one of those in paras (b) to (e) is satisfied. Again, provided that the landlord's requirement for the dwelling house as a residence after his or her retirement or for any of the other purposes in part V is genuine, it need not be reasonable.

7.9.5.5   Case 13: out of season holiday home

Where the dwelling house is let under a tenancy for a term of years certain not exceeding eight months and:

(a)   not later than the start of the tenancy (the relevant date) the landlord gave written notice to the tenant that possession might be recovered under this case; and

(b)   the dwelling house was, at some time within the period of 12 months ending on the relevant date, occupied under a right to occupy it for a holiday.

The fact that the tenancy contains a proviso for forfeiture for non-payment of rent or breach of the terms will not prevent it from being one for a term of years certain but a term allowing the landlord to determine the tenancy on notice (a 'break' clause), will. In other respects this case is very similar to Ground 3 in HA 1988, sch. 2 and the same comments apply: see **5.9.4.3**. The court has no power to dispense with the notice requirement in this case.

7.9.5.6   **Case 14: vacation let of educational accommodation**
Where the dwelling house is let under a tenancy for a term of years certain not exceeding 12 months and:

(a)   not later than the start of the tenancy the landlord gave written notice to the tenant that possession might be recovered under this case; and

(b)   at some time within the period of 12 months ending on the relevant date, the dwelling house was subject to a tenancy within RA 1977, s. 8(1) (a letting to a student by a specified educational institution).

Again, the presence of a forfeiture clause in the tenancy will not prevent it being one for a term of years certain but a 'break clause' will. In other respects this case is similar to Ground 4 in HA 1988, sch. 2 and the same comments apply: see **5.9.4.4**. Again the court has no power to dispense with the notice condition in this case.

7.9.5.7   **Case 15: minister of religion**
Where the dwelling house is held for the purpose of being available for occupation by a minister of religion as a residence from which to perform the duties of his or her office and:

(a)   not later than the relevant date the landlord gave written notice to the tenant that possession might be recovered under this case; and

(b)   the court is satisfied that the dwelling house is required for occupation by a minister of religion as such a residence.

This case is identical to Ground 5 in HA 1988, sch. 2. Again the court has no power to dispense with the notice requirement.

7.9.5.8   **Cases 16 to 18: agricultural**
These cases are all concerned with farm land and apply in varying circumstances where the landlord now wants the dwelling house for either an agricultural employee of his or hers or for his or her tenant farmer and the dwelling house was formerly occupied by an agricultural employee or tenant farmer of the landlord's but is no longer occupied either by such a person or by the widow of such a person.

7.9.5.9   **Case 19: protected shorthold**
This is the mandatory case available against tenants holding under protected short-hold tenancies (PSTs) (see **7.3**). It applies where the dwelling house was let under a PST or is treated as having been so let under the court's discretion to do this: see HA 1980, s. 55 (where the landlord failed to serve the appropriate written shorthold notice before the start of the tenancy).

Case 19 continues to be available in respect of a PST after the expiry of the fixed term whether the tenant remains in occupation as a statutory tenant or whether the landlord grants him or her a further tenancy of the same dwelling house.

Case 19 contains complex provisions as to the notice (the 'appropriate notice') the landlord must serve informing the tenant of the possession proceedings. These must be complied with precisely if the landlord is to succeed.

The proceedings must then be commenced by the landlord after appropriate notice to the tenant and not later than three months after expiry of the notice.

A notice is appropriate for the purposes of Case 19 if:

(i)   it is in writing and states that proceedings for possession under [Case 19] may be brought after its expiry; and
(ii)   it expires not earlier than 3 months after it is served nor, if, when it is served, the tenancy is a periodic tenancy, before that periodic tenancy could be determined by a notice to quit served by the landlord on the same day;
(iii)   it is served—
  (a)   in the period of 3 months immediately preceding the date on which the protected shorthold tenancy comes to an end; or
  (b)   if that date has passed, in the period of 3 months immediately preceding any anniversary of that date; and
(iv)   in a case where a previous [appropriate] notice has been served by the landlord on the tenant in respect of the same dwelling-house, . . .it is served not earlier than 3 months after the expiry of the previous notice.

7.9.5.10   Case 20: armed forces
This case applies where:

(a)   the owner was a member of the armed forces when he or she acquired the dwelling house and when he or she made the letting of the dwelling house; and

(b)   not later than the relevant date the owner gave the tenant written notice that possession might be recovered under this case; and

(c)   the owner has not let the dwelling house on a tenancy where condition (b) above was not satisfied; and

(d)   the court is satisfied either that:

  (i)   the owner requires the dwelling house as a residence; or

  (ii)   one of the conditions (c) to (f) in part V of RA 1977, sch. 15 (see **7.9.5.2**) is made out.

The court may dispense with either or both of the requirements in conditions (b) or (c) if it thinks it just and equitable to order possession despite non-compliance with these conditions.

This case provides a member of the armed forces with a mandatory ground to recover possession of a dwelling house provided that he or she was such a member both at the time when he or she acquired the dwelling house and at the time he or she let it. There is no requirement that he or she ever occupied it as his or her residence. Again there is no need for the landlord's requirement to be reasonable provided that it is genuine.

7.10   Postponement or Suspension of Possession Order

Where the court makes a possession order under any of the mandatory grounds for possession (in RA 1977, sch. 15, part II), the court has no jurisdiction to postpone the giving up of possession for more than 14 days or, in cases of exceptional hardship, for more than a maximum of six weeks from the date of the order: see HA 1980, s. 89 and **20.6**.

Where, however, the order is made under one of the discretionary grounds (in RA 1977, sch. 15, part I), where the court must be satisfied that it is reasonable to make an order, the court has power to adjourn the proceedings or stay or suspend execution of the order or postpone the date for possession: see RA 1977, s. 100. These powers, as well as the conditions that the court should attach to them and their extension in the case of the matrimonial home, are the same as those given to the court by HA 1988, s. 9, already considered at **5.10.2**, **5.10.3**.

7.11 Sub-tenants

The normal common law rule is that on the determination of a tenancy, any sub-tenancy created out of it will automatically determine, although this rule is subject to exceptions, e.g. where the head tenant has voluntarily ended his or her tenancy by surrendering it: see LPA 1925, s. 139.

As in the case of assured tenancies under HA 1988 (see **5.12**), the RA 1977, s. 137 creates a statutory exception to this general rule and provides that a sub-tenancy will survive the determination of the head tenancy if:

(a) the sub-tenancy is itself a protected or statutory tenancy. Note that where the subletting is of part only of the premises comprised in the head tenancy, the sub-tenancy will, in many cases, be subject to the resident landlord exception (see **7.2.1**) and therefore excluded from the protection of RA 1977; and

(b) the sub-tenancy is lawful, i.e. not granted in breach of any of the terms of the head tenancy, though note that a sub-tenancy initially unlawful may later become lawful if the landlord 'waives' the unlawfulness by, e.g., accepting without qualification rent from the head tenant after the landlord has learned of the unlawful subletting; and

(c) the head tenancy is a protected or, possibly, a statutory tenancy under RA 1977.

This third condition is subject to two exceptions:

(a) Where the reason for the head tenancy's exclusion from RA 1977 is only that the dwelling house is too valuable and where the subletting is of part only of the dwelling house with a value within the RA limits: see RA 1977, s. 137(3) and for rateable value limits, see **7.2.3**.

(b) Where the head tenancy is of premises with mixed use, e.g. a shop with a flat above. The head tenancy will usually be a business tenancy and subject to the Landlord and Tenant Act 1954, part 2 but, under RA 1977, s. 137(3) a residential sub-tenancy of the flat may have Rent Act protection against the head landlord: see *Wellcome Trust Ltd v Hamad; Church Commissioners for England v Baines* [1998] 1 All ER 657.

Where these three conditions are satisfied then, after the head tenancy ends, the sub-tenancy continues on the same terms as before but with a new landlord (the former head landlord) as the immediate landlord. The former sub-tenant is entitled to security of tenure under the RA 1977 against his or her new landlord.

7.12 A Rent Act 1977 Possession Claim: General Guide

7.12.1 PRELIMINARY MATTERS

We are here concerned with claims for possession by a landlord against a RA 1977 protected tenant. Again Part 55 of the Civil Procedure Rules applies. Some of the more important grounds for possession are considered. Reference should be had to **20.8** for a general guide to conducting possession actions, and to **7.1** to **7.11** for the substantive law.

7.12.2 THE HEARING

An action under the RA 1977 will be in the County Court. The general rule is that the hearing will be in public, although the judge conducting the hearing has a discretion. A claim by a landlord against one or more tenants or former tenants for possession of a dwelling-house on the ground of non-payment of rent (in this context, a claim pursuant to Case 1 of sch. 15 to the RA 1977) will, in the first instance, be listed in open court, and others for hearing in private. Accordingly, some RA 1977 possession claims will be listed in open court, and others for hearing in private! As to the wearing of wig and gown, the practice differs between courts. In some courts, where the claim is undefended, it is not necessary to wear a wig and gown; in other courts if the claim is heard in public, wig and gown must be worn. If in doubt, bring your wig and gown to court.

7.12.3 CASE 1 CASES

7.12.3.1 Counterclaims

Case 1 cases (rent arrears or breach of other obligations) rarely raise many difficulties for the claimant. Sometimes when you attend at court on a Case 1 rent arrears case you will be met by a counterclaim that the claimant is in breach of repairing covenant, which is usually sufficient to get the claim adjourned on the first hearing with case management directions for the future conduct of the claim being given. If you are representing the defendant in a Case 1 case do not forget that the court must consider it reasonable to make an order, even if the arrears or breach of obligation are proved. As a general rule, the arrears or breach of obligation must be substantial, or the defendant's record on such matters very poor, before an immediate order for possession will be made.

7.12.3.2 Rent

Landlords frequently increase the contractual rent of their regulated tenants during the term. Tenants frequently agree to such increases as they consider it fair that the rent should be increased from time to time. Unless the parties reach agreement in a form prescribed by the RA 1977 (see **7.4.2**), any such increase is irrecoverable from the tenant. This provision is often ignored because landlords and tenants are not aware of it. As counsel for the defendant in a case where the rent, other than a registered rent, has been increased over the years, you should ensure a proper rent agreement has been made between the parties on each occasion the rent was increased. If it has not, the level of rent arrears pleaded by the claimant may be inflated.

As counsel for the defendant, consider your lay client's entitlement, if any, to assistance with payment of rent from the housing authority and/or the Department of Social Security. If the judge is persuaded future arrears are unlikely because of support from local or central government agencies, he or she may be inclined to give your lay client another chance in circumstances where he or she would not otherwise have done so.

7.12.4 CASE 9 CASES

If you are representing the defendant in a claim based upon Case 9 (premises reasonably required for occupation by the landlord or his or her family, see **7.9.4.10**), you should question the claimant very closely on the circumstances under which it has become necessary for him or her, or his or her family, to occupy the premises, as the claim may not be entirely genuine. Disclosure concerning the claimant's financial position is very relevant in such cases, so do not agree to proceed with such a claim unless and until there has been full disclosure. Remember also the greater hardship test, and that it must be reasonable for the court to make an order.

7.12.5 CASE 11 CASES

Provided the claimant can prove each element contained in a Case 11 case (premises required by an owner-occupier, see **7.9.5.3**) there is usually no difficulty.

Sometimes the defendant can only make the claimant prove his or her case. As counsel for the defendant you should ensure the relevant notice has been served, and be satisfied the claimant did in fact live in the premises at some time before the tenancy was granted. If the claimant persuades the court to dispense with the notice requirements, you should insist the court gives its reasons why it has decided so to do.

7.12.6 CASE 19 CASES

Case 19 (mandatory ground for possession against a protected shorthold tenant) frequently causes the claimant problems in respect of the service of the 'appropriate notice' as the provisions are somewhat complex: see **7.9.5.9**. Errors frequently arise where the claimant is seeking to determine the tenancy by relying upon a proviso for re-entry. Always check that the notice has been served at the correct time and gives the correct period of notice.

7.12.7 SUITABLE ALTERNATIVE ACCOMMODATION

7.12.7.1 Order for possession

If the court considers it reasonable to make an order for possession, and the court is further satisfied that suitable alternative accommodation is available for the defendant, or will be available for the defendant when the order takes effect, an order for possession will be made against the defendant: see **7.9.4.1** for this ground.

7.12.7.2 Conditions

It is rare that a claimant can produce a certificate of the housing authority that it will provide the defendant with accommodation, and therefore para. 3 of sch. 15 to the RA 1977 (see sch. 15, part IV, para. 1 at **7.9.4.1**) never has any application in practice. Thus, the claimant will have to show that the defendant will have sufficient security of tenure in the alternative accommodation, and that the alternative accommodation is suitable.

7.12.7.3 Security of tenure

As to security, the simple principle is that the defendant must be provided with security of tenure in the alternative accommodation which is reasonably equivalent to the security which he or she enjoys under the current tenancy. In other words, the security does not have to be precisely the same. There is a *prima facie* presumption that an assured tenancy under the HA 1988 will provide reasonably equivalent security. In practice, provided the defendant is granted an assured tenancy of the alternative accommodation the court will usually be satisfied; it will not insist that another protected tenancy under the RA 1977 be created. Thus, not only does the claimant obtain possession of the current accommodation, he or she weakens the security of tenure of the defendant in the alternative accommodation. There is little a defendant can do to persuade the court a protected tenancy is required. The claimant's big point is that if the defendant behaves, he or she is just as secure under the HA 1988 as he or she is under the RA 1977, and so there is no need for the added security provided by the RA 1977 because, of course, the defendant will behave!

7.12.7.4 Suitability of alternative accommodation

As to suitability, this provides a slightly more fruitful battle ground for the defendant. The RA 1977 describes what is suitable alternative accommodation and reference should be made to substantive provisions: see **7.9.4.1**. In general terms the alternative accommodation does not have to be the same as the defendant's current accommodation, or even nearly the same. Indeed it can be entirely different in extent, location and cost, and still be suitable alternative accommodation. It can even be inferior to the defendant's current accommodation. Again this provides a claimant with an opportunity to make a substantial gain. As counsel for the defendant you should make the most of any interference a move will have with the defendant's employment, or the employment of those living in the current accommodation, and schooling. These are matters which the court considers very important, and quite rightly so.

The crucial question is whether the alternative accommodation is reasonably suitable for the housing needs of the defendant; that is the defendant's need for accommodation in which to live. 'Needs', in this context, does not include the tenant's particular wishes and desires, or particular amenities going beyond his or her housing needs. Thus, a defendant who has enjoyed large accommodation for a number of years can be forced to move to much smaller accommodation, if that smaller accommodation is suitable for his or her housing needs. So, for example, the defendant's inability to store a large library once owned by his or her grandfather in the alternative accommodation will not make the alternative accommodation unsuitable. Large furniture is very frequently an issue in these cases.

7.12.7.5 Reasonableness

However, where claimants often fail on this ground for possession is on the question of whether it is reasonable to make an order for possession. Where the alternative accommodation is inferior, albeit suitable within the meaning of the RA 1977, and the tenant has enjoyed the current accommodation for a long time, the court is often reluctant to force the defendant to move. It is important for counsel for the defendant to make the most of the question of reasonableness; even the defendant's grandfather's library is relevant in this context! There is little prospect of a successful appeal by a claimant against the judge's decision on the question of whether or not it was reasonable to make an order.

7.12.8 REASONABLE TO MAKE AN ORDER

Save in the case of mandatory grounds for possession, the court must consider it reasonable to make an order for possession. Since the HA 1988 came into force, the number of tenancies within the RA 1977 has fallen dramatically, and the majority of those tenants still within the RA 1977 are elderly people living alone.

For reasons that are obvious, the court is often very reluctant to force an elderly tenant to move out of his or her long-term home. Thus the question of whether it is reasonable to make an order has become more and more important, and as stated, counsel for the defendant must make the most of it.

7.12.9 ENFORCING THE ORDER

An order for possession against a regulated tenant is enforced in the same way as in any other possession claim.

EIGHT

SECURE TENANCIES

8.1 Scope

8.1.1 HISTORY

Before 1980 tenants of local authorities and of other providers of public housing had no statutory security of tenure and such tenants had to trust the public body to exercise their powers responsibly. The HA 1980 bestowed on public sector tenants security of tenure similar to that bestowed by the RA 1977 on the tenants of private landlords. This protection was extended to new tenancies and existing tenancies alike.

8.1.2 DEFINITION

A tenancy will be a secure tenancy under HA 1985 (the successor to HA 1980) where:

(a) The dwelling is let as a separate dwelling. This wording is the same as that used in the RA 1977 (see **7.1.1**) and was adopted in the HA 1988 (assured tenancies, see **5.1.2** and **5.1.3**). The purpose of the letting must be residential rather than, e.g., business (see **5.1.3**). The HA 1985, unlike RA 1977 and HA 1988, expressly provides that licences are not excluded from statutory protection (HA 1985, s. 79(3)). However, a licence will be a secure tenancy only if it grants exclusive occupation of a separate dwelling house: see *Westminster City Council v Clarke* [1992] 2 AC 288, HL. In addition, any licence granted as a temporary expedient to a person who entered as a trespasser will not be secure: see HA 1985, s. 79(3), (4).

(b) The landlord is a local authority or one of the other designated public bodies in HA 1985, s. 80(1). If a local authority sells a dwelling house subject to a secure tenancy to a private owner, the tenancy will cease to be secure, though it may become, e.g., an assured tenancy under HA 1988.

(c) The tenant is an individual and occupies the dwelling as his or her only or principal home or, where there are just joint tenants, each is an individual and at least one of them occupies the dwelling house as his or her only or principal home: see HA 1985, ss. 79–81.

Similar wording is used in the HA 1988 but not in the RA 1977. Caution should be exercised therefore when considering Rent Act authorities. A secure tenant may nevertheless occupy as a home two places at the same time. Signs of occupation, such as furniture, together with evidence of an intention to return have been held to be relevant factors when considering which of the two homes is the principal one: *Crawley BC v Sawyer* (1988) 20 HLR 98. If the tenant ceases the necessary occupation, the tenancy will cease to be secure. However, HA 1985, s. 79, provides that a tenancy is a secure tenancy 'at any time' when the landlord and tenant conditions set out in ss. 80 and 81 are satisfied. It appears therefore that a tenant can move in and out of secure status: *Hussey v Camden London Borough Council* (1985) 27 HLR 5, CA.

8.2   Exceptions

Certain tenancies within the above definition are excluded from being secure tenancies. These are set out in HA 1985, sch. 1 and include the following:

(a)   long tenancies, i.e. tenancies for a fixed term exceeding 21 years and others treated as long for this purpose: see HA 1985, sch. 1, para. 1 and s. 115;

(b)   introductory tenancies: see sch. 1, para. 1A and **8.11**;

(c)   tenancies where the landlord (being a local authority or other specified body) is the employer of the tenant and the contract of employment requires the tenant to occupy the dwelling house for the better performance of his or her duties. This head also applies to members of the police force and fire brigade occupying accommodation provided by their employers near the relevant police or fire station. See sch. 1, para. 2;

(d)   tenancies granted pursuant to a local authority's duties to provide temporary accommodation for homeless persons: sch. 1, para. 4;

(e)   tenancies over land held for providing temporary housing accommodation and tenancies granted in various circumstances for this purpose: paras 3, 5, 6, 7;

(f)   tenancies of agricultural holdings and licensed premises: paras 8, 9;

(g)   tenancies granted to students: para. 10;

(h)   tenancies to which the LTA 1954, part II applies (business tenancies): para. 11.

Note that in the HA 1985 there is no exception for high-value dwelling houses or for tenancies at a low or no rent.

8.3   Rent

The HA 1985 imposes no limit on the rent that the landlord may charge nor can the tenant challenge any increase of rent provided that this is permitted by the terms of the tenancy and that the landlord gives notice of increase in accordance with the Act: see HA 1985, ss. 102, 103.

8.4   Implied Terms

8.4.1   LODGERS AND SUBLETTING

It is a term of every secure tenancy that the tenant may take lodgers but will not, without the landlord's written consent, sublet or part with possession of part of the dwelling house. If the tenant parts with possession or sublets the whole of the dwelling house, the tenancy ceases to be secure and cannot subsequently become secure: HA 1985, s. 93.

Consent for this purpose is not to be unreasonably withheld and here the burden of proving that it has not been unreasonably withheld is on the landlord. If unreasonably withheld, the consent is to be treated as given: s. 94. There are detailed provisions (in s. 94) as to the relevant factors to be taken into account on the question of reasonableness, as to the conditions that may be attached to the consent and as to the landlord's duty to give reasons for any refusal or conditions.

8.4.2   ASSIGNMENT

Generally a secure tenancy, whether periodic or for a fixed term, is incapable of being assigned and any purported assignment will vest nothing in the purported assignee: see HA 1985, s. 91.

This rule is subject to three exceptions:

(a)   assignments by way of exchange (see **8.4.3**);

(b)   assignments under property adjustment orders in connection with matrimonial proceedings under Matrimonial Causes Act 1973, s. 24;

(c)   an assignment to a person qualified to be a successor under the statutory succession provisions of the Act: see **8.6**.

8.4.3   ASSIGNMENTS BY WAY OF EXCHANGE

It is a term of every secure tenancy that the tenant may, with the landlord's written consent, assign the tenancy to another secure tenant who satisfies certain conditions or to an assured tenant whose landlord is a registered housing association or charitable housing trust and who satisfies certain conditions: see HA 1985, s. 92 and the conditions set out there.

8.4.4   TENANT'S IMPROVEMENTS

It is a term of every secure tenancy that the tenant will not make any improvements to the dwelling house without the landlord's written consent: HA 1985, s. 97. This provision replaces LTA 1927, s. 19(2) (which makes general provisions in the case of covenants against improvements without consent) in the case of secure tenancies. There are detailed provisions as to the consent required and any conditions attached to the consent, the circumstances in which refusal will be unreasonable, the factors relevant to this question and a definition of 'improvements'.

8.5   Injunctions Against Anti-social Behaviour

In response to complaints about anti-social behaviour on council and other estates, the Housing Act 1996 has given local authority landlords wider powers to stop or prevent such behaviour.

8.5.1   INJUNCTIONS

The High Court and the County Court are empowered to grant injunctions restraining any person who has used or threatened violence which would cause significant harm to a resident or visitor in residential premises subject to a secure or introductory tenancy, from:

(a)   causing nuisance or annoyance to such a resident or visitor or;

(b)   engaging in immoral or illegal use of the premises or;

(c)   entering premises or being in their locality (see HA 1996, s. 152).

8.5.2   POWERS OF ARREST

Further the court may, either in an injunction of the kind just described, or in any other similar injunction against anti-social behaviour sought by specified landlords, including local housing authorities and housing action trusts, attach a power of arrest to any of the provisions in the injunction. A constable may then arrest without warrant any person he or she has reasonable cause to suspect is in breach of any such provision: see HA 1996, ss. 153–157.

8.6   Statutory Succession to Secure Tenancies

8.6.1   SUCCESSION TO PERIODIC TENANCY

Where a secure tenant under a periodic tenancy dies and there is a person qualified (under HA 1985, s. 87) to succeed to the secure tenancy, the tenancy will vest under HA 1985, s. 89, in that person. This may not be the person entitled to the tenancy under the normal rules of testate or intestate succession. A person will be qualified to succeed under HA 1985, s. 89 if three conditions are fulfilled:

(a)   the person is either the tenant's spouse or another member of the tenant's family and, in the latter case, resided with the tenant for the 12 months prior to the tenant's death; and

(b)   the person occupied the dwelling house as his or her only or principal home at the time of the tenant's death; and

(c)   the tenant was not himself or herself a successor under these provisions (only one succession is permitted and that will have been exhausted if the former tenant was himself or herself a successor). See HA 1985, s. 88 for the situations where a tenant is deemed to have been a successor.

'Member of the tenant's family' includes a person living with the tenant as husband and wife and the deceased tenant's homosexual partner: *Fitzpatrick* v *Sterling HA, The Times*, 2 November 1999, HL.

For the meaning of 'resided with', see *Camden LBC* v *Goldenberg* (1996) 28 HLR 727. On occupation 'as his only or principal home', see **8.1.2**.

If there is no one qualified to succeed the tenant, the periodic tenancy will vest in accordance with the normal rules of administration of estates and will, in most cases, cease to be a secure tenancy: HA 1985, s. 89(3), (4).

8.6.2   DEVOLUTION OF FIXED TERM

Where the tenant under a secure tenancy for a term certain dies, there are no statutory succession provisions under HA 1985 and the tenancy will vest in the course of the administration of the tenant's estate. It will then cease to be secure unless either it vests in some one who is qualified to succeed the tenant (under HA 1985, s. 89: see **8.6.1**) when it will be treated as the one permitted statutory succession, or it vests pursuant to an order under the Matrimonial Causes Act 1973: HA 1985, s. 90.

8.7   Security

8.7.1   GENERAL RESTRICTION ON TERMINATION

As with the HA 1988, there is nothing in HA 1985 to prevent the tenant from effectively terminating a secure tenancy by serving a notice to quit if the tenancy is periodic or by exercising a contractual 'break clause' or surrendering the tenancy.

The only way in which the landlord, however, can determine either a periodic secure tenancy or a fixed-term secure tenancy subject to termination by the landlord, is by obtaining a court order for possession. The secure tenancy will then end on the date when the tenant is to give up possession under the terms of the order: see HA 1985, s. 82. Consequently, service of a notice to quit by a landlord in respect of a periodic secure tenancy, whether statutory or not, is of no effect.

8.7.2   FORFEITURE

Where the tenancy reserves a right of re-entry or forfeiture, the court has no power to order possession under the proviso. If satisfied that the landlord has made a valid forfeiture, the court should instead make an order terminating the tenancy on a specified date, after which a periodic tenancy will arise under HA 1985, s. 86 (see **8.7.3**): HA 1985, s. 82.

In order to obtain a termination order of this kind, the landlord must comply with the common law rules relating to forfeiture, such as the need to serve a notice under LPA 1925, s. 146 (see **3.3.3**) and the tenant is entitled to apply for relief against forfeiture in the same way as if the termination proceedings were forfeiture proceedings: HA 1985, s. 86. For the result of a termination order is that the tenant loses the value and security of having a fixed term, becoming a mere periodic tenant.

8.7.3   PERIODIC TENANCY AFTER FIXED TERM ENDS

Where a secure tenancy comes to an end by effluxion of time or on the court making a termination order in pursuance of a proviso for forfeiture (see **8.7.2**), a periodic secure tenancy of the dwelling house arises: HA 1985, s. 86. The terms of this periodic tenancy will be the same as those of the fixed-term tenancy that preceded it so far as these are compatible with a periodic tenancy and do not include any proviso for forfeiture: s. 86(2). The periods of this tenancy are to be the same as those for which rent was last payable under the terms of the fixed-term tenancy.

8.7.4   POSSESSION ORDER

For a practical guide to bringing possession proceedings against a secure tenant, see **8.12**.

8.7.4.1   Service of notice of intention to seek possession
To obtain a possession order the landlord must first serve a notice in prescribed form on the tenant, specifying and giving particulars of the statutory grounds on which the landlord will ask the court to make an order for possession or termination of the tenancy: HA 1985, s. 83, as amended by HA 1996, s. 147.

8.7.4 2   Ground 2 specified
Where the tenancy is periodic and the specified grounds include Ground 2 (nuisance or other anti-social behaviour), the notice must state that possession proceedings may be begun immediately and must specify the date sought by the landlord for the tenant to give up possession: HA 1985, s. 83(3). This date must be no earlier than that on which the periodic tenancy could be determined by notice to quit served on the same day: s. 83(5). The notice will cease to be in force 12 months after the specified date: s. 83(3).

8.7.4.3   Ground 2 not specified
Where the tenancy is periodic but Ground 2 is not one of the grounds specified, the notice must specify the date after which possession proceedings can be started. This date must be no earlier than that on which the periodic tenancy could be determined by a notice to quit served on the same day: HA 1985, s. 83(5).

The landlord must then commence possession proceedings after the date specified in the notice. Again the notice will cease to be in force 12 months after the specified date: s. 83(4).

8.7.4.4   Ground 2A specified
Where the s. 83 notice specifies Ground 2A (domestic violence) and the partner who has left the dwelling house is not a tenant of the dwelling house, there is an additional requirement that the landlord should serve notice or at least take all reasonable steps to serve notice on the partner who has left, informing the partner of the possession proceedings and the ground(s) on which they have been brought: s. 83A. If Ground 2

is also specified in the s. 83 notice, the court has a discretion to dispense with this requirement as to service, where this would be just and equitable: s. 83(5).

8.8 Grounds for Possession

8.8.1 GENERAL

The grounds for possession in HA 1985, sch. 2 fall into three categories:

(a) Grounds 1 to 8, where in addition to the ground being made out, the court must be satisfied that it is reasonable to make a possession order;

(b) Grounds 9 to 11 where, in addition to the ground being made out, the court must be satisfied that suitable alternative accommodation will be available for the tenant; and

(c) Grounds 12 to 16, where, in addition to the ground being made out, the court must be satisfied both that it is reasonable to make an order and that suitable alternative accommodation will be available for the tenant.

The grounds which have been amended and added to by HA 1996 are outlined below.

8.8.2 GROUNDS ON WHICH COURT MAY ORDER POSSESSION IF IT CONSIDERS IT REASONABLE

If the court considers it reasonable, it may order possession on one of the grounds set out in **8.8.2.1** to **8.8.2.9**.

8.8.2.1 Ground 1: rent arrears
Rent lawfully due from the tenant has not been paid or an obligation of the tenancy has been broken or not performed.

8.8.2.2 Ground 2: nuisance etc.
The tenant or a person residing in or visiting the dwelling house has been either:

(a) causing nuisance or annoyance to some one residing, visiting or otherwise engaging in a lawful activity in the locality; or

(b) convicted of:

(i) using the dwelling house or allowing its use for immoral or illegal purposes; or

(ii) an arrestable offence committed in, or in the locality of, the dwelling house.

8.8.2.3 Ground 2A: domestic violence
The dwelling house was occupied by a married couple or a couple living together as husband and wife and one partner has left and is unlikely to return because of violence or threats of violence by the other, either to that partner or to a member of that partner's family.

8.8.2.4 Ground 3: condition of premises
The condition of the dwelling house has deteriorated due to acts of waste or neglect by the tenant or a person residing in the dwelling house. Where that person is a lodger or sub-tenant it must also be the case that the tenant has not taken all reasonable steps to remove the lodger or sub-tenant.

8.8.2.5 Ground 4: condition of furniture
The condition of the landlord's furniture has deteriorated due to ill-treatment by the tenant or a person residing in the dwelling house. Again it must be the case that the

tenant has not taken all reasonable steps to remove the lodger or sub-tenant if one of these is responsible for the damage.

8.8.2.6   Ground 5: false statement
The landlord was induced to grant the tenancy by a false statement made knowingly or recklessly by the tenant or by a person at the tenant's instigation. This ground is only available against the original tenant.

8.8.2.7   Ground 6: exchange
The tenancy was assigned to the tenant by way of exchange under HA 1985, s. 92 (see **8.4.3**) and a premium was paid in connection with the assignment.

8.8.2.8   Ground 7: employment — tenant's conduct
This ground applies where:

(a)   the dwelling house forms part of a building used mainly for purposes other than housing; and

(b)   the tenancy was granted in consequence of the tenant's employment by the landlord; and

(c)   the tenant has been guilty of conduct making it inappropriate for him or her to stay in the dwelling house in view of the purpose for which the building is used.

8.8.2.9   Ground 8: completion of works
Where the tenant accepted the tenancy of the dwelling house while work was being carried out to a previous dwelling house of which he or she had a secure tenancy and on the understanding that on completion of the work, the tenant would give up occupation of this dwelling house, and the works have been completed so that the previous dwelling house is now available.

8.8.3   GROUNDS ON WHICH THE COURT MAY ORDER POSSESSION IF SUITABLE ALTERNATIVE ACCOMMODATION IS AVAILABLE

If suitable alternative accommodation is available, the court may order possession on one of the grounds set out in **8.8.3.1** to **8.8.3.4**.

8.8.3.1   Ground 9: overcrowding
Where the dwelling house is overcrowded in such circumstances that the occupier is guilty of an offence.

8.8.3.2   Ground 10: demolition etc.
The landlord intends, within a reasonable time of obtaining possession of the dwelling house, to demolish, reconstruct or carry out work to the building comprising the dwelling house and cannot reasonably do so without obtaining possession of the dwelling house.

8.8.3.3   Ground 10A: redevelopment
The dwelling house, or part of it, is in an area subject to a statutory redevelopment scheme and the landlord intends, within a reasonable time of obtaining possession, to dispose of the dwelling house, or part of it, under the scheme.

8.8.3.4   Ground 11: charity
The landlord is a charity and the tenant's continued occupation of the dwelling house would conflict with the objects of the charity.

8.8.4   GROUNDS ON WHICH THE COURT MAY ORDER POSSESSION IF IT CONSIDERS IT REASONABLE AND SUITABLE ALTERNATIVE ACCOMMODATION IS AVAILABLE

If the court considers it reasonable and suitable alternative accommodation is available, it may order possession on one of the grounds set out in **8.8.4.1** to **8.8.4.5**.

8.8.4.1   Ground 12: employment

The dwelling house forms part of a building held by the landlord mainly for non-housing purposes and:

(a)   the letting to the tenant was in consequence of his or her employment by the landlord or another specified body; and

(b)   that employment has now ceased; and

(c)   the landlord reasonable requires the dwelling house for another employee of the landlord or of another specified body.

8.8.4.2   Ground 13: premises adapted for disabled

The dwelling house has special features designed to make it suitable for occupation by a physically disabled person, the present tenant is not physically disabled and the landlord wants the house for occupation by a physically disabled person.

8.8.4.3   Ground 14: special housing needs

The landlord is a housing association or housing trust which lets dwelling houses only for occupation by persons with special housing needs and the present tenant either:

(a)   is not such a person; or

(b)   has been offered a secure tenancy of other premises;

and the landlord requires the dwelling house for occupation by another person with special housing needs.

8.8.4.4   Ground 15: special needs

The dwelling house is one of a group which the landlord normally lets to persons with special needs and, close to the group, there is a social service or special facility to assist those special needs, the present occupier is not a person with special needs and the landlord requires the dwelling house for a person with those special needs.

8.8.4.5   Ground 16: succession — size of premises

The dwelling house is larger than the tenant reasonably requires and:

(a)   the tenant is a member of the original tenant's family other than the tenant's spouse and succeeded to the tenancy under the statutory succession provisions (HA 1985, s. 89); and

(b)   the notice of possession proceedings (under HA 1985, s. 83) was served not less than six months nor more than 12 months after the previous tenant's death.

In deciding whether it is reasonable to make an order under this ground, the court is to take into account, *inter alia*:

(a)   the age of the tenant,

(b)   the period he has occupied the dwelling house as his only or principal home, and

(c)   any financial or other support given by him to the previous tenant.

8.8.4.6   Suitable alternative accommodation

Part IV of sch. 2 contains detailed provisions for determining whether alternative accommodation is suitable.

8.9   Postponement or Suspension of Possession Order

8.9.1   ORDER ON MANDATORY GROUND

Where the court makes an order under any of the above grounds in part II of sch. 2 the court has no jurisdiction to postpone the giving up of possession for more than 14 days or, in cases of exceptional hardship, for more than a maximum of six weeks from the date of the order: see HA 1980, s. 89 and **20.6**.

8.9.2 ORDER ON DISCRETIONARY GROUND

Where, however, the order is made under one of the discretionary grounds in parts I or III of sch. 2 where the court must be satisfied that it is reasonable to make an order, the court has power to adjourn the proceedings or, on making a possession order, stay or suspend execution of the order or postpone the date of possession: HA 1985, s. 85. These powers, as well as the conditions that the court should attach to them and their extension in the case of the matrimonial home, are the same as those given to the court in the case of assured tenancies by HA 1988, s. 9: see **5.10.2**, **5.10.3**.

8.10 Sub-tenants

The general common law rule that on the termination of a tenancy any sub-tenancy will also automatically end, applies on the termination of a secure tenancy. The HA 1985 contains no equivalent to HA 1988, s. 18 (see **5.12**). Where, however, the head tenant surrendered his own secure tenancy to a local authority, the former sub-tenant who had a tenancy protected under the RA 1977 against his former landlord, became a direct tenant under a secure tenancy of the local authority: *Basingstoke and Deane BC v Paice* [1995] 27 HLR 433, CA.

8.11 Introductory Tenancies

8.11.1 SCOPE

Any local housing authority or housing action trust may elect to operate an introductory tenancy regime. Once such an election has been made, any periodic tenancy or licence (other than one granted as a temporary expedient to a trespasser (which under HA 1985, s. 79(4) cannot be a secure tenancy at all): see HA 1996, s. 126) granted by the authority or trust, will automatically be an introductory one unless it is granted to a person who is already a secure tenant or an assured tenant of a registered social landlord, whether the new tenancy is of the same or another dwelling house: HA 1996, s. 124. A tenancy will remain an introductory one until the end of the trial period which, in most cases, will be one year from the date of grant: HA 1996, s. 125.

8.11.2 ASSIGNMENT

An introductory tenancy is not capable of being assigned except where:

(a) the assignment is in pursuance of an order made under one of three statutes adjusting property rights in the course of matrimonial proceedings or ordering financial relief against parents; or

(b) the assignment is to a potential successor to the introductory tenancy (see **8.11.3**): HA 1996, s. 134.

8.11.3 SUCCESSION ON DEATH

Where the tenant under an introductory tenancy dies, the tenant's spouse or a member of the tenant's family may succeed to the introductory tenancy if that person satisfied the statutory conditions for qualification which are very similar to those for full secure tenants in HA 1985, ss. 87–89 (see **8.6**). If there is no one qualified to succeed, the tenancy will cease to be introductory unless, on the death, it vests in circumstances amounting to an assignment within **8.11.2**.

8.11.4 SECURITY

8.11.4.1 Possession order
The only way in which the landlord may determine an introductory tenancy is by obtaining a court order for possession and the tenancy will end on the date when the

tenant is to give up possession under the court order: HA 1996, s. 127. Provided that the landlord complies with the statutory procedure, the court must make an order: the landlord does not have to prove grounds for possession or that it is reasonable to make an order, nor does the court have any discretion. If the trial period of one year comes to an end after the landlord has commenced possession proceedings, the tenancy will not become secure but remains an introductory one until the proceedings are determined: HA 1996, s. 130.

8.11.4.2 Notice of proceedings

Before commencing possession proceedings the landlord must serve a notice which:

(i) states the landlord's intention to seek a possession order from the court and the landlord's reasons for seeking an order; and

(ii) specifies a date after which the landlord may begin the possession proceedings: this date must not be earlier than the earliest date on which the tenancy could be determined at common law by a notice to quit served on the same date as the notice of proceedings; and

(iii) informs the tenant, first, of his or her right within 14 days of service of the notice of proceedings, to seek a review of the landlord's decision to seek possession and, secondly, of where he or she can obtain help or advice about the notice: HA 1996, ss. 128, 129.

The court will not hear the possession proceedings unless this notice has been served and the proceedings started after the date specified in the notice.

8.11.4.3 Review of decision to seek possession

Where the tenant seeks a review of the landlord's decision to seek possession, the landlord must, before the date specified in the notice of proceedings, carry out the review and notify the tenant of its reviewed decision and, if that is to confirm its original decision, the reasons for this: HA 1996, s. 129.

8.12 Possession Claim Against a Secure Tenant

8.12.1 ACTING FOR THE CLAIMANT

It is unlikely that you will be instructed on behalf of a claimant in such a case unless your chambers does a lot of work for local authorities or housing associations. Local authorities and housing association landlords usually get the procedure right, as they are involved in a great many such claims, and therefore if you are instructed on behalf of the claimant, it is likely you will be well briefed.

8.12.2 ACTING FOR THE DEFENDANT

8.12.2.1 Errors in procedure

The contrary is often the case if instructed on behalf of the defendant. If you are instructed for the defendant, ensure the correct procedure has been followed, as the case load of local authorities and housing associations may have lead to a minor error. Such an error will usually only result in delay rather than a 'knock-out blow', but delay is an advantage to the person in occupation.

8.12.2.2 Rent arrears

Your main task, assuming there are arrears of rent (the usual ground upon which possession is sought), will be to speak to the representative of the local authority or housing association (often not a lawyer) and try and reach agreement for the discharge of any rent arrears. Such landlords are frequently sympathetic save where it is alleged the defendant has been causing a nuisance to other tenants or has otherwise been acting in an anti-social manner.

If a deal is done, this must be explained to the judge. Judges sometimes take a harsher view of rent arrears than local authorities or housing associations, and express surprise or even reluctance to make the order agreed. At the end of the day, however, there is little the judge can do if the local authority or housing association is prepared to accept the offer made by the defendant.

8.12.2.3 Anti-social behaviour

If the claim against the defendant is based upon anti-social behaviour, expect a very different attitude from the claimant. Those concerned on behalf of local authorities and housing associations often have a certain ideology which sees injustice in a poor person being thrown out of their home, but see good sense in someone guilty of, say, racial harassment of a neighbour, being evicted.

If seeking to defend such a claim offer undertakings, which are neutral as to guilt, in order to avoid a contested hearing which will only work to worsen the situation. If that does not work, it is simply a matter of testing the claimant's evidence.

The best line to take is that the claimant's witnesses are exaggerating, if those are your instructions. Explain to the judge that neighbours, particularly on crowded estates, fall out over small things: a radio being played too loudly, a dog barking, or a child crying. These minor complaints get inflated, leading to unwarranted complaints. Skilful cross examination, and a realistic speech, may be enough to convince the judge that it is not appropriate to make an order for possession, or at least not an immediate order.

Even if the claimant's case is made out, urge the judge to make a suspended order for possession, and offer undertakings as to the future behaviour of your lay client. That should be sufficient to keep your lay client in his or her home provided the anti-social behaviour is not too gross, and it is a 'first offence'. Do not forget to explain to your lay client what the nature of an undertaking is, and what might happen to him or her if the undertaking is broken.

NINE

RESTRICTED CONTRACTS

9.1   Scope

A restricted contract is a contract granting the right to occupy a dwelling house as a residence where the rent includes payment for the use of furniture or for services: RA 1977, s. 19. 'Contract' here includes a licence as well as a tenancy provided that the contract bestows the right to exclusive occupation: see *Luganda* v *Service Hotels* [1969] 2 Ch 209, CA.

Two types of tenancy which do not fall within this definition are also restricted contracts:

(a)   a tenancy which is subject to the resident landlord exception (in RA 1977, s. 12: see **7.2.1**) but would otherwise be a protected tenancy under RA 1977: see RA 1977, s. 20; and

(b)   a tenancy where, under the terms of the contract, the tenant shares living accommodation, e.g. a bedroom or sitting room (see **7.1.3.1**) with the landlord, but where the tenancy would otherwise be a protected tenancy under RA 1977: see RA 1977, s. 21.

No interest granted after 15 January 1989 can be a restricted contract unless granted pursuant to a contract entered into before that date.

9.2   Exceptions

The following contracts cannot be restricted contracts (RA 1977, s. 19):

(a)   a contract which grants the right to occupy the dwelling house for a holiday;

(b)   a contract where the landlord is exempt, e.g. the Crown or a local authority;

(c)   a contract containing terms that the landlord should supply a substantial amount of food or meals;

(d)   a contract which creates a protected tenancy under the RA 1977;

(e)   a contract which creates an agricultural occupancy under the R(Ag) Act 1976;

(f)   a contract to occupy a dwelling house the former rateable value of which exceeds the statutory limit in RA 1977, s. 19(4).

9.3   Rent

Either landlord or tenant may, at any time, apply to the Rent Tribunal (under RA 1977, s. 77) to register a 'reasonable' rent for the dwelling house and the landlord may not lawfully demand rent at a higher rate than that registered even if the contractual rent exceeds the registered rent. The RA 1977 prescribes no formula to be followed but merely directs the Rent Tribunal to register an amount that it may, 'in all the circumstances, think reasonable': RA 1977, s. 78(2).

It is a criminal offence to require the payment of a premium in connection with the grant of rights under a restricted contract: RA 1977, s. 122.

9.4 Security

Security depends on the nature of and the date of creation of the restricted contract.

9.4.1 PERIODIC CONTRACTS ENTERED INTO BEFORE 28 NOVEMBER 1980

In most cases RA 1977 automatically postpones for six months the operation of any notice to quit served, often by way of reprisal, where the tenant has referred the restricted contract to a Rent Tribunal for registration of the rent: RA 1977, ss. 102A, 103. This postponement prolongs the life of the restricted contract.

Further, after service of a notice to quit, the tenant may apply to the Rent Tribunal for an extension or further extension (for up to six months at a time) of the notice to quit: RA 1977, s. 104.

The restricted contract will thus continue until the Rent Tribunal refuses any further extension. When, however, an extension or further extension is refused so that the notice to quit expires, there is no further security of tenure and the landlord is entitled to possession without the need to prove grounds for possession or that it is reasonable to make an order. These provisions do not apply where:

(a) the dwelling house is overcrowded within the statutory definition: see RA 1977, s. 101; or

(b) the landlord formerly occupied the dwelling house as his or her residence and now requires it as a residence for himself or herself or for a member of his or her family who resided with him or her when he or she last occupied the house as his or her residence: RA 1977, s. 105.

9.4.2 FIXED-TERM CONTRACTS ENTERED INTO BEFORE 28 NOVEMBER 1980

A restricted contract granted for a fixed term which is, of course, not determined by a notice to quit, enjoys no security under these provisions.

9.4.3 PERIODIC AND FIXED-TERM CONTRACTS ENTERED INTO ON OR AFTER 28 NOVEMBER 1980

The Rent Tribunal's power of extending notices to quit no longer applies. The landlord's common law rights of determining the contract and of obtaining possession are thus unaffected save that the court, on making a possession order, has, under RA 1977, s. 106A, a discretionary power to suspend execution of the order for up to three months (cf. the general rule that the execution of a possession order cannot be suspended for more than six weeks: HA 1980, s. 89 (see **20.6**)).

TEN

LANDLORD AND TENANT ACT 1954, PART I: LONG RESIDENTIAL TENANCIES

10.1 Scope

This Act applied to certain residential tenancies granted before or pursuant to a contract made before 15 January 1989 (LTA 1954, part I, s. 2; HA 1988, s. 34). The tenancy had to be of a dwelling house for a term exceeding 21 years (a 'long tenancy': LTA 1954, part I, s. 2(4)) at a low rent, i.e. a rent less than two-thirds of the rateable value of the dwelling house on a certain date: LTA 1954, part I, s. 2(5) where:

(a) the circumstances were such that, but for the low rent, the tenancy would have been a protected tenancy under RA 1977; thus the dwelling house must have had a rateable value or rent within the limits of the RA 1977 (see RA 1977, s. 4 as amended by RR(H)R 1990, and see **7.1**), and did not fall within any of the exceptions to Rent Act protection set out in **7.2**; and

(b) the tenant occupied the dwelling house as his or her residence: LTA 1954, part I, s. 2(1).

10.2 Rent

The contractual rent continued to be payable until and unless the long tenancy was replaced by a statutory tenancy (see **10.3**). The landlord and tenant could then agree on a new rent or either of them could apply to the Rent Officer to register a fair rent. The landlord could then, by notice, increase the rent up to the registered rent.

10.3 Security

10.3.1 CONTINUATION

At the expiry of the fixed term, provided that the tenant still occupied the dwelling house as his or her residence, a continuation tenancy arose and continued as an estate in land on broadly the same terms as before the expiry of the fixed term until determined by the landlord or by the tenant: LTA 1954, part I, s. 3. The Act restricted the landlord's right to exercise any right of forfeiture or re-entry reserved by the lease except in respect of terms as to:

(a) payment of rent or rates;

(b) insuring the premises; and

(c) restricting the use of the premises for illegal or immoral purposes.

10.3.2 DETERMINATION

The landlord had first to serve a statutory notice of termination of between six and 12 months' duration (LTA 1954, part I, s. 4) and could then determine the continuation tenancy in one of two ways:

(a) by obtaining a possession order on establishing one of the statutory grounds for possession. For these see LTA 1954, part I, s. 12 — intention of certain landlords to demolish or reconstruct (for these landlords see LRA 1967, ss. 28 and 38) and sch. 3 — grounds corresponding roughly to the discretionary cases in sch. 15 part I to the RA 1977 (see **7.9.4**); or

(b) by 'converting' the continuation tenancy into a statutory tenancy under the RA 1977 (see **7.7**). The terms of the statutory tenancy, if not agreed by the parties were, except for the amount of the rent (see **10.2**), to be determined by the court. The rules prescribed for obtaining the court's settlement of the terms were detailed and imposed strict time limits: LTA 1954, part I, ss. 6–10.

The tenant could determine the continuation tenancy simply by giving to the landlord one month's written notice: LTA 1954, part I, s. 5.

10.4 Change in Protection after 15 January 1999

As from 15 January 1999 the LTA 1954 ceased to apply to long tenancies granted before 15 January 1989 and still in existence on the later date. Instead transitional provisions in the LGHA 1989, s. 186 and sch. 10 now, as from 15 January 1999, apply to any such tenancies a scheme very similar to that under the LTA 1954, part I, the main difference being that any tenancy granted following a statutory notice of termination will be a periodic assured tenancy under HA 1988, rather than a statutory tenancy under RA 1977. For an outline of the scheme, see **Chapter 11**. The only tenancies governed by the 1954 Act after 15 January 1999 will be those which have already expired but are continued by virtue of the LTA 1954, s. 3 and still fulfil the qualifying condition: LGHA 1989, sch. 10, para. 3(2).

ELEVEN

LOCAL GOVERNMENT AND HOUSING ACT 1989: LONG RESIDENTIAL TENANCIES

11.1 Scope

The LGHA 1989, s. 186 and sch. 10, create a scheme which applies to residential tenancies satisfying approximately the same conditions as tenancies within the LTA 1954, part I, i.e., long tenancies of dwelling houses at low rents (see **10.1**) but which were granted on or after 1 April 1990 and would, but for the low rent, have been assured tenancies under the HA 1988. 'Low rent' here means, in most cases, £1,000 a year or less if the dwelling house is in Greater London, and £250 a year or less if it is elsewhere: see RR(H)R 1990, sch., para. 33 for the full definition. The scheme closely resembles that formerly provided by the LTA 1954, part I for long tenancies granted before 15 January 1989 (see **Chapter 10**) and is considered here only in brief outline.

The LGHA 1989 scheme appears only to apply to tenancies granted on or after 1 April 1990, thus apparently leaving most tenancies granted after 15 January 1989, but before 1 April 1990, without the benefit of protection under either the LTA 1954, part I or the LGHA 1989 scheme: see LGHA 1989, s. 186(2).

11.2 Rent

The contractual rent continues to be payable until the expiry of the fixed term. During the continuation tenancy that follows (see **11.3**) the landlord may have an interim rent determined and, if after the landlord determines the continuation tenancy, an assured tenancy under HA 1988 is granted (see **11.3**), the landlord may, in default of agreement, have the rent payable under the assured tenancy determined by a rent assessment committee.

11.3 Security

11.3.1 CONTINUATION

As under the LTA 1954, part I, at the expiry of the fixed term, provided that the tenant still occupies the dwelling house as his or her residence, a continuation tenancy arises and continues until determined by notice served by the tenant or by the landlord.

11.3.2 DETERMINATION

On serving a statutory notice of termination, the landlord may either:

    (a)   obtain a possession order if he or she can establish one of the statutory grounds for possession which are broadly similar to those under LTA 1954, part I (landlord's intention to demolish or reconstruct and most of the discretionary grounds for possession in HA 1988 in respect of assured tenancies); or

(b)   convert the continuation tenancy into an assured periodic tenancy under the HA 1988.

The tenant may determine the continuation tenancy simply by giving to the landlord one month's written notice.

TWELVE

RENT (AGRICULTURE) ACT 1976: PROTECTED OCCUPANCIES OF TIED AGRICULTURAL ACCOMMODATION

12.1   Scope

The Rent (Agriculture) Act 1976 applies in general only to rights to occupy granted before, or pursuant to a contract made before, 15 January 1989: HA 1988, s. 34(4). This subsection provides cases where rights granted after 15 January 1989 will still be protected under R (Ag) Act 1976: see **13.1**. In general, rights to occupy tied agricultural accommodation granted on or after that date may be assured agricultural occupancies under the HA 1988: see **Chapter 13**.

A protected occupancy under the R (Ag) Act 1976 is one where a qualifying worker occupies a dwelling house in qualifying ownership under a relevant tenancy or licence: s. 2(1).

Qualifying worker: one who has worked full time in agriculture for not less than 91 out of the last 104 weeks: R (Ag) Act 1976, sch. 3, part I.

Qualifying ownership: where the occupier of the dwelling house is employed in agriculture and the employer either owns the dwelling house or has arranged with the owner for it to be used as housing accommodation for the employer's agricultural employees: R (Ag) Act 1976, sch. 3, part I.

Relevant licence: one under which a person has exclusive occupation of a dwelling house as a separate dwelling and which, had it been a tenancy, would have been a protected tenancy under the RA 1977 but for a low rent or certain other excluding factors: a relevant tenancy is, correspondingly, one where a dwelling house is let as a separate dwelling and would be a protected tenancy but for a low rent or certain other excluding factors: R (Ag) Act 1976, sch. 2.

12.2   Rent

During the continuance of the contract the rent, normally a low one, is unaffected by the statute. When, however, the protected occupancy becomes a statutory tenancy (see **12.3.1**) then the parties may agree on a rent but, if none is agreed, no rent will be payable until the landlord serves a notice of increase of rent up to either the registered rent, if a rent is registered for the dwelling house, or if none is, then up to one and a half times the rateable value of the dwelling house: R (Ag) Act 1976, ss. 11, 12 and 14. If no rent is registered, either landlord or tenant may apply to have a fair rent registered under the same system that applies to protected tenancies under the RA 1977, here with certain modifications: R (Ag) Act 1976, s. 13.

12.3   Security

12.3.1   STATUTORY TENANCY

On determination of the protected occupancy, whether tenancy or licence, the occupier will become a statutory tenant on broadly the same terms as those of the previous protected occupancy unless his landlord is an exempt one, e.g. the Crown or a local authority: R (Ag) Act 1976, ss. 4, 5 and 10, and sch. 5. On the death of a protected occupier or statutory tenant, his or her spouse or a member of his or her family may, if resident, 'inherit' the protected occupancy or statutory tenancy and become a protected occupier or statutory tenant by succession: R (Ag) Act 1976, ss. 3 and 4.

12.3.2   POSSESSION

The owner can recover possession against a protected occupier or statutory tenant only on proof of one or more of the statutory grounds for possession in the R (Ag) Act 1976, s. 6 and sch. 4. They are of two types: discretionary grounds, where the court must be satisfied that it is reasonable to make an order (these resemble closely the discretionary grounds available against tenants protected under the RA 1977: **7.9.4**), and three mandatory grounds where there is no requirement of reasonableness (landlord's requirement, notified to the occupier at the start of the contract, of the dwelling house as a residence or a retirement home, or cases where the dwelling house is overcrowded). The court has wide powers, under R (Ag) Act 1976, s. 7 to adjourn the proceedings or suspend the execution of any possession order made on any of the discretionary grounds: an exception to the general rule in HA 1980, s. 89 (six weeks maximum).

12.3.3   REHOUSING

As an alternative to a possession order, the owner may be able to procure the rehousing of a protected occupier or statutory tenant by the local housing authority, if the owner cannot himself or herself provide alternative accommodation but can show that the dwelling house is needed for another agricultural employee and that it is in the interests of efficient agriculture for the present occupier to be rehoused: R (Ag) Act 1976, ss. 27 and 28.

12.3.4   SUB-TENANTS

A sub-tenant who is a protected occupier or statutory tenant under the R (Ag) Act 1976 may, in some circumstances, claim the protection of that Act against a superior landlord on the determination of his own landlord's tenancy: R (Ag) Act 1976, s. 9. This is an exception to the common law rule that on the determination of a tenancy, any sub-tenancy falls in with it.

THIRTEEN

HOUSING ACT 1988: ASSURED AGRICULTURAL OCCUPANCIES (AAO)

13.1   Scope

A licence to occupy or tenancy of tied agricultural accommodation granted on or after 15 January 1989 may be an assured agricultural occupancy (AAO) although the transitional provisions in the HA 1988, s. 34 prevent licences and tenancies granted after 15 January 1989 from being AAOs if:

(a)   the right was granted pursuant to a contract made before 15 January 1989; or

(b)   it was granted to a previous protected occupier or statutory tenant under the R (Ag) Act 1976 by his or her previous landlord or licensor.

An AAO is a licence or tenancy of a dwelling house where the agricultural worker condition is fulfilled, i.e. that a qualifying worker (which has the same meaning as in the R (Ag) Act 1976: see **12.1**) occupies a dwelling house in qualifying ownership (also with the same meaning as under the R (Ag) Act 1976: **12.1**): HA 1988, s. 24(1), sch. 3. Only a tenancy or licence which:

(a)   is an assured tenancy other than an assured shorthold tenancy, or

(b)   only fails to fall within (a) because of its low rent or because it is comprised in an agricultural holding, or

(c)   is a licence conferring exclusive occupation which, if a tenancy, would fall within (a) or (b) above,

is qualified to be an AAO: HA 1988, s. 24(2).

Tenancies of agricultural holdings within the Agricultural Holdings Act 1986 and farm business tenancies within the Agricultural Tenancies Act 1995 cannot be AAOs: HA 1988, s. 24(2A) inserted by HA 1996, s. 103(3).

13.2   Rent

An AAO is, for most purposes, to be treated under the HA 1988 as an assured tenancy: s. 24(3). Where an AAO is periodic then, as in the case of an assured tenancy, the landlord may serve notice to increase the rent and the occupier may require the Rent Assessment Committee to determine the rent. See HA 1988, ss. 13, 14 and 24(4) and **5.5**.

13.3   Security

If the AAO is one for a fixed term then, at its expiry, the statutory periodic tenancy that arises under the HA 1988, s. 5 (see **5.7.2**) is to be an AAO so long as the agricultural worker condition is satisfied: HA 1988, s. 25(1)(a). The rules governing the landlord's rights to possession are the same as those for other assured tenants (see **5.8**), subject to the minor modifications in HA 1988, s. 25.

The right of a landlord of a protected occupier under the R (Ag) Act 1976, s. 27 to require the local housing authority to rehouse a protected occupier or statutory tenant (see **12.3.3**) applies also to the landlord of an occupier under an AAO: HA 1988, s. 26.

FOURTEEN

HOUSING ACT 1985: RIGHT TO BUY

14.1 Scope

Part V of the HA 1985 entitles a tenant who has a secure tenancy of a dwelling house (see **8.1.1**) and who has been in occupation of it for at least two years, to acquire the freehold or a long lease (maximum 125 years) of the dwelling house depending on whether the dwelling house is a house or flat and also on the nature and length of the landlord's interest in the dwelling house: HA 1985, ss. 118, 119 and 139, sch. 6, para. 12. There are some secure tenancies which are excepted from the right to buy provisions altogether: see HA 1985, s. 120, sch. 5, and some cases in which a particular secure tenant may not exercise the right to buy: see HA 1985, s. 121.

14.2 Price

The purchasing tenant, whether acquiring the freehold or a long lease, is to pay the market value of the dwelling house on a vacant possession basis as determined by the district valuer who is to make certain statutory assumptions and disregards: HA 1985, s. 127. The purchasing tenant is entitled, however, to a discount of an amount varying between 32 per cent and 60 per cent of the market value in the case of a house and between 44 per cent and 70 per cent of the market value in the case of a flat, in both cases depending on the length of time he or she has been a secure tenant. The purchasing tenant formerly had a right to a mortgage on the security of the dwelling house in order to help him or her pay the purchase price. The amount of the mortgage was limited by the size of the tenant's available annual income: HA 1985, s. 133. This right has been abolished with effect from 11 October 1993 and has been replaced with the right to acquire the dwelling house on rent to mortgage terms: HA 1985, s. 143 as substituted by LRHUDA 1993, s. 108.

FIFTEEN

LEASEHOLD REFORM ACT 1967: LEASEHOLD ENFRANCHISEMENT OF HOUSES

15.1 Scope

The 1967 Act, which has been amended by LRHUDA 1993 and by HA 1996, chapter III, applies to tenancies of houses whose values do not exceed certain statutory limits, but not of flats, granted by private landlords. It gives the right to a tenant who occupies the house as his or her residence to acquire the freehold or an extended lease (usually a term of 50 years) of the house when the following conditions are satisfied:

(a) The tenancy is a long one, i.e. for a term exceeding 21 years.

(b) The tenancy is at a low rent, i.e. where the tenancy was granted or contracted for before 1 April 1990, a rent less than two-thirds of the rateable value of the house on a certain day and where it was granted on or after 1 April 1990, the annual rent does not exceed £1,000 if the house is in Greater London or £250 if it is elsewhere. Note that even if the tenancy fails the low rent test, provided that the term exceeds 35 years or fulfils certain other conditions, the tenant has the same right to acquire the freehold (though not an extended lease) as if the tenancy had been at a low rent: LRA 1967, s. 1AA inserted by HA 1996, s. 106, sch. 9, para. 1.

(c) In the case of a tenancy:

    (i) *either* granted before 1 April 1990 *or* granted after that date pursuant to a contract made before then provided that the house had a rateable value on 31 March 1990, then the rateable value of the house did not exceed the statutory limit.

    (ii) granted on or after 1 April 1990 and not falling within (i) above, then the premium payable on the grant of the tenancy does not exceed an amount calculated in accordance with a complicated formula.

(d) The tenant has occupied the house as his residence for at least three years.

LRA 1967, ss. 1, 3 and 4 as amended by RR(H)R 1990, sch., paras 5–8.

If the tenancy does not satisfy condition (b) above, it may, nevertheless, be treated as one at a low rent if it satisfies the less stringent additional 'low rent' test introduced with effect from 1 November 1993 by LRA 1967, ss. 1A(2) and 4A (added by LRHUDA 1993, ss. 63 and 65). If the tenancy fails to satisfy condition (c) above, the tenant is, with effect from 1 November 1993, given the same right to acquire the freehold as if condition (c) were satisfied: LRA 1967, s. 1A(1) (added by LRHUDA 1993, s. 63). Both these relaxations apply only to the right to acquire the freehold and not to the right to an extended lease.

There are many special cases where, although the tenancy satisfies the above conditions, the right to acquire the freehold or an extended lease is nevertheless excluded altogether, postponed, determined or restricted. The reasons range from the landlord's identity or needs for the house to the tenant's behaviour or the type of lease.

15.2   Price

The price for the freehold is to be the open market value of the house and premises on the basis that they are being sold subject to the tenancy (not their value with vacant possession) and subject to a number of statutory assumptions: LRA 1967, s. 9. Different statutory assumptions more favourable to the landlord are to be made and compensation is to be payable in the case of tenancies which do not satisfy conditions (b) and (c) in **15.1**, and were brought within the right to acquire the freehold under the provisions of LRHUDA 1993, referred to in **15.1**: LRA 1967, s. 9(1A), as added by LRHUDA 1993, s. 66. An extended lease is to be granted at a ground rent representing the letting value as at the date when the original lease would have expired of the site alone (ignoring the value of the buildings on the site) for the uses to which the house and premises have been used since the start of the long tenancy: LRA 1967, s. 15.

SIXTEEN

LEASEHOLD REFORM, HOUSING AND URBAN DEVELOPMENT ACT 1993: COLLECTIVE ENFRANCHISEMENT OF FLATS AND INDIVIDUAL RIGHTS TO NEW LEASES

16.1 Scope

The 1993 Act, which came into force, so far as is relevant here, on 1 November 1993, gives long leaseholders of flats the right collectively to acquire, at market value, the freehold of their flats, or, individually, to the grant of an extended lease. The provisions of the Act are complex and only a brief outline is given here. For collective enfranchisement, which is considered first, the following conditions must be satisfied:

(a) The premises must be within the Act, i.e., the premises must be a self-contained building or part of a building. Premises are excluded from the Act if 10 per cent or more of their floor area is occupied for non-residential purposes, or where different parts of the premises are owned by different freeholders and any of those parts is a self-contained part of a building, or they consist of a building converted into no more than four flats and the landlord is resident: LRHUDA 1993, ss. 3, 4 and 10, as amended by HA 1996, s. 107.

(b) The premises must contain at least two flats held by qualifying tenants.

(c) The total number of flats held by qualifying tenants must be at least two-thirds of the total number of flats in the premises: LRHUDA 1993, s. 3.

A 'qualifying tenant' must have a long lease (exceeding 21 years: s. 7) either at a low rent (as defined by reference to former rateable value or rent in s. 8) or for a 'particularly long term' (one exceeding 35 years) or satisfy other conditions in LRHUDA 1993 s. 8A, inserted by HA 1996, sch. 9, para. 3, and his or her lease must not be a 'business tenancy' within the meaning of the LTA 1954 (LRHUDA 1993, s. 5).

16.2 Claim to Purchase

A claim to exercise the right to collective enfranchisement is made by notice given to the freehold reversioner, in respect of no less than half of the total number of flats, by the qualifying tenants who must number at least two-thirds or the total number of tenants. At least half of the qualifying tenants who give the notice (the 'participating tenants') must satisfy the residence condition in s. 6 (as amended by HA 1996, s. 111), i.e., that the tenant has occupied the flat as his or her only or principal home either for the last 12 months, or for periods amounting to three out of the last 10 years (s. 13).

16.3 The Purchaser

The participating tenants must appoint a nominee purchaser, both to conduct the enfranchisement procedure and to take the conveyance of the freehold: s. 15. The nominee purchaser may be one or more of the participating tenants, but will more usually be a limited company formed by the tenants for the purpose of taking the conveyance.

16.4 The Price

The purchase price payable by the nominee purchaser is laid down in LRHUDA 1993, sch. 6, as amended by HA 1996, s. 109. At its simplest, the price is the aggregate of three elements:

(a) the market value of the freeholder's reversion subject to the participating tenants' existing leases;

(b) the freeholder's share (approximately 50 per cent) of the 'marriage value', i.e. the amount by which the total value of the participating tenants' interest after enfranchisement (which will reflect the tenants' potential ability to have new leases of any length granted to them without payment of a premium), exceeds the sum obtained by adding the value of the freeholder's reversion (see (a) above) to the market value of the tenants' present leasehold interests (ignoring their right to enfranchise);

(c) compensation for any detrimental effect of the enfranchisement on the value of any interest of the freeholder in other property.

16.5 Individual Right to Extended Lease

An individual tenant who is both a qualifying tenant (see **16.1**) and satisfies the residence condition (see **16.2**), may, as an alternative to collective enfranchisement, acquire a new lease of his or her flat: LRHUDA 1993, s. 39, as amended by HA 1996, s. 112. The new lease is to be for a term of 90 years commencing from the end of the present lease, at a peppercorn rent and in consideration of a premium calculated by reference to similar factors as for collective enfranchisement (see **16.4**), i.e.:

(a) the loss in value of the landlord's reversionary interest caused by the grant of the extended lease;

(b) the landlord's share of the 'marriage value';

(c) compensation for any diminution in value of any interest in other property of the landlord as a result of the grant of the extended lease: s. 56, sch. 13, as amended by HA 1996, s. 110 which enacts new principles for calculating the 'marriage value'.

SEVENTEEN

LANDLORD AND TENANT ACT 1954, PART II: BUSINESS TENANCIES

17.1 Scope

The LTA 1954 applies to tenancies where the tenant occupies the premises or part of the premises for the purposes of a business carried on by him or her other than:

(a) tenancies of agricultural holdings and formerly of licensed premises (other than those where the sale of alcoholic drinks was only subsidiary to the main business, e.g. a restaurant or hotel): LTA 1954, part II, s. 43(1) (note that tenancies of licensed premises are protected by the LTA 1954, part II as from 11 July 1992: see the Landlord and Tenant (Licensed Premises) Act 1990, s. 1);

(b) tenancies granted to an employee of the landlord by reason of his or her employment and coterminous with it: s. 43(2);

(c) tenancies for a short term certain: s. 43(3);

(d) tenancies whose terms prohibit business use for the whole of the premises: s. 23(4).

17.2 Rent

During the tenancy, the LTA 1954, part II in no way affects the rent reserved under the terms of the tenancy. After notice to terminate the tenancy has been given by the landlord or the tenant, the landlord may apply to the court for the determination of a reasonable rent for the tenant to pay during the tenancy's statutory continuation: s. 24A. Any new tenancy granted will be at a rent determined by the court as being that obtainable on the open market, after hearing expert valuation evidence and disregarding certain matters such as the value of the goodwill of the tenant's business and the value of voluntary improvements made by the tenant: s. 34.

17.3 Security

17.3.1 CONTINUATION TENANCY

After the expiry of the contractual term, the tenancy, but not the term, continues as to the whole of the premises until terminated by service of one of the statutory notices of termination, which must be of between six and 12 months' duration, by either the landlord or the tenant: s. 24. (Note that this statutory continuation does not affect any right of the landlord to forfeit the tenancy: s. 24(2).)

17.3.2 NEW LEASE

On termination of the continuation tenancy, the tenant is then entitled to a new lease under the Act unless the landlord can establish one or more of the seven statutory grounds of opposition to a new tenancy, based on some fault of the tenant's, or the landlord's own need for the premises, or the fact that the landlord has offered suitable alternative accommodation: s. 30.

Where the granting of a new lease is not successfully opposed, the new lease will comprise only so much of the premises in the former lease as is actually occupied by the tenant and will be at a rent and on other terms determined by the court in default of agreement by the parties. The Act lays down strict time limits for the service of notices and counter-notices to terminate tenancies within the Act and for applications by tenants for new tenancies. Failure to observe these time limits is a fruitful source of professional negligence claims.

17.3.3   COMPENSATION

If the tenant is refused a new tenancy on one of three of the statutory grounds (that the landlord wishes to let larger premises, of which these premises form part, as a whole; that the landlord wishes to demolish or reconstruct the premises; or that the landlord himself or herself wishes to occupy the premises for business or residential purposes), then the tenant is entitled to statutory compensation for disturbance: s. 37. The tenant may also, at the end of the current tenancy, claim compensation for improvements to the premises carried out by him or her: LTA 1927, s. 1; LTA 1954, s. 47.

17.4   Practical Advice on Bringing Simple Possession Claim Against a Business Tenant

17.4.1   INTRODUCTION

Simple possession claims against business tenants arise where it is alleged the provisions of the LTA 1954, part II, do not apply to the tenancy in the first instance, or where the tenancy has been determined in accordance with the provisions of the LTA 1954, part II, and the tenant has failed to take the steps required under that Act to ensure his or her tenancy continues until the court grants a new tenancy. In either case, if you represent the claimant, all you need show is that the tenancy has come to an end. You do not need to show any grounds for possession, unless of course the tenant claims to have security of tenure under some other statute.

Business tenants sometimes lose the protection of the LTA 1954, part II, when they start to operate their business through a company. The tenancy is still vested in the individual, but it is the company that is carrying on the business. In such circumstances the LTA 1954, part II, does not apply to the tenancy. This is often not appreciated.

17.4.2   THE CLAIM

The statement of case in such a case could not be more simple. It must comply with the requirements of Part 55 of the Civil Procedure Rules 1998, but apart from that all that need be said is that the tenancy has come to an end, and the defendant has failed to vacate.

Mesne profits are recoverable from the tenant in respect of his or her occupation from the date the tenancy came to an end. If a landlord serves notice on his or her tenant demanding possession and the tenant wilfully refuses to give up possession, a claim for double rent can be made. This is a distinct cause of action from the claim for mesne profits.

17.4.3   THE HEARING

The course of the hearing is the same as in any civil claim save that if the claim has not been allocated to the fast track or multi-track, facts may be proved in writing.

17.4.4   ENFORCEMENT OF THE ORDER

An order for possession against a former business tenant is enforced in the same way as in any other possession claim: see the practical guide at **20.8.11**.

EIGHTEEN

AGRICULTURAL HOLDINGS ACT 1986: AGRICULTURAL TENANCIES

18.1 Scope

The Act applies to agricultural tenancies, i.e. tenancies and some licences (AHA 1986, s. 2(2)) granted before 1 September 1995 (and to some granted on or after that date: see ATA 1995, s. 4) to tenants who are independent farmers and not employees of the landlord, of land to be used under the terms of the tenancy as agricultural land, i.e. land used for agriculture (which is widely defined in the Agriculture Act 1947, s. 109) and so used for the purpose of a trade or business: AHA 1986, s. 1.

18.2 Rent

After the fixed term, if any, has expired the landlord or the tenant may, not more frequently than once in every three years, demand that the amount of the rent payable in respect of an agricultural holding should be referred to arbitration by an arbitrator appointed by agreement or, in default, by the President of the RICS: AHA 1986, s. 12. In determining the rent 'properly payable' the arbitrator is directed to have regard to some factors, e.g. evidence of rents of comparable agricultural holdings disregarding any element of 'scarcity' value in such rents, and is to disregard other factors, e.g. the effect of voluntary improvements made by the tenant: AHA 1986, sch. 2. Any increase or decrease in the rent will take effect from the date on which the tenancy could next have been determined by a notice to quit served on the date when arbitration was demanded: AHA 1986, s. 12(4).

18.3 Security

18.3.1 CONTINUATION TENANCY

A tenancy granted for a term of two years or more will, in general, continue after the term expires as a tenancy from year to year on broadly the same terms as those of the original tenancy: AHA 1986, s. 3. Also a tenancy granted for an interest less than a tenancy from year to year (e.g., a tenancy for 365 days) is deemed (by s. 2(2)(a)) to be a tenancy from year to year as is any licence which qualifies under the AHA 1986 (s. 2(2)(b)). A tenancy, however, granted for a fixed term exceeding one year but less than two years, e.g. a term of 15 months, is not treated as a tenancy from year to year and thus, gaining no security under the AHA 1986, expires on its term date.

An agricultural tenancy from year to year, under either the terms of its original grant or under the deeming provisions just mentioned, continues until terminated in accordance with the Act.

18.3.2   TERMINATION

In general the landlord must serve a notice to quit expiring no earlier than 12 months after the end of the current year of the tenancy: s. 25(1). The tenant may then serve a counter-notice claiming security of tenure (s. 26(1)) and if he or she does so the notice to quit will not take effect unless the Agricultural Lands Tribunal consents to its operation on one or more of the statutory grounds, which are connected broadly with the landlord's own needs for the land or reasons of good husbandry or sound management: ss. 26(1) and 27.

The tenant has no right to serve a counter-notice and the Tribunal's consent to the operation of the notice to quit is not required where the landlord can establish one or more of the cases in AHA 1986, sch. 3, part I, s. 26(2). The cases are based mostly on some default of the tenant's or his or her age, insolvency or death.

18.4   Compensation

On quitting, an agricultural tenant may be entitled to claim compensation under a number of heads including compensation for disturbance and for improvements. A landlord may also claim compensation for deterioration of the holding: for all these see AHA 1986, part V.

NINETEEN

AGRICULTURAL TENANCIES ACT 1995: FARM BUSINESS TENANCIES

19.1   Scope

The Act applies to most tenancies which fulfil the two conditions set out below and are granted on or after 1 September 1995: ATA 1995, s. 1. Some tenancies granted on or after this date will nevertheless be subject to the Agricultural Holdings Act 1986 (see **Chapter 18**), e.g. where granted pursuant to a written contract of tenancy entered into before 1 September 1995 the terms of which indicate that the tenancy is to be subject to the AHA 1986: ATA 1995, s. 4. The two conditions are that at least part of the land comprised in the tenancy must, since the start of the tenancy, be farmed for the purposes of a trade or business and the character of the tenancy must be wholly or primarily agricultural: ATA 1995, s. 1.

19.2   Rent

Any provision in the tenancy either that there shall be no rent review during the tenancy or that there shall be one at a specified time in accordance with a specified formula, provided that this formula does not preclude a reduction in the rent, will take effect: s. 9. In the absence of any such provision, either party may initiate a rent review by serving a notice on the other party specifying a review date and requiring the rent payable from the review date to be referred to arbitration: s. 10. The review date specified must be at least 12 months and not more than 24 months from the date of the notice and, unless the parties agree otherwise, not less than three years from the start of the tenancy or from the date when a previous rent review took effect, and must comply with the other provisions in s. 10. The arbitrator is to determine a rent at which the holding might reasonably be expected to be let in the open market by a willing landlord to a willing tenant having regard to all relevant factors including specifically the terms of the tenancy and disregarding specified factors such as the effect of voluntary improvements made by the tenant and that of dilapidations caused by the tenant: s. 13.

19.3   Security

19.3.1   CONTINUATION TENANCY

A tenancy granted for a term of more than two years will, in general, continue after its term date as a tenancy from year to year but otherwise on broadly the same terms as those of the original tenancy: s. 5. Either party may, however, by written notice given at least 12 months and not more than 24 months before the term date, terminate the tenancy on the term date: s. 5. The tenant is given no right to serve any counter-notice.

19.3.2   TERMINATION

Where a farm business tenancy is a tenancy from year to year whether by original grant or by the operation of the provisions in **19.3.1**, any notice to quit must be of at least 12 and not more than 24 months duration and must take effect at the end of a year of the tenancy: s. 6. Again the tenant is given no right to serve any counter-notice.

19.4   Compensation

On quitting, a farm business tenant is entitled to compensation for any improvements made to or benefits obtained for the holding provided that these were made or obtained with the landlord's written consent: ss. 15–18. Compensation under this Act is payable in respect of a wider range of matters than under the AHA 1986 and includes intangible benefits obtained for the holding by the tenant such as planning permission. If the landlord refuses his or her consent the tenant may refer the question of whether this was reasonable to arbitration: s. 19. Claims for compensation are to be settled by arbitration at amounts calculated in accordance with principles laid down in the Act: ss. 20–27.

TWENTY

POSSESSION CLAIMS: MISCELLANEOUS PROVISIONS

20.1   Jurisdiction to Make a Possession Order

The County Court now has jurisdiction to make a possession order in respect of any land irrespective of its rateable value: County Courts Act 1984, s. 21 as amended by the High Court and County Courts Jurisdiction Order 1991, sch., part I (which removed the former limit of County Court jurisdiction to cases where the rateable value of the land did not exceed £1,000).

20.2   Legal Services Commission Funding

The tenant or, rarely, the landlord may be eligible for LSC funding in bringing or defending a possession action or other landlord and tenant proceedings. LSC funding is considered in the *Civil Litigation Manual*, **Chapter 35**. The particular implications of a Community Legal Service certificate in landlord and tenant proceedings are considered in **Chapter 27** below.

20.3   Tenant's Claim for Possession Against Landlord

If a tenant is wrongly evicted by the landlord during the term granted by his or her tenancy, this is a trespass and the tenant can maintain an action for possession against the landlord and, amongst other remedies, obtain an interim mandatory injunction restoring the tenant to possession.

Some of the residential statutory codes, e.g. HA 1988, RA 1977 and HA 1985, prolong the life of the tenancy by providing for a statutory tenancy of some sort to arise after the term has ended, e.g. by effluxion of time. In such cases, too, the landlord will be guilty of trespass if he or she evicts the tenant during the statutory continuance and the same remedies will naturally be available to the tenant.

In other cases if the landlord evicts the tenant after the tenancy or, in some cases, a licensee after the licence, has come to an end without a court order this, although no trespass, will be statutory tort under PEA 1977, s. 3 (see **3.4**). The tenant or licensee may, in respect of this tort, claim a mandatory injunction for reinstatement, or where the eviction is threatened, a prohibitory injunction to prevent it happening, in addition to damages: *Warder* v *Cooper* [1970] 1 Ch 495.

See **Chapter 26** for a guide to conducting proceedings for a mandatory injunction of this sort and **3.9** for a practical guide to conducting proceedings on behalf of an unlawfully evicted residential occupier.

20.4   Possession Claim for Non-payment of Rent or Service Charges

Where the premises consist of or include a dwelling and the tenancy is not one within the LTA 1954, part II (a business tenancy), then if the landlord fails to give notice to the tenant of an address in England and Wales at which notices (including notices in proceedings) may be served on the landlord by the tenant, any rent or service charge otherwise due to the landlord is to be treated for all purposes as not being due to the landlord at any time before the landlord does provide such an address: LTA 1987, s. 48.

The notice must be written (*Rogan* v *Woodfield Building Services* [1995] 1 EGLR 72, CA) but need not necessarily state expressly that it is the address at which such notices may be served on the landlord. Thus where the tenancy agreement contains the landlord's name and address (being an address in England and Wales) and there is nothing to suggest that the address is not one at which such notices can be served, that will of itself comply with s. 48: *Rogan* v *Woodfield Building Services* (above).

Where, however, the current landlord was not the original landlord named in the tenancy agreement and had no address in England and Wales, then a letter from the current landlord's solicitors in England and Wales demanding rent, which did not expressly state that notices including notices in proceedings could be served on the landlord at the solicitors' address, failed to comply with s. 48: see *Dallhold Estates (UK) Pty Ltd* v *Lindsey Trading Properties Inc.* [1994] 1 EGLR 93, CA.

Failure to comply with s. 48 does not mean that the landlord is for ever barred from recovering the rent/service charges or claiming possession for their non-payment. The bar is removed as soon as the landlord complies with s. 48: see *Rogan* v *Woodfield Building Services* (above).

20.5   Forfeiture for Failure to Pay Service Charges

Where premises are let as a dwelling, the landlord may not exercise any right of re-entry for the tenant's failure to pay a service charge unless the amount:

(a)   is agreed or admitted by the tenant; or

(b)   has been determined by the court or by arbitration: HA 1996, s. 81(1).

This restriction does not apply where the tenancy is a business tenancy within the LTA 1954, part II, a tenancy of an agricultural holding within the AHA 1986, or a farm business tenancy within the ATA 1995: HA 1996, s. 81(4).

Where the reasonableness of service charges is an issue the landlord or the tenant may apply to a leasehold valuation tribunal (LVT) for a determination: LTA 1985, s. 19, as amended by HA 1996, s. 83. The court also has the power to transfer a claim to a LVT if the issue arises during court proceedings: LTA 1985, s. 31C.

Further where the amount of the service charge has been determined as in (b) above, the landlord may not exercise his or her right of re-entry before 14 days from the date of the decision: HA 1996, s. 81(2).

The landlord's right to serve a notice under LPA 1925, s. 146 in respect of unpaid service charges (if these are not payable as rent) is not affected by the above restriction but the s. 146 notice will be ineffective unless it complies with new statutory requirements in HA 1996, s. 82 (notice must state that s. 81 applies and set out its effect in letters of a certain size).

20.6   Restriction on Court's Discretion in Making Possession Orders

The general rule is that, on making a possession order, the court is not to postpone the giving up of possession for more than 14 days or, in cases of exceptional hardship, for more than a maximum of six weeks from the date of the order: HA 1980, s. 89(1).

There are important cases (in HA 1980, s. 89(2)) where this restriction does not apply, including the following which are relevant to this course:

(a) The order is made in forfeiture proceedings.

(b) The court has power to make an order only if satisfied that it is reasonable to do so. This head includes possession orders made under the discretionary grounds in respect of assured tenancies (HA 1988), protected tenancies (RA 1977) and secure tenancies (HA 1985).

(c) The order is made in respect of a dwelling-house occupied under a restricted contract (under RA 1977).

In addition, on making a possession order in respect of a licence or tenancy of tied accommodation against certain agricultural employees, their spouses or other members of their families, the court must, as a general rule, suspend execution of the order for six months from the end of the former tenancy or licence on appropriate terms as to, e.g., payment of rent arrears and mesne profits, and has further discretionary powers of suspension: PEA 1977, ss. 4, 8. These provisions do not apply to excluded licences: PEA 1977, s. 4(2A).

20.7 Warrants of Possession

In order to enforce an order for possession the landlord must apply for a warrant of possession: CCR, O. 26, r. 17 (preserved in CPR, sch. 2). The landlord will be given an appointment when the bailiff will call at the premises to execute the warrant. Where the warrant is issued pursuant to an order made following proof of discretionary grounds for possession, the tenant may apply for execution of the order to be stayed or suspended, or the date for possession to be postponed, at any time before execution of the order. Where a possession order is made in the absence of the tenant, under CPR, r. 39.3, the tenant may apply to have the order set aside, if there are grounds for doing so.

20.8 Possession Claims: General Guide

20.8.1 INTRODUCTION

We are here concerned with court proceedings in which (inter alia) an order for possession of land is sought. Herein, the person claiming possession is called 'the claimant', and the person against whom the order is sought is called 'the defendant'.

Since 15 October 2001, the relevant rules of court are those prescribed by Part 55 of the Civil Procedure Rules and the Practice Direction which supplements Part 55. Part 55 is entitled 'Possession Claims' and that expression is defined as being a claim for the recovery of possession of land (including buildings or parts of buildings).

The procedure contained in Part 55 must be used where the claim includes a claim for possession brought by a landlord (or former landlord), a mortgagee, or a licensor (or former licensor). It must also be used where a possession claim is made against trespassers. Part 55 covers all the types of possession claims with which you will be concerned.

A possession claim must be commenced in the County Court for the district in which the land is situated. To this there are two exceptions: first, if a statute otherwise provides, the claim may be commenced in the High Court; secondly, the claim may be commenced in the High Court if the criteria set out in PD 55 are satisfied. Exceptional circumstances must be shown. The value of the property and the amount of any financial claim are relevant, but these factors alone will not normally justify starting the claim in the High Court. It follows that in the vast majority of cases, you will find yourself issuing the claim in, and appearing in, the County Court.

A good deal of what appears below merely reflects that which is required by Part 55. It is important to check whether Part 55 (and/or PD 55) make specific provision for the type of case you are concerned with; it is safe to assume they do! It is easy to be distracted by the substantive law (which of course is important, and which the beginner will know all about) and forget the mechanics of the litigation; something that will be new to the beginner.

20.8.2 TYPE OF CLAIM AND STARTING THE CLAIM

20.8.2.1 The claim
A claim form must be in form N5 or form N5B and must be verified by a statement of truth. The particulars of claim must be filed and served with the claim form. As counsel you will usually only be concerned at this stage with settling the necessary particulars of claim and, perhaps, witness statements.

20.8.2.2 Particulars of claim
The CPR, Part 16 and PD 16 contain detailed provisions as to what the particulars of claim must contain where possession of land is sought. If you are instructed to settle the particulars of claim make sure they comply with the rules; no more, no less.

20.8.2.3 Parties to the claim
In a possession claim against a former tenant it is the person in whom the immediate reversion is vested who should be the claimant; he or she may or may not be the freehold owner, although he or she will inevitably hold a legal estate. In other cases, it is the person with an interest immediately superior to that of the defendant occupier who should be the claimant.

It is of course important that the right persons are joined as defendants: the right persons are those in actual possession of the premises. Indeed the new rules expressly provide that the particulars of claim must contain details of every person who, to the best of the claimant's knowledge, is in possession of the property. Thus all those in physical occupation of the premises, or at least all adults, should be joined as defendants. The husband might be the former tenant but is living in the premises with his wife; the wife should be a defendant. The same applies to grown up children living at home. Although the bailiffs can remove any one they find on the premises when they attend to execute the warrant, it is clearly wise to have all the occupiers before the court. Joining all occupiers in the first instance reduces the risk of a dispossessed occupier making an application without notice to be allowed back into the premises thereby delaying matters and increasing costs.

If a tenant has sublet the whole of the premises, the tenant or sub-tenant, or both, may be made defendants. However it is advisable to join them both in most cases. Sometimes the premises are vacant, but an order for possession is required in case the occupier moves back in, or in order to satisfy a purchaser of the premises that vacant possession can be given. In such circumstances the defendant should be the person who would be the defendant if physical occupation had not been given up.

If you are merely instructed to appear at a hearing of a claim for possession it will be too late to do very much about joining additional defendants and still go ahead on the hearing date. If you arrive at court and the named defendant says his or her husband or wife and/or child is also living in the premises, then provided that other occupier is not alleging a right to remain in occupation other than that based upon the named defendant's alleged right to occupy, the judge will probably allow you to amend the claim to join the additional occupiers and order that service of the claim on them be dispensed with.

20.8.3   SERVICE OF PROCEEDINGS AND INTERIM MATTERS

20.8.3.1   Service

Like most actions in the County Court, claim forms seeking possession are usually served by the court. Where a claim form is served by the court, the court must send the claimant a notice which will include the date when the claim form is deemed to be served. This notice will prove service. If the claimant has served the proceedings, and it is his or her choice, he or she must file a certificate of service, and service must be proved. Ask your solicitor before the hearing how proceedings were served.

20.8.3.2   Case management

When the court issues the claim form it will fix a date for the hearing. At that hearing, the court will decide the claim or give case management directions. If the defendant fails to serve a defence, he or she may nevertheless take part in the hearing. Unless the defendant raises a genuine dispute which cannot be decided at the first hearing, there is no reason why the court should not decide the claim.

What frequently happens in practice is that if the defendant does not file a defence, the claimant's case is listed in a general possession list to be heard by the circuit or district judge. If the defendant does not attend at the date fixed for the hearing, the claimant can prove his or her case and obtain the orders sought, or not as the case may be. It follows that if instructed on behalf of the claimant on the hearing you must be prepared to prove the tenancy has been determined, all pre-proceedings notices have been served, title and the necessary grounds for possession. It is now expressly provided in CPR, Part 55 that except where the claim is allocated to the fast track or the multi-track (which will not have happened prior to the first hearing) or the court considers otherwise, any fact that needs to be proved by evidence of the witnesses at the first hearing may be proved by evidence in writing. To that end it is also provided that all witness statements must be served at least two days before the hearing, save where the claim is against trespassers in which case the witness statements must be filed and served with the claim form.

Even if no defence has been served it is frequently the case that the defendant and his or her lawyers will attend at court, and if the claim is to be contested, case management directions will be given and then the claim will be adjourned. Where the claim is genuinely disputed on grounds which appear to be substantial, the case management directions given will include the allocation of the claim to a track or directions to enable it to be allocated. If you are counsel for the claimant and this happens, you should consider asking for the costs of the hearing in any event, or at least for the costs of counsel attending.

If case management directions are given at the first hearing consideration must be given to the directions needed for the proper prosecution of the claim and any counterclaim; that is what case management is all about. The appropriate directions will vary depending upon the nature of the claim. In a Case 1 possession claim under the RA 1977 it is unlikely experts will be required, but an order that there be an exchange of witness statements will be needed.

Typical directions in a claim for possession based upon non-payment of rent might be as follows:

(a)   that the defendant do file and serve a full defence and counterclaim, if so advised, by (a specified date);

(b)   that the claimant do file and serve a reply, if so advised, and defence to counterclaim by (a specified date);

(c)   that there be standard disclosure by (a specified date);

(d)   that there be inspection by (a specified date);

    (e)   that the parties shall exchange 14 days after inspection written statements of all witnesses of fact whose evidence will be relied upon by (a specified date);

    (f)   that the claim be set down for hearing on the first open day after (a specified date) to be heard by a circuit judge with a time estimate of one day.

It is rare now for such directions to provide that steps be taken within a specified period, a number of days for example. The norm now is for dates to be specified in the order. Such a modest claim is likely to be allocated to the fast track.

A claim involving an allegation of breach of repairing obligation, and counterclaims in possession claims often do, will require further directions dealing with the exchange of experts' reports.

It is very common for directions to be agreed, thereby dispensing with the need for an attendance at the court. If there is an actual hearing, the order for costs is usually costs in the case. If sensible directions were rejected by one side, thereby requiring an attendance at court, an application for costs should be made.

Save where the possession claim is against a residential occupier and the ground for possession is non-payment of rent, the first hearing will be in open court and wig and gown should be worn.

20.8.3.3   Interim payments

The claimant in a possession claim should consider making an application for an interim payment. Frequently landlords are reluctant to accept money from the person in occupation as they fear it will prejudice their case. This fear may or may not be misplaced depending upon the nature of the case, but all risk is eliminated if there is an order for an interim payment.

The reality of it is that whether the defendant wins or loses, he or she will have to pay for having enjoyed the use of the premises during the pendency of the claim; it will either be rent, if the defendant wins, or damages if the claimant wins. Such being the case, an order for an interim payment is inevitably made.

20.8.3.4   Interim applications generally

Depending upon the nature of the claim, and the circumstances of the particular case, it may be necessary to make other types of interim applications. Thus, landlords often fear that the premises will be damaged by the occupier during the pendency of the claim. If there are grounds to support such a fear, an application for an interim injunction can be made restraining any untoward conduct. If an order is made it will make a delinquent occupier think twice before damaging the premises, and if there is a breach of the order, the occupier can be committed.

However, care must be taken when one is forfeiting a lease. The right to forfeit may be waived if an order seeking compliance with the tenant's covenants is sought.

20.8.4   THE HEARING

20.8.4.1   Generally

Claims in the County Court in which possession of residential accommodation is claimed last, on average, 90 seconds! An ideal first court appearance perhaps. On the other hand this reflects the fact that judges wish to deal with such actions quickly, and therefore it is important that you are able to match the pace set by the judge.

It is an unlucky beginner who, attending on his or her first possession claim, finds his or her case listed first in a long possession list. If you are not so unlucky, it is a great help to spend a short period in court watching how others, perhaps more experienced, are doing it. As, if not more, important is the benefit you receive from seeing how the judge is dealing with his or her list. If you are unsure about something about your case, or how the judge is dealing with the cases before him or her, have a word with someone in the robing room. However, make sure that person is not your opponent!

20.8.4.2 Proving the case

If counsel for the claimant, you must ensure that you are able to prove your case. CPR, Part 55 now provides that witness statements must be filed two days before the first hearing and these can be relied upon without calling the witnesses in many cases. It is important to check that the witness statements filed (which were probably drafted by someone other than counsel) prove all the necessary elements of your claim. Most obviously, this means the witness statements must prove that the claimant 'owns' the premises. It is only those with superior title to the land occupied by the defendant who may be entitled to possession. It is therefore important to ensure the claimant has such title and that you are in a position to prove it. If the witness statements are not up to scratch, it may be necessary to adjourn the first hearing. However, if you have a live witness at court, invite the judge to hear oral evidence.

Frequently, there will be no issue between the parties on the question of title; for example, the defendant tenant will admit the claimant is his or her landlord or be estopped from denying it. Almost as frequently, the occupier fails to attend at trial, and you, as counsel for the claimant, will be asked by the judge to 'prove your case'. Unless title can be shown, the claim is bound to fail before it gets going.

Generally on the question of proof, you should approach a brief for the claimant in a possession claim on the basis that it is entirely possible the defendant will not attend, and each and every part of the claimant's case will have to be strictly proved. Some of the more important elements are now considered.

20.8.4.3 Registered land

If the claimant is the owner of the freehold interest in registered land, or a lease of registered land granted for a term of more than 21 years, title can be proved by producing office copy Land Registry entries. The property register will describe the property and the proprietorship register will contain the claimant's name. In the case of a claimant who owns a registerable leasehold title, it is not strictly necessary to produce the head lease unless of course it is relevant to some other issue in the claim. Office copy land registry entries are admissible in evidence in all claims and matters to the same extent as the originals would be, so the originals, which are often locked away in the vaults of a bank or building society, need not be produced at trial.

It sometimes happens that the claimant who says he or she 'owns' registered land is not registered as proprietor. This sometimes happens where, for example, the claimant has recently purchased the premises and wishes to re-sell them immediately after gaining vacant possession. The claimant may not have applied to be registered as proprietor (it is not necessary to be so registered to effect a valid disposition of registered land), or the land registry may simply have not registered him or her as proprietor by the time the action comes on for trial. In such cases, it is sufficient if title from the last registered proprietor can be deduced. In the example given, you would need to produce office copy land registry entries showing the claimant's vendor as registered proprietor, and an executed transfer by that person to the claimant.

The leasehold owner under a lease not capable of substantive registration proves his or her title by producing his or her lease or tenancy agreement. The original should be produced. In theory the court will only accept secondary evidence of the lease if there are grounds for so doing, for example if the original is lost or destroyed.

20.8.4.4 Unregistered land

If the land is unregistered, the claimant must deduce title, but it is not necessary to provide an epitome of title as a vendor would do on a conveyance of unregistered land. If the claimant's interest is freehold, the conveyance to him or her is sufficient. If leasehold, the head lease is sufficient, or if the claimant is an assignee of the term, the head lease and the assignment. Again, originals of such documents should be available for the trial. The stock of unregistered land is decreasing, and it is rare these days to be concerned with unregistered land, particular where the land is situated in a city or large town.

20.8.4.5 Eliminating confusion

The title to a piece of land can sometimes become confusing. If a number of derivative leasehold interests have been carved out of the freehold over the years, and there have been assignments of the various terms, assignments of the reversion, and the odd concurrent lease granted from time to time, it is sometimes difficult to know how the claimant comes to be the claimant. It is essential that you understand precisely how your lay client comes to be the claimant, and are in a position to explain it to the judge. A simple line diagram will often assist you.

20.8.4.6 In practice

In practice you will more often than not find you do not have the title documentation referred to above. You might only have a copy of the claimant's lease, or your solicitors will have not taken the trouble to obtain office copy entries and formed the view it will be enough if the claimant states in his or her witness statement that he or she 'owns' the premises in question. It is often possible to get by with such evidence of title, especially in a simple case in the County Court, but there is no guarantee a particular judge will accept secondary evidence of title, particularly if the defendant does not attend. You should therefore insist, if it is not too late when you receive the brief, that proper evidence of title is available at court. Your solicitor may think you are a 'fussy beginner', but if you have not warned him or her of this potential problem, and the case goes badly, you may be criticised. It is better to be safe than sorry.

20.8.4.7 The position of the occupier

It will also be necessary for the claimant to prove the terms, if any, upon which the defendant occupied the premises. This will involve producing some form of written agreement, or producing oral evidence of an oral agreement.

If the claimant is the assignee of the reversion, it is not necessary to adduce evidence from the person who granted the lease, provided the claimant can give evidence to the effect that he or she acquired the freehold or headlease subject to the tenancy granted to the defendant.

20.8.4.8 Other elements of the claimant's case

All the other elements of the claimant's case must be proved. For example, that the defendant's right to occupy has come to an end, the grounds upon which possession is sought, if grounds need be shown. It is not enough to show the defendant has failed to pay rent, or has otherwise acted in breach of his or her obligations.

20.8.4.9 Rent arrears

Problems often arise concerning rent arrears, as the person who can prove title is not always the same person who was concerned with the collection of rent. You must avoid the trap of being left with nothing but hearsay evidence. Ensure there is direct evidence at court concerning the non-payment of rent.

What is extremely useful, and much appreciated by the court, is a clear schedule of the alleged arrears. Such a schedule should show the current rent payable, the dates payments were due, the payments made on those dates, if any, and the cumulative total of arrears. The computers of managing agents produce schedules of rent arrears, but often these are unintelligible, so before you put one before the court make sure you, as counsel for the claimant, know what it all means. Such a schedule should be exhibited to a relevant witness statement.

The prescribed form of particulars for claims against occupiers of dwellings requires full particulars of the rent arrears to be set out, so a schedule is not necessary in such cases.

Remember, rent payable in advance is not apportionable, so if the tenancy comes to an end during a rent period, the whole of the rent for that period can be claimed.

20.8.4.10 Interest

Interest is payable on the rent arrears provided the claimant has a contractual right to the same, or a claim is made under s. 69 of the CCA 1984, and the claim for interest is pleaded. As counsel for the claimant you should have prepared an interest figure to present to the judge. Large landlords often have computers which calculate the interest due on the rent arrears and produce schedules, and in such cases life is made easy. In other cases it will be necessary to calculate the interest due on the accumulating rent arrears in order to produce a figure. This can be a very tedious exercise, but it must be done. Judges often have long possession lists and wish to deal with each case quickly. A claim for interest may be lost if a figure is not given to the judge at once. There is no need to prove how the calculation was done; the court will invite the parties to agree the figure, and provided the arithmetic is correct, or nearly correct, there is rarely an issue. If the defendant does not attend, the court will inevitably take the interest figure from counsel for the claimant, so bring a calculator to court.

20.8.4.11 Mesne profits

Mesne profits is the name given to damages for trespass when the trespasser is a former tenant holding over. Until his or her tenancy has come to an end, the tenant is obliged to pay rent. Once the tenancy has come to an end, if the now former tenant remains in possession of the premises, he or she will be liable to pay mesne profits.

The amount of mesne profits is usually equal to the letting value of the premises during the period of unlawful occupation. In many cases mesne profits at the rate of the last rent reserved is claimed, but if there has been a change in the value of the premises, another figure may be appropriate. A claimant can claim mesne profits without proving he or she would have re-let the premises but for the unlawful occupation of the defendant: see **21.5**.

An order for mesne profits will be for mesne profits calculated up to the date the claimant obtains possession. In other words, the claimant will be able to obtain an immediate judgment for sums which have not yet accrued. This ability to obtain a judgment for mesne profits which have not yet accrued removes the need for the claimant to come back to court to obtain a second judgment.

20.8.4.12 Putting the claimant to proof

A defendant can often defeat a claim simply by not admitting anything and sitting back where the claimant is unable to prove his or her case. If counsel for the defendant makes the claimant prove his or her case, as indicated above, claimants often find themselves in difficulty proving the level of rent arrears. An inability to prove termination of the relevant tenancy is also a common problem for claimants.

Of course if the defendant has a substantive defence, this must be pleaded in the normal way. If instructed for a defendant to attend at this first hearing in a case where a defence has not been filed or served, you must have some idea of what defence your lay client has and be able to explain it in a convincing manner to the judge. Do not make the mistake of sounding as if *you* do not believe that what you are saying is an arguable defence. In an ideal world a draft defence should be put before the court at that first hearing, but in many cases you will not see your lay client until you arrive at court. If such is the case, you will have to do the best you can.

20.8.5 ORAL EVIDENCE

The general rule is that any fact which needs to be proved by the evidence of witnesses is to be proved at trial by their oral evidence given in public, and at any other hearing by their evidence in writing, which should be by witness statement, but can be by affidavit. However, as stated in a possession claim witness statements must be filed two days before the first hearing, and these statements can be relied upon unless the case is allocated to the fast track or the multi-track or unless the court otherwise orders.

If a witness who has made a witness statement does not attend the trial for some reason, and the circumstances are such that the written evidence cannot be relied upon as the primary source of evidence, his or her evidence, as reflected in the witness statement may nevertheless be relied upon provided the court so orders. Further, if the party whose witness has not turned up does not wish to rely upon the witness statement of the missing witness, any other party can put the witness statement in as hearsay evidence.

There are express provisions in PD 55 which allow oral evidence to be given at trial in order to bring the amount of rent or mortgage payments in arrear up-to-date. Such 'up-to-date' evidence can also be given in writing on the day of the hearing.

20.8.6 FAILURE OF WITNESS TO ATTEND HEARING

It not infrequently happens that you arrive at court to discover one of your vital witnesses has failed to attend. If there is no prospect of the witness being brought to court that day, you should ask for the hearing to be adjourned. If the defendant has not attended, the court will probably agree to this course, although it might strike out the claim. If the defendant attends and is represented, it is likely such an application will be resisted.

If there is some good reason for the failure of the witness to attend, for example a sudden illness or transportation strike, the court is likely to adjourn the hearing, but the claimant will have to pay the costs in any event.

If there is no good reason for the witness's failure to attend, you may be in some difficulty if the court refuses to adjourn the hearing; an ever more likely event in the current climate. To have the claim struck out is an expensive nuisance only; fresh proceedings can be issued the same day. What you must avoid is having the case dealt with on its merits, as this would prevent the claimant commencing a fresh claim based upon the same cause of action. If the judge decides not to adjourn the case and insists you proceed with the claim, you can rely upon the witness statement of the missing witness, but the value of that evidence may be much reduced by the fact that the evidence cannot be tested by cross-examination. A claimant in the County Court is no longer able to enter a non-suit.

It is now also expressly provided that if a witness fails to attend at court, and the other side seriously disputes his or her evidence, the court will normally adjourn the hearing so the oral evidence can be given.

20.8.7 THE FORENSIC COURSE OF THE HEARING

20.8.7.1 Introduction
No two possessions will take the same forensic course, even if they are very similar in nature. Much depends on the judge, the state of the list, the skill of the advocates and the performance of the witnesses. Having said that, as counsel for the claimant in a possession claim against a former tenant you should proceed as follows.

20.8.7.2 Usual course of hearing
Once your case is called on (and wait for that), introduce yourself and your opponent (or the defendant in person) and briefly indicate the nature of the claim. If the defendant admits the claim, which sometimes happens, explain this to the judge, and he or she will proceed to make an order provided the defendant has confirmed this is the case.

If the case is to fight, next refer the judge to the statements of case (he or she may indicate this is unnecessary) and then proceed to call your evidence. If the case is one where witness statements are to stand as the evidence, you should invite the judge to read the statements. Establish the claimant's title, the terms of the letting, the determination of the tenancy, and the other elements, for example the amount of rent arrears, needed to prove the claimant's claim. Ask the witness(es) to produce any relevant documents: the tenancy agreement, notice to quit, rent demands, etc. If there are witness statements, the elements that have to be proved should all be dealt with in them.

As in any other civil claim, the defendant will then have the opportunity to cross-examine the claimant's witnesses and call evidence at the close of the claimant's case. Even if the defendant in person has no defence, the judge will ask him or her if he or she wants to ask questions. Instead of asking questions, the defendant in person usually starts to make a speech at this stage, and the judge will have to tell him or her that this is not the right time for that, but that they will get their say.

It is usually unnecessary to refer the judge to the substantive law in simple possession claims as he or she will be very familiar with it. You should, however, be prepared to refer the judge to the relevant statutory provisions if necessary. The defendant has the opportunity to make any submissions to the court at the end of the defence case. The claimant then has the final opportunity to address the court if this is necessary.

As counsel for a successful claimant, you must be able to inform the judge of the order you seek. In particular, if your claim involves a claim for rent or other money, ensure you have the correct figure to give to the judge. As stated, if you are claiming interest, make sure you have calculated the amount you claim in order that you can make an immediate response when the judge asks for the figure.

In contested hearings it is very common these days for counsel to prepare written submissions or a skeleton argument for use by the judge. There are extensive rules which apply to skeleton arguments to be used in the Court of Appeal and the High Court, and some County Courts have local protocols, but even when written submissions/skeleton arguments are not required by the rules, they are a worthwhile exercise. At the very least they ensure the judge has a written record of what your submissions are. Unless the rules or a local protocol otherwise provide, you need not serve a copy of your written submission on the other side until the hearing is due to commence.

20.8.7.3 Variations
Although this is the usual course of events, do not be surprised if the judge invites you, counsel for the claimant, to proceed in a different manner. Some judges will have read the papers and will simply want to hear the evidence. Some will not only allow you, but encourage you, to lead your witness in order to maintain the 90 second average! There is a great deal of variation between judges. Whatever the judge says, do not panic. Provided you know the elements of your lay client's case, you should be able to adapt to whatever approach the judge adopts without too much trouble.

20.8.7.4 Inadequate brief
It is fair to say that some solicitors do not prepare a brief for what they consider to be a simple possession claim with the care and attention which it requires. Frequently, by the morning of the hearing, you will still not be entirely clear how you are going to prove your case, or resist the claim made against your lay client, as the case may be. You will not understand, because your papers will contain no explanation, how a rent arrears figure has been calculated. Even as a beginner, it is likely you will have some criticisms to make of the statements of case.

Do not assume you are the first to have received such a brief and keep calm. Speak to your solicitor the night before or in the morning before the hearing; you may catch him or her in the office before he or she leaves for court. In any event, be at court in good time in order to take further instructions. Your team may not arrive until 10.28 a.m. If you need more time, and your case is near the top of the list, inform the usher that you are not quite ready, and invite him or her to drop you a little way down the list. If the usher feels unable to do this, ask the judge for more time. It is vital that you fully understand your case before you stand up before the judge, so do not feel embarrassed to ask for time.

20.8.8   COMPROMISE

20.8.8.1 Ageement between parties
It sometimes happens that agreement is reached between the parties. Often the defendant agrees to leave the premises in return for a monetary payment, or because

the claimant agrees to waive a money claim. Sometimes the claimant will agree not to proceed with his or her claim for possession if the defendant does not pursue his or her counterclaim for damages for breach of repairing covenant. Frequently the defendant merely wants an order for possession made against him or her in order that it can be presented to the housing authority.

20.8.8.2 Regulated tenancies

As counsel for the claimant you should always take a realistic view of your case. Even if the case can be proved, the net result is often that the occupier remains in possession. To prove a regulated tenant is in arrear with his or her rent is unlikely to result in an immediate order for possession being made; at best the court will suspend the order provided the defendant pays the arrears plus the current rent. The position is now somewhat different under the provisions of the HA 1988.

It frequently happens that agreement is reached between a landlord and a regulated tenant under which the tenant agrees to vacate the premises in return for a capital sum. As counsel for the claimant, you should take great care; the basic rule is that one cannot contract out of the Rent Acts.

Accordingly, an agreement by a tenant to vacate premises which are subject to a regulated tenancy cannot be enforced by the landlord, even if the tenant has accepted the money. The fact the agreement may be supported by an order for possession made by the court may make no difference.

The court cannot make an order for possession against a regulated tenant otherwise than under s. 98 of the RA 1977. Accordingly, if it is desired to reach an effective agreement under which the defendant will vacate the premises, the court must be given jurisdiction under this section. This is done by the tenant admitting, which admission should be recorded in the body of the order, the elements of the claimant's claim which will give the court jurisdiction. For example, the defendant should admit the rent is in arrears and that it is reasonable to make an order for possession (although that is, strictly speaking, a matter for the court); or admit that suitable alternative accommodation is available. Similar care should be taken in cases under the HA 1988. Such a form of compromise will not arise in cases to which the HA 1985 applies.

20.8.8.3 Consequences of agreement

If you are counsel for the defendant, you should take care that the defendant is fully aware of the consequences of any agreement made. It is too simple to say that if an order for possession is made the housing authority has a duty to re-house the defendant. Housing authorities have a duty to house the homeless who have a priority need. A single man in good health is unlikely to fall within this class. Even where the defendant is likely to have a priority need, for example a young unmarried mother, you should explain that the type of accommodation made available to the homeless is often very uncomfortable, especially for a family. Further, there is always the risk that if a claim for possession is not contested where there is an arguable defence, the housing authority may take the view the defendant has become intentionally homeless, and in such circumstances, the housing authority is under no duty to re-house the defendant even if he or she does have a priority need.

If you are representing a legally aided defendant who agrees to compromise the claim on terms which involve the payment of a sum of money to him or her, you should ensure your lay client is fully aware of the consequences of the legal aid board's charge.

20.8.9 ORDERS FOR POSSESSION

20.8.9.1 Discretion whether or not to make order

If the claimant proves his or her case, it does not necessarily follow that an order for possession will be made. In some instances the court has a discretion whether or not to make an order for possession notwithstanding that the claimant has made out his or her case. See **5.9.1** (discretionary grounds for possession against assured tenants), for example.

20.8.9.2 Suspended orders

If an order for possession is made, the court has jurisdiction to suspend the order in some instances. judges often need assistance as to the extent of their powers to suspend orders. Further, it is not uncommon for judges who have made orders for possession to try and indulge the defendant a little by giving him or her a long period of suspension; they feel it tempers the main order they have made. If your lay client is happy with the period of suspension, all well and good, but if not you must be in a position to remind the judge that there are statutory limits on his or her jurisdiction to suspend orders for possession: see **20.6**.

20.8.9.3 Prescribed forms

There are prescribed forms of orders for possession in the County Court (Forms N26 to N28): see Forms N27, N27(1) and N27(2), although you will need an old Green Book to find these forms. These will be used in most cases, but they are not always appropriate, particularly if a claim is compromised on terms, and may need to be adapted. Even if they are not used, they provide a beginner with guidance as to what an order for possession should contain.

20.8.10 COSTS

20.8.10.1 Generally

The usual rules concerning costs apply equally to possession claims as they do to other types of civil claim. A successful party will usually be awarded his or her costs. Detailed and fundamental changes were introduced by the Civil Procedure Rules 1998 to the manner in which costs are dealt with, both in the County Court and the High Court. One change of substance is that the court is much more likely to take into account all the circumstances including the conduct of the parties, success on some or all of the issues and any payments into court or any admissible offer when deciding the question of costs. Thus there will be more split or partial orders as to costs. For example, even if successful and awarded costs, a claimant who has spent time and money on producing bundles of irrelevant or unnecessary documents may not get the cost of preparing those bundles. Similarly, if the claimant succeeded on one ground, but lost on three other grounds, it is unlikely he or she will get all his or her costs.

20.8.10.2 Assessed costs

As to the new procedures, it is sufficient to note that in possession claims which go to hearing, the costs awarded will be the subject of an assessment, either a summary assessment, or a detailed assessment.

A summary assessment will be undertaken by the judge at the end of the hearing. In an undefended possession hearing, the assessment will be undertaken in the 'rough and ready' way that judges have been doing it for years. As counsel for the party who is awarded costs, you will invite the judge to assess the costs. In many courts there is a 'going rate', but these days the amount of the assessment should be what the successful party has actually had to spend.

Where there has been a defended trial which has lasted less than a day, each party who intends to claim costs must prepare and lodge at court, and serve on the other side, a written statement of the costs intended to be claimed. This is a job for your solicitors. This statement, which should follow a form and be signed, will contain details of the number of hours spent on the case, the hourly rate charges, the grade of fee earner, disbursements, counsel's fee and VAT. At the end of the hearing, and once the judge has awarded costs, he or she will consider the costs statement of the party awarded his or her costs, and hear submission on it from the other party.

If you are counsel for the paying party, do not be slow to take issue with the items referred to in the statement; for example, the time spent on the case by the other side's solicitors is often excessive, or the hourly rate too high. As a beginner you will probably need assistance from your solicitors on these matters. If you are counsel for the party who has been awarded costs, be prepared to defend the amount set out in your lay client's statement.

In other cases, the judge will order that there be a detailed assessment. This means the costs will be assessed by an officer of the court at a later stage. As counsel you will not be concerned with this.

20.8.10.3 Trespassers

In claims against trespassers there is no reason why the successful claimant should not obtain his or her costs against a named defendant. Where, however, the proceedings have been commenced against unidentified occupiers, the court will not award the successful claimant his or her costs.

20.8.10.4 Publicly-funded cases

If you are representing a publicly-funded lay client you should remember:

(a)   there should be a detailed assessment of costs;

(b)   the client needs to be advised about the statutory charge (i.e. the sums expended by the Legal Services Commission will be a first charge on any property recovered or preserved for the assisted party).

20.8.11   ENFORCING THE ORDER

As counsel for the claimant you will consider your job done, and well done, when the judge makes an order for possession against the defendant. For the most part that is correct; your job is done. However, it is often the case that the claimant will want to know what happens next, and how long it will take to get the defendant out of the premises.

An order for possession is enforced by a warrant of possession. So if the defendant has not left the premises by the date specified in the order for possession, the court will issue a warrant upon a request being made for the same by the claimant. As counsel it is very unlikely you will ever be involved in making such a request; it is an administrative step. Once the warrant is issued, the bailiffs, who enforce the warrant, will make an appointment to attend at the premises to enforce the warrant. As indicated above, a warrant covers all persons who are found on the premises at the time of execution. There is no certainty as to when the bailiffs will attend at the premises; it depends upon how busy they are. In some busy courts, it may be a number of weeks before the bailiffs attend. Notification will be sent to the defendant and other occupiers of the date upon which the bailiffs are to attend.

It will be seen therefore that even after the date for the delivery up of possession has passed, there may still be a significant delay before the defendant is removed from the premises. Your lay client will not be too happy about that, but he or she will be grateful to counsel for informing them of the fact.

20.9   Possession Claims Checklist

20.9.1   THE CIVIL PROCEDURE RULES

Although the Civil Procedure Rules 1998 were introduced in April 1999, landlord and tenant procedure in the High Court and the County Courts continued until 15 October 2001 to be governed by the Rules of the Supreme Court and the County Court Rules (which were significantly different). On 15 October 2001, Parts 55 and 56 were added to the Civil Procedure Rules, for the first time introducing a uniform code for possession claims and landlord and tenant procedure in the High Court and the County Courts. Claims issued before that date are still governed by the old procedure, and practitioners seeking guidance on that procedure should look in an edition of the White Book (or its equivalent) published prior to Autmn 2001. The sub-paragraphs below deal with the new procedure.

20.9.2   ON RECEIPT OF BRIEF

(a)   Open papers immediately and read instructions.

(b)   Check the statements of case. Has Form N5 been used for the claim form? Has the statement of truth been filled in correctly? Do the particulars of claim set out all the material matters, together with the ingredients prescribed by CPR, r. 16.4 and PD 55, para. 2.1? Has all the appropriate relief (possession, money claim, interest) been claimed? If not, and if defect is potentially fatal, ring solicitors with a view to adjourning the matter or putting the other side on notice (if there is time) that permission will be sought to amend at the hearing. Does the Claim Form contain a statement of truth?

(c)   Check whether materials in instructions support the matters set out in the particulars. In particular check whether (as appropriate):

   (i)   the lease is stamped and signed;

   (ii)   there is a properly worded proviso for re-entry;

   (iii) the service charge is recoverable as rent in arrears;

   (iv)   there is a properly worded s. 146 notice;

   (v)   there is proof that the defendant is the assignee of the term of the lease;

   (vi)   there appears to be sufficient compliance with (as appropriate), ss. 47 and 48 of the LTA 1987, s. 17 of the Landlord and Tenant (Covenants) Act 1995 and s. 82 of the HA 1996.

(d)   In the case of forfeiture proceedings for non-payment of service charge, ensure that the amount of the service charge has already been agreed by the defendant or determined by a court or arbitral tribunal (see s. 81 of the HA 1996).

(e)   Check whether a schedule of costs has been included.

(f)   Resist the temptation to ring your solicitors immediately if there appears to be an omission or mistake — read right through the papers carefully first, and then consider the problem afresh.

20.9.3   DAY BEFORE HEARING

Reopen your brief and prepare for the hearing. In particular:

(a)   Highlight or otherwise mark those parts of the tenancy agreement which are relevant, for easy reference (date, parties, premises, term, covenants and proviso for re-entry).

(b)   Calculate the outstanding sums due (arrears of rent, mesne profits, interest, etc.) as at the date of the hearing.

(c)   Marshal your papers in the correct order for presentation to the court (particulars of claim and then in order, those documents referred to in the particulars).

20.9.4   ATTENDANCE AT COURT

(a)   Arrive at the court at least half an hour before the time of the hearing.

(b)   Check where your case is on the list. Find the usher, give in your name, and note whether there is anyone on the other side. (Ask the usher to inform you if the defendant's representatives subsequently appear.)

(c)   Use the time before the hearing:

   (i)   to take any further instructions that are necessary;

   (ii)   to check your monetary calculations; and

   (iii)   to ensure that the originals of the documents necessary to prove your claim are available.

   If the defendant turns up, ascertain whether he or she is or is to be legally represented. If so, it may be appropriate to discuss the case with those representatives. If not, ask whether the defendant is prepared to indicate what stance is to be taken in relation to the proceedings (are they to be defended?), remembering to indicate first that the defendant is under no obligation to say anything at all to you.

(d)   Ensure that you are at hand when your case is called on.

20.9.5   PRESENTATION OF CASE

(a)   Open your case with the words: 'May it please [Your Honour] [you Sir] I represent the claimant in this matter ...'. If the defendant is present or represented, add: 'and my [learned] friend ... represents the defendant'/'and the defendant is here in person'. If not, add: 'as far as I am aware, the defendant is neither present nor represented', or words to that effect.

(b)   Give the judge a brief outline of the nature of the proceedings (for example: 'This is a forfeiture claim for possession of residential premises held under a long lease on the ground of arrears of rent and service charges amounting as at the date of issue of proceedings to £...').

(c)   Refer the judge to the statements of case. Some prefer to go through the particulars of claim in detail (and have them read out) whilst others prefer to go straight to the evidence after your brief introduction. Get to know your judge's style and preferences by sitting in the court beforehand (where the proceedings are in public) listening to the cases before you in the list.

(d)   Call your evidence. In a simple possession claim, this will consist of asking the witness to produce the lease or tenancy agreement, the relevant provisions of which you will then take the judge through. If the proceedings are not forfeiture proceedings, the witness will then have to produce the means of termination of the tenancy or other notice served as a statutory prerequisite to the proceedings. It may be necessary, in a contested case, for the witness not merely to produce a copy of the notice to quit served, but also to confirm that it was put in an envelope and actually sent to the defendant. Finally, your witness will have to give evidence as to the current amount outstanding, broken down into arrears of rent, mesne profits and so forth, and will need to show that the statutory requirements (see **20.9.2**(c)(vi) and (d)) have been complied with.

(e)   Closing submissions. This will often be limited to asking the judge for the relief sought. Ensure that you have yourself checked the monetary calculations and that you are in a position to supply the judge with the figures broken down in the way he or she prefers.

TWENTY ONE

DRAFTING LANDLORD AND TENANT STATEMENTS OF CASE

21.1 General

Before attempting to draft a landlord and tenant statement of case you should look back at the advice on this skill in the **Drafting Manual, Chapters 1** to **8**. In that Manual, **4.1** to **4.8** are particularly important. Directly relevant, also, are the passages in **7.6** and **7.7** of that Manual on the structure of a contract particulars of claim, since a tenancy is a contract. Thus, it will, for instance, generally be appropriate to give brief details of the lease or tenancy agreement in the first paragraph of the particulars of claim. Furthermore, in order to comply with CPR, PD 16 (Statements of Case), para. 9, where the claim is based upon a written agreement, a copy of the lease or tenancy agreement should be attached or served with the particulars of claim and the original should be available at the hearing. Where the agreement was oral, the particulars of claim should set out the contractual words used and state by whom, to whom, when and where they were spoken. The particulars of claim must also be verified by a statement of truth: CPR, r. 22.1(1)(a). In addition, there are certain matters peculiar to landlord and tenant claims which you may need to include and these are considered in the following paragraphs.

21.2 Parties

The parties to a landlord and tenant claim are frequently not the original parties to the lease or tenancy agreement, who may have assigned the term created by the lease and the reversion respectively long before the events causing the present proceedings occurred. In such a case it is unnecessary to draft all the details of dealings with term and reversion between parties who are in no way concerned with the present litigation. It is sufficient, after setting out the terms of the tenancy, to state that at all times material to the present proceedings, the term and reversion were vested in the claimant and defendant respectively. For an example, see **29.1, para. 3**. This paragraph in the statement of case is unnecessary when the parties to the current proceedings are the original landlord and tenant. See also **21.3**.

21.3 Possession Claims

21.3.1 GENERAL

CPR, Part 55 governs all possession claims and the procedure set out in this Part must be followed where the claim includes:

(a) a possession claim brought by a—

   (i)   landlord (or former landlord),

   (ii) mortgagee,

(iii)   licensor;

(b)   a possession claim against trespassers; or

(c)   a claim by a tenant seeking relief from forfeiture.

The claim form and defence must be in the forms annexed to PD 55. For most possession claims the forms to be used are N5 and N11 respectively. However, for the accelerated possession procedure, form N5B must be used (see **5.11**).

PD 55 provides that in a possession claim the particulars of claim must:

(a)   identify the land to which the claim relates;

(b)   state whether the claim relates to residential property;

(c)   state the ground on which possession is claimed;

(d)   give details about any mortgage or tenancy agreement; and

(e)   give details of every person, who to the best of the claimant's knowledge, is in possession of the property.

Where the claim relates to residential property let on a tenancy and the claim includes a claim for non-payment of rent, the particulars of claim must set out:

(a)   the amount due at the start of the proceedings;

(b)   in schedule form, the dates when the arrears of rent arose, all amounts of rent due, the dates and amounts of all payments made and a running total of the arrears;

(c)   the daily rate of any rent and interest;

(d)   any previous steps taken to recover the arrears of rent with full details of any court proceedings; and

(e)   any relevant information about the defendant's circumstances, in particular:

(i)   whether the defendant is in receipt of social security benefits; and

(ii)   whether any payments are made on his behalf directly to the claimant under the Social Security Contributions and Benefits Act 1992.

If the claimant knows of any person (including a mortgagee) entitled to claim relief against forfeiture as underlessee under LPA 1925, s. 146(4) (or in accordance with the Supreme Court Act 1981, s. 38, or the County Courts Act 1984, s. 138(9C)):

(a)   the particulars of claim must state the name and address of that person; and

(b)   the claimant must file a copy of the particulars of claim for service on him.

The requirements set out in CPR, Part 55 and PD 55 came into force on 15 October 2001 and must be read in conjunction with CPR, Part 16 and PD 16 (Statements of Case).

21.3.2   SUBTENANTS

In addition to joining the tenant as defendant, you should normally join any sub-tenants in case they claim protection under one of the statutory codes which give sub-tenants an independent right to remain in the dwelling house after the determination of the head tenancy, e.g. HA 1988, s. 18: see **5.12**. The tenant's spouse, too, should normally be joined if the tenant has left the dwelling-house but the spouse remains. See **20.8.2.3** and *Megarry*, vol. 1, p. 365.

21.3.3 MESNE PROFITS

There may well be a gap of some months between the termination of the lease where the life of the tenancy is not extended by any of the statutory codes and the date when the ex-tenant actually gives up possession. During this time the ex-landlord is not entitled to rent (as the lease has ended) but can claim mesne profits (i.e. compensation for the loss of use of his or her land while it is occupied by the ex-tenant). If the statement of case is silent as to the value of the land, the ex-landlord will recover mesne profits at the rate of the rent under the former lease. Frequently the value of the land will have risen and if the ex-landlord proves that the current open market letting value exceeds the former rent, then mesne profits will normally be awarded at that higher rate. The current value must be expressly stated (on instructions) to give the ex-tenant the opportunity to adduce his or her own valuation evidence at trial. If the land is worth less than its full market value to the tenant, e.g. where the letting was at a concessionary rent, then the value of the benefit of its occupation may be less than its market value: *Ministry of Defence* v *Ashman* [1993] 2 EGLR 102, CA. The ex-tenant may be liable to pay a reasonable rent even where he or she derived no benefit from his or her occupation: see *Inverugie Investments* v *Hackett* [1995] 3 All ER 841, PC, where holiday apartments were left vacant by the landlord after wrongfully evicting the tenant who recovered the notional rent they would have earned.

21.3.4 FORFEITURE PROCEEDINGS

A landlord wanting to forfeit for a cause other than non-payment of rent must serve a notice under LPA 1925, s. 146 (see **3.3.3** and *Megarry & Wade*, pp. 831–5 and precedents in **29.7** and **29.8**). In order to establish a valid forfeiture, the landlord must state and prove that the tenant failed to comply with the s. 146 notice by remedying any remediable breaches complained of. For examples see **29.6** and **29.11**.

In all forfeiture cases the landlord, in order to obtain a possession order, must show that he or she has exercised his or her right to re-enter the premises, thus determining the lease. The most common way of effecting this re-entry is by serving possession proceedings on the tenant (see *Canas Property Co. Ltd* v *KL Television Services Ltd* [1970] 2 QB 433, CA), and for a suggested draft of this notional re-entry see **29.11**). Where, however, the premises are unoccupied, the landlord may physically re-enter them and the fact that this has been done should be specified in the statement of case.

21.3.5 LP(R)A 1938

In a case where this Act (considered at **23.6.1**) applies, a landlord claiming possession and/or damages should state whether the defendant, on receipt of the appropriate notice under the Act, claimed the protection of the Act, and, if so, the date when the court gave permission to the landlord to bring proceedings. For an example, see **29.6**.

21.3.6 PRECEDENTS

For precedents of possession claims, see **29.6, 29.9, 29.10, 29.11, 29.12** and **29.13**.

For particulars of claim relating to rented residential premises, form N119 is used where grounds for possession include rent arrears. For an example of form N119, see **21.3.7**. For a guide to completing form N119, see **21.3.8**.

21.3.7   FORM N119

Particulars of claim
for possession
(rented residential premises)

In the

Claim No.

Claimant

Defendant

1.   The claimant has a right to possession of:

2.   To the best of the claimant's knowledge the following persons are in possession of the property:

About the tenancy

3.   (a) The premises are let to the defendant(s) under a(n)   tenancy
     which began on

     (b) The current rent is £   and is payable each (week) (fortnight) (month).
     (*other*   )

     (c) Any unpaid rent or charge for use and occupation should be calculated at £   per day.

4.   The reason the claimant is asking for possession is:
     (a) because the defendant has not paid the rent due under the terms of the tenancy agreement.
     (Details are set out below)(Details are shown on the attached rent statement)

     (b) because the defendant has failed to comply with other terms of the tenancy.
     Details are set out below.

     (c) because: (including any (other) statutory grounds)

5. The following steps have already been taken to recover any arrears:

6. The appropriate (notice to quit) (notice of breach of lease) (notice seeking possession) (*other* ....) was served on the defendant on   20

About the defendant

7. The following information is known about the defendant's circumstances:

About the claimant

8. The claimant is asking the court to take the following financial or other information into account when making its decision whether or not to grant an order for possession:

Forfeiture

9. (a) There is no underlessee or mortgagee entitled to claim relief against forfeiture.

or (b)   of

is entitled to claim relief against forfeiture as underlessee or mortgagee.

What the court is being asked to do:

10. The claimant asks the court to order that the defendant(s):

(a) give the claimant possession of the premises;

(b) pay the unpaid rent and any charge for use and occupation up to the date an order is made;

(c) pay rent and any charge for use and occupation from the date of the order until the claimant recovers possession of the property;

(d) pay the claimant's costs of making this claim.

Statement of Truth

'(I believe)(The claimant believes) that the facts stated in these particulars of claim are true.
' I am duly authorised by the claimant to sign this statement.

signed _____ date _____

'(Claimant)(Litigation friend*(where claimant is a child or a patient)*)(Claimant's solicitor)
'*delete as appropriate*

Full name _____

Name of claimant's solicitor's firm _____

position or office held _____
(if signing on behalf of firm or company)

21.3.8   GUIDE TO COMPLETION OF FORM N119 (PRESCRIBED FORM OF PARTICULARS OF CLAIM)

Use of Form N119 (for a blank form see **21.3.7**) is required by CPR, Part 4, in all County Court cases where possession of land which consists of or includes a dwelling house is claimed because of non-payment of rent.

Note:

(a)   the form should be used even if the claimant landlord also relies on other (non-rent-related) grounds for possession; and

(b)   strictly speaking, the form should be used where the claim is for forfeiture for non-payment of rent of a business lease where the demised premises comprise a shop with residential accommodation above.

General advice:

(a)   Do not be afraid to include additional relevant information (over and above that specifically requested on the form), if necessary by using continuation sheets.

(b)   In complex cases, for instance where non-payment of rent is only one of a number of alternative/cumulative grounds for possession, consider drafting a traditional particulars of claim and incorporating Form N119 by reference thereto.

Specific advice:

Para. 3:   This may be considered an appropriate place to include many of the matters which would have been included within an ordinary statement of case but in respect of which Form N119 makes no express provision.

Examples:

(a)   particulars of lease (e.g. date, term, parties, interest clauses, insurance rent provisions, rent review details, other material leasehold covenants [but see also para. 4(b)], proviso for re-entry);

(b)   devolution of title (if reversion and/or term assigned);

(c)   rateable value (if relevant to a statutory exception); and

(d)   if necessary, a statement as to status of tenancy.

Para. 4(a):   Insert accurate particulars of the rent arrears. Do not omit to state the outstanding total. Also, provide details of all instalments (partly) unpaid by the tenant. Attach a schedule and ensure that it starts at a time when the rental account showed a nil or credit balance; if there has been a long history of default, it may be necessary to go back a long way! The schedule must set out the dates when the arrears arose, all amounts of rent due, the dates and amounts of all payments made and a running total of the arrears: PD 56, para. 2.3(2).

Particularly in cases involving residential long leases at low rents, if there is unpaid service charge (reserved as rent by the lease) and it is sought to forfeit the lease by reason of the same, it is advisable to include a statement that, for the purposes of HA 1996, s. 81, the service charge (a) has been agreed or admitted by the tenant, or (b) has been the subject of determination by a court or by an arbitral tribunal. Of course, in such event full particulars of the relevant supporting facts should be provided.

Para. 4(b):   Here include details of all breaches other than the failure to pay rent, e.g. breach of a covenant against the commission of nuisance. Presumably the very covenant in question could itself be pleaded here. This would also appear to be an appropriate place to particularise any claim for damages.

        If there is unpaid service charge (*not* reserved as rent by the lease) and it is sought to forfeit the lease by reason of the same, it is advisable to include a statement that, for the purposes of HA 1996, s. 81, the service charge (a) has been agreed or admitted by the tenant, or (b) has been the subject of determination by a court or by an arbitral tribunal. Of course, in such event full particulars of the relevant supporting facts should be provided.

Para. 4(c):   Where reliance is placed on statutory grounds for possession (tenancies within RA 1977 or HA 1985 and 1988) specify, rather than merely identify, the grounds. In other words, repeat the statutory text verbatim.

Para. 6:   Identify which option, if any, applies to your case and then insert (as appropriate) the date of service of any notice to quit (periodic protected tenancies under RA 1977 or periodic tenancies falling outside any of the statutory codes), notice seeking possession (HA 1985, s. 83 or HA 1988, s. 8) or s.146 notice (forfeiture of fixed-term tenancies, whether protected under RA 1977 or otherwise).

        For the sake of completeness, you may also wish to include at this point failure to remedy the breach(es) in accordance with the s. 146 notice and also the fact of the landlord's forfeiture by service of these particulars of claim (although it is probably unnecessary to do so).

Para. 10:   You may well desire to plead other heads of relief claimed. For example, these may include:

        (a)   damages;

        (b)   interest, pursuant to contract and/or statute.

TWENTY TWO

SUMMARY POSSESSION PROCEEDINGS

22.1 Disadvantages in Normal Possession Claim

Where premises are unlawfully entered and occupied by trespassers ('squatters'), a possession claim of the sort used between landlord and tenant has two main disadvantages:

(a) It is usually difficult or impossible to identify any of or all the trespassers so as to name them as defendants and serve them with proceedings.

(b) Obtaining a normal possession order usually takes several months.

22.2 Special Procedure

Part 55 of the CPR, which came into force on 15 October 2001, provides for all possession claims, including those against trespassers. A trespasser includes a person who entered or remained upon the land without the consent of the owner, but does not include a tenant, whether the tenancy has been terminated or not. Consequently, a claim will start in the same way as other possession claims (see **Chapter 21**). However, where the claimant does not know the name of the person in occupation, as is common in claims against squatters, the claim must be brought against 'persons unknown' in addition to any named defendants: CPR, r. 55.3(4). The defendant must be served with the claim form, particulars of claim and any witness statements on which the claimant seeks to rely, in the case of residential property, not less than five days and, in the case of any other land, not less than two days before the hearing date. The particulars of claim should be set out in form N121. Where the claim has been issued against 'persons unknown', copies of the claim form, particulars of claim and witness statements must be attached to the main door or some other part of the land so that they are clearly visible and, if practicable, inserting copies in a sealed transparent envelope addressed to 'the occupiers' through the letter box: CPR, r. 55.6(1)(a). Alternatively, service may be effected by placing stakes in the land in places where they are clearly visible and attaching to each stake copies of the documents in a sealed transparent envelope addressed to 'the occupiers': CPR, r. 55.6(1)(b). Where the claimant effects service, a certificate of service must be produced at the hearing: CPR, r. 55.8(6).

22.3 Interim Possession Order

The interim possession procedure was introduced in 1995 to help landowners to remove squatters more quickly. The relevant rules are set out in CCR Order 24, Part II (CPR, sch. 2) and they have survived the introduction of CPR, Part 55. Where an application for an interim possession order is to be made, CPR, r. 55(2)–(7) do not apply: CCR, r. 24.10. Instead, claim form N130 is used, together with an application notice: form N131. There must also be a witness statement or affidavit in support. The claim may be made against any person who entered as a trespasser, providing it is made within 28 days of the owner learning of the trespasser's occupation. This procedure may not be used against a person who originally entered with the consent of the owner and it may only be used in respect of premises, not land. At the hearing of the application, the court may order the respondent to vacate the premises within 24 hours of service of the order. The applicant may be required to give undertakings, e.g. as to reinstatement of the respondent or damages, if the order is ultimately held to have been wrongly made.

If the respondent does not comply with the order the applicant must seek police help and produce to the police a copy of the interim order and affidavit of service, showing that the period of 24 hours has elapsed. It is a criminal offence for the respondent to disobey such an order or to return to the premises within 12 months, and a constable may arrest without warrant any one he or she reasonably suspects to be guilty of such an offence: Criminal Justice and Public Order Act 1994, s. 76. It is also a criminal offence to give false information in order to obtain or resist an interim possession order: ibid, s. 75.

At the hearing the court will also fix a return date when the interim possession order will expire. At the hearing on the return date the judge may make a final possession order, or dismiss the claim or order that the claim should continue under CCR, O. 24, part I as if no interim possession order had been sought. A respondent who vacates pursuant to an interim order may apply to the court to have it set aside before the return date.

22.4   Criminal Liability

It is now also a criminal offence for a 'squatter' to remain in residential premises if required to leave by the freehold owner or tenant of the premises who wishes to occupy them as a residence: Criminal Law Act 1977, s. 7, as substituted by the Criminal Justice and Public Order Act 1994, s. 73.

22.5   Possession Claims Against Trespassers: A Practical Guide

(a) Since 15 October 2001, the procedure applicable to possession claims against trespassers (including those who were originally licensees) is prescribed by CPR, Part 55 and PD 55.

(b) Note that this procedure cannot be used against tenants holding over, and, unlike the procedures it replaces (namely RSC O. 113 and CCR O. 24), it cannot be used by a landlord against unlawful sub-tenants. Such proceedings are so simple that although a beginner, you may well be instructed to appear in the High Court in such a case. Having said that, as a result of the changes made by CPR, Part 55 it will be a rare case that will now be commenced in the High Court.

(c) If instructed to settle the appropriate claim form and witness statement, a choice has to be made between the High Court and the County Court. As stated above, save in exceptional circumstances possession claims, including claims against trespassers, should be commenced in the local County Court. PD 55 contains the criteria to be applied when deciding whether or not such a possession claim should be started in the High Court or the County Court.

(d) Confusingly in the County Court, there remains a procedure for obtaining interim possession orders: see **22.3**. The procedure is only available in respect of premises, not land. If an interim possession order is obtained, and there are detailed requirements which must be satisfied, the burden is, in effect, placed on the defendant to show why a final order should not be made. It is a criminal offence to fail to obey such an order, and a criminal offence to return to the premises within 12 months of an order being made.

(e) Provided the words of the orders are followed exactly, there should be no difficulty from the claimant's point of view. There tend to be two areas where mistakes are made. The first concerns service on those in occupation not named in the proceedings. You should ensure the prescribed means of service are followed precisely; solicitors often think their means of service is better! The requirement that the claim form and witness statement in support be sealed in a transparent envelope is often not followed. Frequently an ordinary, opaque envelope is used. This is not sufficient.

(f) Mistakes are frequently made in the witness statement in support. The witness statement must contain the averments required by the rules. The requirement under the former rules that the witness statement contain an averment that the witness does not know the name of any person occupying the land who is not named in the summons is not required by CPR, Part 55, but best practice suggests it should still be averred.

(g) This procedure is to be used in straightforward cases only. If there are serious issues as to title, the summary procedure is inappropriate. Where a defendant raises a genuine dispute on grounds which appear to be substantial, the court will treat the first hearing as a case management conference and give directions. Having said that, if there is court time available, and the relevant witnesses are in attendance (both of which may infrequently be the case) the court has power to decide the claim.

(h) In the County Court claims under CPR, Part 55 will be heard in open court and wig and gown are worn. Having said that, the practice may vary from court to court. If in doubt, bring your robes! In the High Court, the hearing will be before a Master in chambers.

(i) It is not uncommon for the defendant or defendants to attend and raise a number of points which have nothing to do with their alleged rights to stay in the premises. Premises are often occupied in order to prevent them being demolished or redeveloped, and the complaints of the occupiers are really aimed at the local planning authority or some government department. Although these points are raised, they are never enough to defeat a claim under this procedure. The area where real issues do arise is whether a tenancy or licence has been created.

(j) As to costs, there is no reason why the successful claimant should not obtain his or her costs against a named defendant. Where, however, the proceedings have been commenced against unidentified occupiers, the court will not award the successful claimant his or her costs.

22.6   Summary Possession Claims Checklist

22.8.1   THE CIVIL PROCEDURE RULES

Although the Civil Procedure Rules 1998 were introduced in April 1999, procedure governing possession claims against trespassers in the High Court and the County Courts continued until 15 October 2001 to be governed by the Rules of the Supreme Court and the County Court Rules (which were significantly different). On 15 October 2001, Part 55 was added to the Civil Procedure Rules, for the first time introducing a uniform code for the conduct of possession claims against trespassers in the High Court and the County Courts. Claims issued before that date are still governed by the old procedure, and practitioners seeking guidance on that procedure should look in an edition of the White Book (or its equivalent) published prior to Autumn 2001. The sub-paragraphs below deal with the new procedure.

22.8.2   ON RECEIPT OF BRIEF

Check that the statements of case and evidence comply with the rules.

In particular:

(a)   Check that the claim form is in Form N5.

(b)   Check that the claim has not been brought against a 'tenant or subtenant holding over after the termination of the tenancy'.

(c)   Each party should wherever possible include all the evidence he wishes to present in his statement of case, verified by a statement of truth (see PD 55, para. 5.1). Accordingly, it should rarely be necessary for a witness statement to be provided to support the particulars of claim. A working guide to the requirements for the particulars of claim is provided by Form N121. In particular, the claimant must state his interest in the land and the circumstances in which it was occupied without licence or consent (see CPR, r. 55.1(b)).

(d)   Any fact that needs to be proved by the evidence of witnesses at a hearing may be proved by evidence in writing. It will be good practice to attempt to ensure that hearsay evidence is not included in the written evidence.

(e)   Check that the relevant time limits have been complied with (see CPR, r. 55.5(2)). In the event of non-compliance, check that you have instructions to apply to abridge time and consider whether circumstances equivalent to those set out in PD 55, para. 3.2 apply.

(f)   As to jurisdiction in cases involving licences, see Protection from Eviction Act 1977.

Note that CCR, O. 24 (which has been retained in sch. 2 to the CPR) provides for an 'interim possession order' in certain circumstances: see **22.3**. If your instructions are to seek such an order, then follow through the requirements of part II of O. 24, ensuring that each condition has been complied with to the letter.

22.8.3   AT THE HEARING

It is rare for a defendant to appear at the hearing of possession proceedings against trespassers. For that reason, the court may be anxious to scrutinise the proceedings with especial care. Ensure, therefore, that you are thoroughly familiar both with the rules and with your brief. In the event that you are successful, remember that you are not entitled to costs against persons unknown. In the event that you are unsuccessful, it may be that you will be able to persuade the court that the proceedings should continue rather than be dismissed, under CPR, r. 8.1(3).

TWENTY-THREE

REPAIRING COVENANTS

23.1 Implied Covenants by Tenants

The only obligation generally imposed on a tenant in the absence of express stipulations in the lease is that of tenant-like user of the premises. The tenant must take proper and reasonable care of the premises, e.g. do the odd jobs around the house which a reasonable tenant would do: *Warren v Keen* [1954] 1 QB 15. He or she must also repair damage caused by himself or herself, his or her family or guests, but has no duty to effect repairs to counter the effects of fair wear and tear and the passage of time.

23.2 Implied Obligations of Landlords

23.2.1 OBLIGATIONS IMPLIED BY COMMON LAW

23.2.1.1 Fit for occupation
In letting a furnished house or flat a landlord impliedly covenants that the premises shall be fit for occupation at the start of the tenancy, e.g. not infested with bugs or having defective drains: *Collins v Hopkins* [1923] 2 KB 617. No warranty is, however, implied that the premises will continue fit during the term.

23.2.1.2 Ancillary property
A landlord is under a duty to repair his or her own property ancillary to the demised premises where its maintenance in proper repair is necessary for the safe enjoyment of the demised premises by the tenant, e.g. the roof or a staircase of a block of flats. This duty is to take reasonable care that the premises retained by him or her are in a state of repair such that they will not cause damage to the tenant or to the demised premises: see *Cockburn v Smith* [1924] 2 KB 119, approved in *Duke of Westminster v Guild* [1985] QB 688, CA.

23.2.1.3 Business efficacy
The court will sometimes imply a repairing obligation by the landlord to give business efficacy to the agreement under the contractual doctrine discussed in *Miller v Hancock* [1893] 2 QB 177. In *Liverpool City Council v Irwin* [1977] AC 239, HL, a landlord let parts of a block of flats to a number of different tenants and retained essential means of access (stairs, lifts, rubbish chutes). There was no express obligation on the tenants or on the landlord to repair these means of access and the landlord was held to be under an obligation to take reasonable care to keep those essential means of access in reasonable repair. This principle obliged a local authority landlord to repair a path retained by it over which the tenant had an easement to use it as a necessary rear access to the premises: *King v South Northants DC* [1992] 06 EG 152. See also *Barrett v Lounova* [1988] 2 EG 54, where the tenancy agreement obliged the tenant to repair the interior but was silent as to any obligation to repair the exterior. The court implied an obligation by the landlord to repair the exterior in order to give business efficacy to the agreement.

23.2.2   OBLIGATIONS IMPLIED BY STATUTE

23.2.2.1   Low rent: fit for human habitation

LTA 1985, s. 8 implies into certain leases, notwithstanding any stipulation to the contrary, a condition that a house let at a low rent for human habitation is reasonably fit for that purpose at the start of the tenancy and an undertaking that the landlord will keep it so fit during the tenancy. Low rent here means, if the tenancy was granted after 6 July 1957, a rent not exceeding £80 per annum if the house is in London and not exceeding £52 per annum if the house is elsewhere. The rent limit is even lower if the tenancy was granted before that date. Few tenancies are subject to this implied obligation!

23.2.2.2   LTA 1985, ss. 11 and 12

LTA 1985, ss. 11 and 12 contain the most important of the landlord's implied repairing obligations.

(a)   Application: the obligation is implied in leases of dwelling-houses granted on or after 24 October 1961 for a term of less than seven years: LTA 1985, s. 13(1). In determining whether a lease satisfies this condition the following rules apply:

    (i)   any part of the term which falls before the date of the grant shall be ignored and the lease is treated as one commencing on the date of the grant;

    (ii)   a lease which can be determined at the option of the landlord sooner than seven years from the start of the term is treated as a lease for less than seven years;

    (iii)   a lease which gives the tenant the option to renew the lease for a term which together with the original term exceeds seven years is treated as a lease for seven years or more: s. 13(2).

(b)   Exceptions: the obligation is not implied in leases granted to certain tenants, e.g. local authorities: s. 14(4) and (5). It is not implied in certain leases: s. 14(1), (2) and (3) and s. 32(2).

(c)   The obligation: the covenant implied in such leases is:

    (i)   to keep in repair the structure and exterior of the dwelling house (including drains, gutters and external pipes) (for a definition of 'structure and exterior of the dwelling-house', see *Campden Hill Towers v Gardner* [1977] QB 823, CA, *Douglas Scott v Scorgie* [1984] 1 All ER 1056, CA, and *Irvine v Moran* [1991] 1 EGLR 261, QB);

    (ii)   to keep in repair and proper working order the installations in the dwelling house for the supply of water, gas and electricity and for sanitation (including basins, sinks, baths and sanitary conveniences, but not other fixtures, fittings and appliances for making use of the supply of water, gas or electricity); and

    (iii)   to keep in repair and proper working order the installations in the dwelling house for space heating and heating water: s. 11(1).

The covenant does not oblige the landlord:

    (i)   to carry out works or repairs for which the tenant is liable under his or her duty to use the premises in a tenant-like manner, or would be so liable but for an express covenant on his or her part; or

    (ii)   to rebuild or reinstate the premises in the case of destruction or damage by fire, or by tempest, flood or other inevitable accident; or

(iii) to keep in repair or maintain anything which the tenant is entitled to remove from the dwelling house (tenant's fixtures): s. 11(2).

In determining the standard of repair required by this covenant, regard is to be had to the age, character and prospective life of the dwelling house and the locality in which it is situated: s. 11(3).

(d) Wider obligation in new leases: where a dwelling house forming part only of a larger building is let after 15 January 1989, the landlord's repairing obligation under s. 11(1) is not confined to the dwelling house itself but is extended to any part of the building in which the landlord has an interest and also to installations serving the dwelling house in such parts of the building: s. 11(1A).

This wider obligation arises only where the lack of repair affects the tenant's enjoyment of either the dwelling-house or of common parts the tenant is entitled to use under the terms of the lease: s. 11(1B). Further, the landlord is given a defence to liability, if despite reasonable efforts, he or she is unable to obtain such rights over other parts of the building as are necessary to enable him or her to comply with his or her obligation: s. 11(3A).

(e) Tenant's covenant: any covenant in the lease obliging the tenant to carry out or pay for repairs or work falling within s. 11(1) is void and of no effect: s. 11(4) and (5).

(f) Limited right to opt out: any provision in a lease purporting to exclude the landlord's liability under s. 11 or to penalise a tenant who seeks to rely on the statute is void (s. 12(1)), unless the inclusion of the provision was authorised by the County Court. The County Court may, with the consent of both parties, authorise the inclusion of a term in the lease excluding or modifying the landlord's liability under s. 11 if satisfied that it is reasonable to do so: s. 12(2).

(g) Right to inspect: any lease in which this landlord's repairing covenant is implied is also subject to an implied covenant by the tenant to permit the landlord to enter the dwelling house to view its condition and state of repair: s. 11(6).

23.2.2.3 Defective Premises Act 1972, s. 4

A duty under s. 4 is owed first where the landlord is under an obligation in the lease, express or implied, to maintain or repair the premises. It is owed secondly, where, although under no obligation to do so, the landlord has the right to enter the premises to carry out maintenance or repair. Such a right has been implied into a tenancy agreement to give it business efficacy: see *McAuley v Bristol City Council* [1992] 1 All ER 749, CA.

The duty on a landlord is owed to all persons (including the tenant) whom the landlord might reasonably expect to be affected by defects in the state of the premises to take reasonable care to ensure that they are reasonably safe from personal injury or damage to property caused by a 'relevant defect' — a defect caused by the landlord's failure to comply with his or her repairing obligations. This statutory duty is not strictly a repairing covenant and the landlord may, in some circumstances, be able to satisfy the duty simply by erecting warning signs or notices of any defects or danger although frequently performance of the duty will necessarily involve carrying out the repair: see *McAuley v Bristol City Council.*

23.3 'Repair' Interpreted by the Courts

23.3.1 CONSTRUCTION

The construction of an express covenant or implied term depends largely on the words used in the lease or statute, but it is possible to give some general guidelines as to the court's approach.

23.3.2   STANDARD OF REPAIR

The obligation to repair is usually to keep the premises in 'good', 'habitable' or 'tenantable' repair. These all mean much the same thing, i.e. such repair as, having regard to the age, character and locality of the house, would make it reasonably fit for the occupation of a reasonably minded tenant of the class who would be likely to take it at the time of the demise: *Proudfoot* v *Hart* (1890) 25 QBD 42; *Calthorpe* v *McOscar* [1924] 1 KB 716. Note that a covenant to keep premises in repair entails an obligation to put them in repair first, if at the time of the demise they are out of repair: *Proudfoot* v *Hart* (above).

23.3.3   REPAIR DISTINGUISHED FROM RENEWAL AND IMPROVEMENT

A covenant to repair does not oblige the covenantor either to renew or to improve the premises, though the dividing line between repair on the one hand and renewal or improvement on the other, is often a difficult one to draw. Repair, it has been said, is restoration by renewal or replacement of subsidiary parts of a whole, whereas renewal is reconstruction of the entirety, meaning not necessarily the whole but substantially the whole of the subject-matter: *Lurcott* v *Wakely* [1911] 1 KB 905; cf. the facts in *Lister* v *Lane* [1893] 2 QB 212.

A further test has been suggested: do the works required involve giving back to the landlord a wholly different thing from that which was demised?: see *Ravenseft Properties* v *Davstone (Holdings)* [1980] QB 12, DC, where the court found it helpful to contrast the cost of the works required with the replacement cost of the building. But the question is always one of degree: can the necessary works be properly described as repair?: *Post Office* v *Aquarius Properties Ltd* [1987] 1 All ER 1055, CA. The judgments in both the *Ravenseft* and *Post Office* cases are essential reading on this difficult question.

23.3.4   NO DUTY TO CURE STRUCTURAL DEFECT

A repairing covenant does not oblige the covenantor to replace a defective part of a building unless the part has deteriorated from some former better condition and can thus be said to be out of repair: *Quick* v *Taff Ely Borough Council* [1986] QB 809, CA; *Post Office* v *Aquarius Properties Ltd* (above). Where the structural defect existed in its present form from the start of the tenancy there is no duty to cure it. If, however, the defect has caused a state of disrepair in other parts of the premises within the repairing covenant, the covenantor will be liable to repair those: *Quick* v *Taff Ely Borough Council* (above).

23.3.5   REPAIR CONTRASTED WITH IMPROVEMENT

The duty to repair does not normally oblige the covenantor to carry out improvements to the premises such as curing inherent defects, e.g. waterproofing outside walls built without any water protection (*Pembery* v *Lamdin* [1940] 2 All ER 434), or installing a damp-proof course in premises built without one. If the lack of a damp-proof course results in dry rot the covenantor must deal with the dry rot as a matter of repair but will not normally be obliged to install a damp–proof course (though see *Elmcroft Developments* v *Tankersley-Sawyer* (1984) 270 EG 140, CA, where on the particular facts, the repairing covenant was construed as obliging the landlord to install a damp-proof course rather than keep patching up damp plaster).

This general rule is subject to the qualification that in many cases performing a repair will necessarily involve making an improvement: see the *Ravenseft* case where current building practice would not allow the necessary repair work to be carried out without making an improvement — it was the only safe way of carrying out the repair; and see also *Lurcott* v *Wakely* (above), *Brew Bros* v *Snax* [1970] 1 QB 612 and *Elmcroft Developments* v *Tankersley-Sawyer* (above).

23.3.6   WORDS OTHER THAN 'REPAIR'

Note, however, that a sufficiently widely worded covenant to repair can oblige the covenantor to rebuild virtually the whole of the premises: *Smedley* v *Chumley* &

Hawkes (1982) 44 P & CR 50, CA and see *Credit Suisse* v *Beegas Nominees Ltd* [1994] 4 All ER 803, ChD: obligation 'to renew and amend'. See also *Welch* v *Greenwich LBC* [2000] 3 EGLR 41 (maintaining the dwelling in good condition and repair).

23.3.7 DESTRUCTION BY FIRE OR OTHER CALAMITY

A tenant may, under a general repairing covenant, be obliged to rebuild the whole of the premises if they are destroyed by fire or some other calamity or by the tenant's own act: *Redmond* v *Dainton* [1920] 2 KB 256. Therefore it is common to insert words such as 'damage by accidental fire or by tempest or other inevitable accident excepted' — see clause 2(3) of the draft specimen lease in **Chapter 25** — to avoid this.

23.4 Need for Notice

Where the landlord is obliged, whether by an implied or an express term, to repair the demised premises themselves, the obligation to remedy any lack of repair will not arise until the landlord has been notified of the want of repair: *Torrens* v *Walker* [1906] 2 Ch 166 and *O'Brien* v *Robinson* [1973] AC 912. This rule applies even where the lease contains a right for the landlord to enter to inspect the premises and so could discover the defect himself or herself. There is no obligation to give notice, however, where the lack of repair is in the common parts of a building in multiple occupation or in a part of the premises retained by the landlord. Where the covenant is to keep common or retained parts in repair, the landlord will be in breach as soon as a defect occurs and not at the possibly later time when the landlord discovers the existence of the defect: *British Telecom* v *Sun Life Assurance Society* [1995] 4 All ER 44, CA.

23.5 Further Reading

For a full consideration of repairing covenants, see *Woodfall*, vol. 1, pp. 13/1–13/52 and for a practical guide to a tenant's claim for breach of repairing obligation, see **23.10**.

23.6 Landlord's Remedies for Tenant's Breach of Repairing Covenant

23.6.1 FORFEITURE

23.6.1.1 Preliminary
This remedy is only available if the lease reserves a right to forfeit or re-enter. Of the many strict rules which must be complied with to effect a valid forfeiture (see *Megarry & Wade*, pp. 811–46), only those relevant to forfeiture for breach of a repairing covenant are considered below.

23.6.1.2 The rules

(a) LPA 1925, s. 146: the landlord must serve a notice informing the tenant of the breaches of covenant complained of, calling on him or her to remedy them within a reasonable time and, if relevant, pay monetary compensation in respect of them. Section 146 should be studied in detail: see *Megarry & Wade*, pp. 678–83, and **29.7** and **29.8** for examples of such a notice.

(b) LTA 1927, s. 18(2): the landlord must prove that the tenant knew that the s. 146 notice had been served and had had sufficient time to comply with it since acquiring that knowledge.

(c) LP(R)A 1938, s. 1: applies only to leases for terms of seven years or more of which at least three years remain unexpired at the date of service of the s. 146 notice. This section requires the landlord in his or her s. 146 notice to inform the tenant of his or her rights under the 1938 Act and how to claim them.

If the tenant does claim the benefit of the Act, then the landlord cannot commence forfeiture proceedings without the court's permission. Permission will only be given if the landlord can prove in accordance with the balance of probabilities the existence of one or more of the five grounds (which relate to proof of the genuine gravity of the consequences of the breaches): s. 1(5). As to the standard of proof required to make out these grounds, see *Associated British Ports* v *C H Bailey plc* [1990] 2 AC 703, HL.

23.6.2 SPECIFIC PERFORMANCE

The court will not compel a tenant by a decree of specific performance or by a mandatory injunction to carry out his or her repairing covenant: *Hill* v *Barclay* (1810) 16 Ves 402. This principle has been doubted and it has been said that specific performance might, in rare cases where it was appropriate, be granted against a tenant, e.g. where the nature of the work to be carried out was clear and the landlord might have difficulty in carrying out the repairs (in a case where the landlord has no rights of access): *Rainbow Estates* v *Tokenhold Ltd* [1998] 2 All ER 860. Specific performance will not be granted where this would circumvent the protection given to tenants by the LP(R)A 1938: see **23.6.1.2** and **23.6.3.1**.

23.6.3 DAMAGES

23.6.3.1 Procedural requirement where landlord sues

LP(R)A 1938 again applies if at least three years of a term exceeding seven years remain. The landlord must serve a notice complying with LPA 1925, s. 146 and informing the tenant of his or her rights under the 1938 Act and how to claim them. The court's permission to bring proceedings for damages without any forfeiture claim is necessary if the tenant claims the Act's protection. Note that permission will not be given in a case where the landlord has already remedied the breach (i.e. carried out the repairs) before service of the s. 146 notice: *SEDAC Investments* v *Tanner* [1982] 1 WLR 1342, ChD.

23.6.3.2 Measure of damages at common law for non-repair by the tenant

(a) During the term: the measure will be the amount by which the market value of the reversion is depreciated due to the lack of repair. This is a matter for expert evidence and will be affected by the length of time the lease has still to run.

(b) At the end of the term (because the lease has either expired or been forfeited for breach of covenant): the measure is the difference between the value of the property as it stands and the value it would have had if the tenant had carried out his or her obligations under the contract: *Hanson* v *Newman* [1934] Ch 298. Where the landlord has re-entered, the tenant cannot claim a reduction in the damages on the ground that the landlord has had his or her property back sooner than he or she would otherwise have done: *Hanson* v *Newman* (above).

The landlord is also entitled to compensation for the loss of use of the premises while being repaired due to the tenant's breach. The landlord may, instead of claiming the fall in the value of the property, be entitled to the cost of carrying out the work necessary to remedy the breach in a case where he or she has carried out or is about to carry out those repairs: *Jones* v *Herxheimer* [1950] 2 KB 106.

23.6.3.3 Statutory 'ceiling' on damages

The common law measure of damages discussed in **23.6.3.2** is subject to the ceiling on damages imposed by LTA 1927, s. 18(1). This provision limits the damages recoverable by the landlord in respect of a breach of the tenant's repairing covenant to the amount by which the value of his or her reversion is reduced, rather than the probably higher figure of the cost of carrying out the repairs. In practice, however, if the landlord has actually carried out the repairs or satisfies the court that he or she is about to do so, then the cost involved will be taken as evidence of damage to the reversion and the landlord will recover that cost: *Jones* v *Herxheimer* (above). See also *Culworth Estates Ltd* v *Society of Licensed Victuallers* (1991) 62 P & CR 211, CA, where a landlord who did not intend to carry out the repairs, recovered their cost on proving that the diminution in the value of the reversion exceeded that cost and *Crewe Services and Investment Corporation v Silk, The Times*, 2 January 1998 (cost of repairs heavily discounted in absence of evidence they would be executed). When the landlord's reversionary interest had a negative value, the diminution was calculated as the difference between the sum the landlord had to pay the transferee with the premises in their unrepaired state and the lesser sum the landlord would have had to pay had the premises been repaired in accordance with the tenant's covenant: *Shortlands Investments Ltd v Cargill plc* [1995] 1 EGLR 51.

LTA 1927, s. 18(1), proviso, precludes the landlord from recovering any damages at all where, at the end of the lease, he or she intends to demolish the premises or carry out structural works which would render valueless the repairs covered by the covenant.

23.6.4 TERM ENTITLING LANDLORD TO DO REPAIRS AND RECOVER COST

A well drafted lease will reserve to the landlord the right, on the tenant's failure to comply with his or her repairing obligations, to carry out the repairs and claim the cost of doing so from the tenant as a debt: see the specimen draft lease, clause 2(7) (**Chapter 25**). Such a claim is one in debt rather than a claim for damages for breach of covenant and is therefore not 'caught' by LP(R)A 1938: *Hamilton v Martell Securities* [1984] Ch 266, *Jervis v Harris* [1996] 1 All ER 303, CA.

23.7 Tenant's Remedies for Landlord's Breach

23.7.1 PROCEDURAL CONSIDERATIONS

A Draft Pre-Action Protocol for Housing Disrepair has been published which is likely to form the basis of a formally adopted Protocol.

As with other Pre-Action Protocols, sanctions will be applied where there is failure to follow the Protocol.

Under the CPR, r. 26.6, claims by a tenant of residential premises against the landlord will be allocated to the small claims track where:

(a) the tenant is seeking an order requiring the landlord to carry out repairs or other work;

(b) the cost of the repairs or other work is estimated to be not more than £1,000; and

(c) the financial value of any claim for damages is not more than £1,000.

23.7.2 SPECIFIC PERFORMANCE

The court (and, in the County Court, this includes a district judge sitting in a small claims case: *Joyce v Liverpool CC* [1995] 3 All ER 110, CA) has power to decree specific performance of a landlord's repairing covenant both at common law (see *Jeune v Queen's Cross Properties Ltd* [1974] Ch 97) and, in relation to dwellings, under statute: LTA 1985, s. 17. In exceptional cases, such as where there is a real risk to the tenant's health, the court may grant an interim mandatory injunction to carry out the repairs, especially where the nature of the work to be done is clear and it can be easily carried out: *Parker v Camden LBC* [1986] Ch 162.

23.7.3 DAMAGES

23.7.3.1 Measure of damages
These will depend on the facts of the individual case but, where the tenant has remained in the premises during the period of the breach, the following is a useful guide. The measure is:

(a) the difference in value to the tenant, starting from the date when the tenant notified the landlord of the need for repair up to the date of assessment of damages, between the house in its unrepaired condition and the house in the condition in which it would have been if the landlord, on receipt of the notice, had fulfilled his or her repairing obligations; plus

(b) any damage to the tenant's property during that period: *Pembery v Lamdin* [1940] 2 All ER 434.

This formula has been interpreted in *Calabar Properties v Stitcher* [1984] 1 WLR 287, CA (which is essential reading on this area) and also in *McGreal v Wake* (1984) 269 EG 1524, CA, *Mira v Aylmer Square Investments* [1990] 1 EGLR 45, CA, *Branchett v Beaney* [1992] 3 All ER 910, 916 and *Wallace v Manchester City Council* (1999) 30 HLR 1111. For heads of loss, see **23.10.5.1.**

23.7.3.2 Tenant's right to equitable set-off against rent claim

A tenant sued for unpaid rent may rely on any counterclaim he or she has for damages for breach of the landlord's repairing covenant as a defence by way of equitable set-off to the claim for rent: *British Anzani (Felixstowe) Ltd v International Marine Management (UK) Ltd* [1980] QB 137. It is immaterial that the tenant's counterclaim has not been quantified at the start of the landlord's proceedings: *Televantos v McCulloch* [1991] 1 EGLR 123. Clear words must, however, be used to exclude this right of set-off and an obligation to pay rent 'without any deduction' is not sufficiently clear, by itself, to do so: *Connaught Restaurants Ltd v Indoor Leisure Ltd* [1994] 1 WLR 501, CA.

A clause in a lease barring such a right of set-off is part of a contract relating to the creation of an interest in land and does not, therefore, fall within the scope of the Unfair Contract Terms Act 1977: *Electricity Supply Nominees Ltd v IAF Group Ltd* [1993] 1 WLR 1059. However, it may fall foul of the Unfair Terms in Consumer Contracts Regulations 1999 (SI 1999 No. 2083): see *Draft Guidance on Unfair Terms in Tenancy Agreements* published by the Office of Fair Trading.

A landlord may be restrained by injunction from exercising the remedy of levying a distress to satisfy a claim for unpaid rent against which the tenant asserts a defence by way of equitable set-off. For it would be 'contrary to principle that a landlord should be able to recover more by distress that he [could] by action': *Eller v Grovecrest Investments Ltd* [1994] 4 All ER 845 at 850, CA, per Hoffman LJ.

23.7.4 TENANT'S RIGHT TO RECOUP COST OF REPAIRS FROM RENT LIABILITY

Where the landlord is in breach of his or her repairing obligations and the tenant carries out the repairs, the tenant is entitled to have his or her expenditure treated as though it had been a direct payment of the rent. The tenant may, by a process of recoupment, not equitable set-off, claim credit for that expenditure in assessing his or her liability for rent: *Lee-Parker v Izzet* [1971] 1 WLR 1688, *Connaught Restaurants Ltd v Indoor Leisure Ltd* [1994] 1 WLR 501 at 507, CA.

23.7.5 LANDLORD'S REPUDIATORY BREACH OF COVENANT

If the breach of a repairing covenant is severe, it may amount to a repudiatory breach which, if accepted by the tenant, will terminate the lease and the tenant's obligations under it. In a case where the breaches of the landlord's repairing covenant under LTA 1985, s. 11 were so grave as to render the house unfit to be lived in, it was held that the landlord's refusal to carry out repairs showed an intention not to be bound by his repairing covenant and amounted to a repudiatory breach of covenant. The tenant's action in returning the keys and vacating the house was an acceptance of that breach and terminated the three-year lease. The tenant was accordingly relieved of any liability for rent accruing after that date and recovered damages for breach of covenant: *Hussein v Mehlman* [1992] 2 EGLR 87.

23.8 Statutory Nuisance: Criminal Sanction

Where the premises are in such a state as to be prejudicial to health, this will constitute a statutory nuisance under the Environmental Protection Act 1990 (EPA 1990), s. 79. Where this state is the landlord's responsibility, e.g. where it is due to a breach of the landlord's repairing covenant, or where it is due to a defect of a structural character in the premises, then the landlord is guilty of an offence: EPA 1990, ss. 80(2) and 82.

The tenant, as a person aggrieved by this statutory nuisance, may, after giving (usually) 21 days' notice to the landlord both of the matters he or she complains of and his or her intention to bring proceedings, make a complaint against the landlord to a magistrates' court: EPA 1990, s. 82.

If satisfied that the statutory nuisance exists, the magistrates may:

(a) order the landlord to abate the nuisance, if necessary by executing works to the premises: EPA 1990, s. 82;

(b) impose a fine: ibid.;

(c) order compensation for any personal injury, loss or damage resulting from the statutory nuisance: Powers of Criminal Courts Act 1973, s. 35.

If the landlord fails to comply with any order under (a) above, a further fine may be imposed under EPA 1990, s. 82(8) and compensation awarded: Powers of Criminal Courts Act 1973, s. 35. This procedure, like that of its predecessor (Public Health Act 1936, s. 99), has been frequently used against local authority landlords, e.g. over 630 summonses in two years against one local authority (see *Sandwell Metropolitan BC* v *Bujok* [1990] 3 All ER 385, 392, HL).

23.9 Further Reading

For a full consideration of the remedies for non-repair, see *Woodfall*, vol. 1, pp. 13/52–13/74, 13/41–13/44 and for a practical guide to conducting a tenant's claim for breach of repairing obligation, see **23.10**.

23.10 A Tenant's Claim for Breach of Repairing Obligation

23.10.1 INTRODUCTION

We are here concerned with a tenant who claims that his or her landlord is in breach of a repairing obligation. The repairing obligations of landlords, express and implied, are described earlier in this chapter, and the remedies available to tenants are described in **23.7**, to which reference should be made. It is sufficient here to emphasise that there must be a want of repair, that is a deterioration from a previous physical condition, and that which is alleged to be out of repair must be the subject matter of the landlord's obligation. It is vital to remember that not all defects constitute wants of repair.

23.10.2 THE TENANT'S CHOICE OF REMEDIES

A tenant has a choice of remedies. Which remedy, or combination of remedies, is appropriate turns, of course, on the circumstances and immediate needs of the tenant, but the circumstances of the landlord are also important. Estate landlords and local authorities, for example, are likely to comply with an order for specific performance (see **23.7.2**) (although local authorities can be slow), and are good for the money if damages are claimed. A £100 limited company with no assets is a different matter. An award of damages may well not be met, and the company may not have the finances to undertake the necessary repairs. In such a case the remedy of self-help, together with non-payment of future rent may be the appropriate course for the tenant: **23.7.3.2**, **23.7.4**. Think about what is best in practical terms for your tenant client.

23.10.3   ESTABLISHING A BREACH OF OBLIGATION

23.10.3.1 Condition of premises

Whatever the remedy sought, the first step is to establish the breach of obligation. This will involve legal input of course, but perhaps more important is establishing, as a matter of fact, the condition of the premises in respect of which complaint is made.

A lay person can readily identify a hole in a roof the size of a pool table, but frequently things are not that simple. All the tenant will know, for example, is that water is running down the walls of his or her bedroom, or whatever the case may be. Whilst that suggests something is wrong, it is not enough for the tenant merely to prove water is entering the premises in order to succeed; the subject matter of the landlord's obligation must be shown to be out of repair.

23.10.3.2 Qualified surveyors

The point is that the tenant should obtain, as soon as possible, a detailed report of the alleged wants of repair. Ideally this should be prepared by a building surveyor. Of course many tenants are reluctant or unable to engage a suitably qualified surveyor; like many professionals their services are often not cheap, but a claim will not get off the ground unless the tenant can prove there are wants of repair, and that is best done by engaging a surveyor as soon as possible. Quite apart from the forensic advantage this provides if the dispute gets to court, a landlord is very much more likely to take seriously a claim by a tenant if that tenant has engaged a surveyor. Further, there can be no question of a landlord not having the notice necessary to give rise to an obligation to repair if he or she is presented with a detailed schedule of wants of repair. If money must be spent, it should be spent on a good surveyor.

Such cases are often compromised. A landlord will know the premises are out of repair and that something has to be done. The main debate is often what precisely needs to be done. This being the case, a tenant is very much better off having a surveyor negotiate with the landlord's surveyor. Surveyors require assistance with the law, but they are far better qualified to deal with questions concerning the condition of the premises and what is required to put them right.

23.10.3.3 Standard of repair

Tenants often criticise the standard of repair carried out by their landlords; they understandably believe they are entitled to the very best. Such is not the case. The standard of repair required turns upon the age, character and location of the premises; there is no universal standard. Thus, the standard of repair necessary to comply with a repairing obligation in a lease of modest accommodation in a run-down part of town will be lower than the standard required in respect of high-class accommodation in the West End of London. This is important to have in mind when advising on whether a landlord has been in breach of his or her obligation, and the input of a surveyor is often very useful when undertaking this analysis.

23.10.4   WHAT THE TENANT CAN DO

There is also much a tenant can do to assist his or her case. The tenant should be encouraged to keep an accurate record of when the want of repair arose, the consequences of the alleged want of repair, and the complaints made to the landlord, e.g. how often water enters the premises or how often the water heater breaks down. Damage caused to the premises and the tenant's belongings should be recorded, and if repairs are carried out, for example repainting a room or cleaning soiled clothes or furniture, receipts should be kept. Keeping such records often eliminates accusations of exaggeration on the part of the tenant, and the records are very helpful to the court when it comes to the quantification of the tenant's damages claim. Photographs are also useful in this respect.

23.10.5   THE TENANT'S TRUE LOSS

23.10.5.1 Heads of loss

It is important to include all heads of loss in any claim. *Prima facie* the measure of damages for breach of a repairing obligation by a landlord is the difference between the value of the premises to the tenant in their defective condition, and the value of the premises in the condition required by the landlord's obligation during the period the premises are out of repair. In addition, a tenant can claim damages under the following heads:

(a)   damages for inconvenience and discomfort;

(b)   damages for ill-health caused by the breach of obligation;

(c)   damages for damage caused to personal property;

(d)   damages for damage caused to the premises (for example to decorations);

(c)   if the tenant carries out the necessary remedial works, damages equal to the cost of the works;

(f)   if the tenant moves out of the premises because of the wants of repair, damages equal to the cost of alternative accommodation, together with the cost of moving to the alternative accommodation.

23.10.5.2 Limitation of claims

Whilst all legitimate claims must be made on behalf of a tenant, tenants often believe their landlord's failure to repair is the cause of all that is wrong in the world. Be careful; a solid claim can be prejudiced by claiming that which is irrecoverable. Explain to the tenant that the loss in respect of which recovery may be had is limited.

For example, tenants often allege their health, or the health of others residing in the premises, has been prejudiced, or a pre-existing condition worsened, by the want of repair. As stated, damages for ill-health caused by a want of repair are recoverable, but the problem is often one of proof. A letter from the tenant's GP which says no more than that the tenant has told the doctor his or her health has deteriorated as a result of the want of repair is insufficient. It must be proved that the ill-health has been caused by the want of repair. A claim for damages for ill-health, if properly prosecuted, very much enlarges the nature of the dispute between the parties, as it will involve expert evidence from at least one doctor. The tenant should be warned that such a claim will inevitably add substantially to the costs of the proceedings, and if the case is lost, or that element of the claim not made out, the burden of those extra costs may fall on the tenant.

A claim for damages for mental distress and general anxiety caused by the landlord's failure to repair is also a favourite of tenants. The better view is that damages are not recoverable for such loss in a claim based upon a landlord's breach of repairing obligation. Further, before advising a tenant to move out of the premises, be sure the wants of repair are sufficiently substantial to justify such a step. The tenant will have to show it was reasonable for him or her to vacate. If it was reasonable, the cost of the alternative accommodation is recoverable.

23.10.6   KEEPING UP THE PRESSURE

The landlord must be given notice of the want of repair and a chance to put it right. Frequently landlords temporise even if faced with a good claim. They know the onus is on the tenant who is living or working in premises which are out of repair, and they know, perhaps, that the tenant's finances are often not such as to permit a full scale legal assault. However it is important to keep the pressure on the landlord. Make sure the tenant does nothing which the landlord might rely upon to support an argument that he or she was denied access to the premises; this is a common allegation by landlords.

If the landlord does not make good the wants of repair, or does not carry out the repairs to the required standard, commence proceedings. Withholding of rent often forces the landlord to take the initiative, in which case there will be a counterclaim. Either way, once the litigation has started it is important to keep the case moving forward; as stated, in many cases it is in the landlord's interest to delay.

23.10.7 INTERIM APPLICATIONS

The court is often sympathetic to interim applications by tenants for orders that temporary repairs be carried out: see **23.7.2**. Be prepared to apply as it will often be your lay client's home that is out of repair.

23.10.8 GENERALLY

If the ground work, in terms of establishing a cause of action, obtaining a surveyor's report and choosing the appropriate remedy or remedies, is done, then life will be made very much easier for the tenant by the time the matter gets to trial. Once the breach of duty is established, the remedies sought usually follow without difficulty. Quantum is sometimes a tricky area, especially if the judge is not experienced in this area. *Current Law*, and other publications, contain cases on quantum, and an appropriate selection of these should be presented to the court as a guide in any given case.

It is a sad reality that even an order for specific performance of the landlord's obligation is not necessarily the end of the matter. As indicated, some landlords will not, or cannot, comply with such an order. Ultimately therefore self-help and the withholding of rent is often the only solution, but if there is a substantial want of repair, even this may not provide a satisfactory solution.

TWENTY FOUR

COVENANTS RESTRICTING THE RIGHT TO ASSIGN OR SUBLET AND COVENANTS AGAINST CHANGE OF USE

24.1 General

24.1.1 NEED FOR EXPRESS INSERTION

A tenant may assign or sublet freely (for the distinction between these, see **1.3**) unless a covenant restricting the right to do so is expressly inserted in the lease or unless such a term is implied by statute (e.g. HA 1988, s. 15 and HA 1985, s. 93). It is very common to insert such a covenant; see, for example, the specimen draft lease, clause 2(10) in **Chapter 25**. Such a covenant is not implied: *Chester* v *Buckingham Travel* [1981] 1 WLR 96, ChD. Note the fundamental changes in the position of the original tenant and the original landlord after assignment of the lease and reversion respectively, made by the Landlord and Tenant (Covenants) Act 1995 with effect from 1 January 1996.

24.1.2 STRICT CONSTRUCTION

This covenant is strictly construed; for example, an express restriction on the right to assign will not cover an equitable assignment (unless expressly mentioned) nor a sublease. Nor will such a restriction apply to involuntary assignments such as occur on the death or bankruptcy of an individual tenant or on the liquidation of a company tenant.

24.1.3 EFFECT OF ALIENATION IN BREACH

An assignment or subletting in breach of this covenant is nevertheless effective to vest the lease in the assignee or create a sublease: *Old Grovebury Manor Farm* v *Seymour Plant Sales and Hire (No. 2)* [1979] 1 WLR 1397. This is subject to any right of the landlord to forfeit the lease for breach of covenant if a right to forfeit is reserved by the lease: no such right is implied. In a clear case a mandatory injunction has been granted ordering the subtenant to surrender to the tenant a sublease granted, to the knowledge of both parties, in breach of covenant: *Hemingway Securities* v *Dunraven* [1995] 1 EGLR 61, ChD.

24.2 Covenant not to Assign, Sublet, etc. Without Consent

24.2.1 THE COVENANT: EFFECT OF LTA 1927, s. 19(1)(a)

It is common to find the covenant against assigning or subletting made subject to obtaining the landlord's consent, as is the one in the specimen draft lease (clause 2(10)) (**Chapter 25**). LTA 1927, s. 19(1)(a) inserts into such a covenant the proviso that the landlord will not unreasonably refuse his or her consent. The statute does not apply and this proviso is not inserted where the covenant is absolute, i.e. where the words 'without the consent of the landlord' are not included: *F. W. Woolworth & Co. Ltd* v *Lambert* [1937] Ch 37 at 59–60, CA; *Bocardo SA* v *S & M Hotels Ltd* [1980] 1 WLR 17, CA.

24.2.2 NEED TO SEEK CONSENT FIRST

Where alienation is permitted subject to the landlord's consent, then even where the circumstances are such that consent could not reasonably be refused, the tenant must first seek consent before assigning or subletting. Failure to do this will be a breach of covenant, possibly giving rise to a right to forfeit.

24.2.3 EFFECT OF UNREASONABLE REFUSAL

Where the landlord unreasonably withholds consent, the effect is that the statutory proviso is not satisfied and the covenant is removed, so that the tenant can assign without consent: *F. W. Woolworth & Co. Ltd* v *Lambert* (above) at 53. Thus a tenant faced with a clearly unreasonable refusal can safely proceed with the assignment without consent. Where there is any doubt about the reasonableness of the refusal, the tenant's safer course is to seek a declaration (in the county court: LTA 1954, s. 53) that consent has been unreasonably refused. The onus of proving this was formerly on the tenant but has now been apparently reversed by LTA 1988: see s. 1(6) and *Midland Bank plc* v *Chart Enterprises Inc.* [1990] 2 EGLR 59, ChD. In many cases now the tenant will, in addition to seeking a declaration, also be claiming damages under LTA 1988 (see **24.2.4**). This combined claim for damages and a declaration must be brought by Part 8 claim (Form N208): for precedents see **30.1**, **30.2**.

24.2.4 EFFECT OF LTA 1988

This Act, which came into force on 28 September 1988, applies to covenants against assigning, subletting or otherwise dealing with a lease without consent. It imposes on a landlord whose consent is sought after 28 September 1988 a duty within a reasonable time to give written notice of his or her decision whether or not to give consent. If the consent is conditional, the conditions must be specified in writing within a reasonable time and if consent is refused, the reasons for the refusal must be given in writing within a reasonable time. The landlord cannot rely on reasons only given orally: *Footwear Corp. Ltd* v *Amplight Properties Ltd* [1998] 3 All ER 52. Breach of this duty is a statutory tort for which damages or an injunction may be awarded. The onus of proving that consent was reasonably refused is expressly imposed on the landlord: LTA 1988, s. 1(6), *Midland Bank plc* v *Chart Enterprises Inc.* [1990] 2 EGLR 59, ChD.

For a consideration of this Act, see *Woodfall*, vol. 1, pp. 11/72–11/77.

24.2.5 NO CONTRACTING OUT

Subject to **24.2.6**, a landlord cannot contract out of LTA 1927, s. 19(1)(a), e.g. by providing in the lease that certain circumstances will make refusal reasonable, for the test is an objective one. A landlord can, however, avoid the impact of s. 19 in the following ways:

(a) By imposing an absolute covenant against alienation, i.e. omitting the words 'without consent'. Section 19 does not apply to an absolute covenant: see **24.2.1**.

(b) By inserting in the covenant restricting alienation a condition precedent to the effect that, if the tenant wishes to assign or sublet, he or she must first offer to surrender the lease to the landlord. In such a case the proviso that the landlord will not unreasonably refuse consent will only operate if the landlord first refuses the offer to surrender: *Adler* v *Upper Grosvenor Street Investment* [1957] 1 WLR 227, QB and see *Bocardo SA* v *S & M Hotels Ltd* (above). Note that this condition precedent needs registration as an estate contract under the Land

Charges Act 1972 if it is to bind third parties: *Greene v Church Commissioners for England* [1974] Ch 467, CA.

24.2.6 CONTRACTING OUT UNDER LANDLORD AND TENANT (COVENANTS) ACT 1995

The parties to a non-residential lease granted after 1 January 1996 may agree either that in specified circumstances the landlord may withhold his or her consent to an assignment or that such consent may be granted subject to specified conditions. The landlord is then not to be regarded as unreasonable if he or she later withholds consent in those specified circumstances or makes consent subject to any of those specified conditions: LTA 1927, s. 19(1A) and (1E) inserted by the 1995 Act, s. 22.

24.3 When is it Reasonable to Refuse Consent?

24.3.1 GENERAL

This is a prolific source of litigation and you are likely to be asked to advise on this question in your early years at the Bar. The law has been developed through the cases rather than by statute. Familiarity with a fair number of these cases, so that you are aware of what view the court took previously of similar circumstances, is necessary to enable you to advise whether or not consent has been reasonably refused in any given case.

24.3.2 ONUS OF PROOF

Before the LTA 1988 the onus was on a tenant seeking a declaration that consent had been unreasonably withheld to prove the unreasonableness of the refusal: *Pimms Ltd v Tallow Chandlers Co.* [1964] 2 QB 547, 564, CA and most of the cases cited in **24.3.2** to **24.3.6** were decided when this was the position. The landlord was not obliged to accompany his or her refusal with reasons; in some cases the reasons might have been too obvious to need stating. Nor was the landlord confined to relying on reasons given at the time when consent was sought; he or she could rely at the hearing on any reasons which in fact influenced his or her decision: *Bromley Park Garden Estates v Moss* [1982] 1 WLR 1019, CA. The LTA 1988 has reversed the burden of proof as to the reasonableness of refusal and the onus is now on a landlord defending a claim under the Act to show that his or her refusal was reasonable: *Air India v Balabel* [1993] 2 EGLR 66, CA. The Act imposes a duty on a landlord who refuses consent to state in writing within a reasonable time his or her reasons for refusal and a landlord who fails to do this may be liable in damages under the Act: see **24.2.4**. It seems that the landlord is now barred, when defending a claim under the Act that he or she has unreasonably withheld consent, from asserting grounds for refusal other than those he gave in writing at the time consent was sought or within a reasonable time thereafter: *Footwear Corp. Ltd v Amplight Properties Ltd* [1998] 3 All ER 52. He or she clearly cannot rely on grounds which did not, in fact, influence his or her decision at the time he or she refused consent: *CIN Properties Ltd v Gill* [1993] 2 EGLR 97, QB. If the landlord wants further information about the proposed transaction, he must seek this promptly and will be in breach of the statutory duty if he seeks even clearly relevant information (e.g. as to the financial standing of the proposed assignee) only after a reasonable time for giving consent has elapsed. The tenant is under no duty to supply such information unless promptly requested for it by the landlord: *Norwich Union Life Insurance Society Ltd v Shopmoor Ltd* [1998] 3 All ER 32.

24.3.3 GENERAL TESTS OF REASONABLENESS

If the landlord has acted as a reasonable person might do in the circumstances, he or she will not be held to have refused consent unreasonably even though some persons might have taken a different view: *Re Town Investments Underlease* [1954] Ch 301; *Pimms Ltd v Tallow Chandlers Co.* (above) at 564.

This general rule must be qualified by the principle that a refusal of consent will be unreasonable if the ground does not relate to either the personality of the proposed assignee or subtenant or to the effect of the proposed assignment or sublease on the use or occupation of the demised premises: *Houlder Bros & Co. v Gibbs* [1925] Ch 575, and see *Bromley Park Garden Estates v Moss* (above), where consent was held to have been unreasonably withheld since the purpose of the refusal was to force the tenant to surrender the lease — a purpose unconnected with the terms of the lease and *Norwich Union Life Insurance Society v Shopmoor Ltd* [1998] 3 All ER 32 where the refusal of consent to a sublease was due to the landlord's fear of a possible detrimental effect on future rents of other properties it owned nearby. The landlord is not generally bound to be altruistic and is entitled to consult his or her own interests in deciding whether or not to give consent, except where:

(a)   The reason for refusal is to achieve some purpose totally unconnected with the lease: *Bromley Park Garden Estates v Moss* (above), and see *F W Woolworth plc v Charlwood Alliance Properties Ltd* [1987] 1 EGLR 53.

(b)   There is such a disproportion between the benefit to the landlord and the detriment to the tenant that would be caused by a refusal of consent, that it would be unreasonable for the landlord to refuse consent: *International Drilling Fluids v Louisville Investments* [1986] Ch 513, CA.

24.3.4   OBJECT OF THE TRANSACTION

It may be reasonable for the landlord to refuse consent where the motive for the assignment is not the 'normal' or 'proper' one of the assignee's desire to enjoy the lease itself but an ulterior motive, e.g. to enable the assignee to force his or her way into a redevelopment scheme using the nuisance value of the lease: *Pimms Ltd v Tallow Chandlers Co.* (above); or to enable the assignee to claim the statutory protection that the lease will attract rather than the lease itself: *Swanson v Forton* [1949] Ch 143, CA; or to achieve by an indirect route a determination of the lease in circumstances where that was expressly barred by the lease: *Olympia & York Canary Wharf v Oil Property Investments* [1994] 2 EGLR 49, CA.

24.3.5   CONSTRUCTION APPROACH

In some cases the wording of the lease itself, either in the covenant dealing with alienation or elsewhere, may show clearly what the purpose of the covenant restricting alienation was. In such a case, the court should construe the covenant or other term in the lease in order to determine the intention of the parties at the start of the lease. It will, in most cases, be reasonable for a landlord to refuse consent to a transaction which would defeat those intentions: *Bickel v Duke of Westminster* [1977] QB 517, CA; *West Layton Ltd v Ford* [1979] QB 593, CA. The court will not, however, readily imply into a lease terms which aid one party's argument on its construction: *Olympia & York* (above).

24.3.6   ANTICIPATION OF BREACH OF USER CLAUSE

In general it will be unreasonable to withhold consent because the landlord apprehends that the assignee will breach a user clause in the lease, for the landlord's right to enforce the user covenant will be unaffected by the assignment: *Killick v Second Covent Garden Property Co.* [1973] 1 WLR 658, CA. A refusal may, however, be reasonable where the landlord may be unable to enforce the user covenant against the assignee, e.g. because the covenant is a positive one or because the assignment will necessarily lead to a breach of the user covenant so that if the landlord consents to the assignment, he may be estopped from later suing on the user covenant: *F W Woolworth plc v Charlwood Alliance Properties Ltd* (above), *Warren v Marketing Exchange for Africa* [1988] 2 EGLR 247, CA.

24.3.7   REFUSAL ON GROUND OF RACE, SEX OR DISABILITY

It is unlawful to refuse consent to assign or to sublet premises to a person by reason of his or her race, sex or disability: Race Relations Act 1976, s. 24; Sex Discrimination Act 1975, s. 31; Disability Discrimination Act 1995, s. 22. This rule is subject to an exception in the case of small dwellings where the landlord resides on the premises.

24.3.8   NO FINE OR OTHER PECUNIARY CONSIDERATION FOR CONSENT

Where the covenant restricting alienation is qualified by the words 'without consent', then, unless the lease contains an express provision permitting this, the landlord is prohibited from demanding money as a condition of giving his or her consent except that he or she may require a reasonable amount to cover any costs incurred by him or her in connection with the consent, e.g. legal costs: LPA 1925, s. 144. The provision does not make a contract to pay such money illegal but merely unenforceable: *Comber* v *Fleet Electrics* [1955] 1 WLR 566; *Waite* v *Jennings* [1906] 2 KB 11.

24.4   Reading the Cases

You should be familiar with the facts of all the cases mentioned in **24.3.1** to **24.3.8** before you attempt any exercises on this topic. *International Drilling Fluids* v *Louisville Investments* (above), in particular, contains an extremely helpful general consideration of the subject, discussing many of the cases and explaining the various approaches to this difficult question. It is therefore a good starting-point.

24.5   Further Reading

See *Woodfall*, vol. 1, pp. 11/59–11/94 for a full account of these covenants.

24.6   Covenants against Change of Use

24.6.1   THE COVENANT

It is common for a lease to restrict the use that may be made of the demised premises, e.g. to use only as a private dwelling house: see specimen draft lease, clause 2(12) **(Chapter 25)**. The restriction may be absolute or qualified, i.e. permitting change of use subject to the landlord's consent.

24.6.2   LTA 1927, S. 19(3)

Where the lease forbids a change of use without the landlord's consent, s. 19(3) bars a landlord from demanding the payment of a capital sum of money as a condition of giving that consent, though the landlord may require the payment of compensation for any financial loss he or she suffers as a result of the change of use, and is also entitled to recover any legal or other costs incurred in connection with the consent. The prohibition only applies where the change of use involves no structural alterations to the premises.

It is important to note that this provision differs in effect from LTA 1927, s. 19(1), which, in respect of covenants restricting the right to assign or sublet without consent, inserts the proviso that such consent is not to be unreasonably withheld: see **24.2.1**. Section 19(3), by contrast, only prevents the landlord from demanding money for consent; he or she can be as unreasonable as he or she wishes in any other respect.

24.6.3   EXPRESS CONDITION OF REASONABLENESS

Sometimes the covenant expressly provides that consent is not to be unreasonably withheld. In such a case, even where the change does involve structural alteration so that s. 19(3) does not apply, it is probably unreasonable for the landlord to demand money for consent unless it is to compensate him or her for loss caused by the change of use or to reimburse his or her expenses.

In determining generally whether consent has been unreasonably withheld the same considerations will apply as in the case of consent to an assignment or subletting: see **24.3**. For an example of this, see *Anglia Building Society v Sheffield County Council* (1983) 266 EG 311, CA, where the landlord was held to have refused consent in an attempt to secure a collateral advantage for himself wholly unconnected with the terms of the lease and for a reason wholly extraneous to the intention of the parties at the time when the lease was entered into. Therefore, by analogy with the case of *Bromley Park Garden Estates v Moss* [1982] 1 WLR 1019, CA (see **24.3.2**), his consent was unreasonably withheld.

24.6.4 EFFECT OF UNREASONABLE REFUSAL

The effect of an unreasonable refusal and the choices of action open to the tenant if it happens are the same as in the case of covenants restricting assigning and subletting: see **24.2.3** and **24.3**. Note that the LTA 1988 (**24.2.4**) does not apply to this covenant.

24.6.5 FURTHER READING

See *Woodfall*, vol 1, pp. 11/95–11/128 for a full account of these covenants.

TWENTY FIVE

SPECIMEN DRAFT LEASE

This Draft Lease is reproduced with a few minor amendments by the kind permission of His Honour Judge Colyer QC.

DRAFT LEASE

Parties

(1) PREMISES (see also Schedule Part I)

THIS LEASE is made the ... day of ... BETWEEN [lessor] of [address etc] (hereinafter called the landlord which expression shall where the context so admits include the person for the time being entitled to the reversion immediately expectant on the determination of the term hereby created) of the one part and [lessee] of [address etc.] (hereinafter called the tenant which expression shall where the context so admits include his successors in title) of the other part.

RECITALS

WHEREAS

(1) The landlord and the tenant had by an agreement in writing made the 1st day of April 2000 agreed to grant and to take respectively a lease of "Blackacre".

(2) The landlord and the tenant now desire in substitution for Blackacre to grant and to take a lease of "The Laurels" . . ..

DEMISE

(2) HABENDUM

NOW THIS DEED WITNESSETH as follows:

1. The landlord demises unto the tenant the premises described in the first part of the schedule hereto (hereinafter called the demised premises) subject to the exceptions and reservations specified in the second part of the schedule TO HOLD the same unto the tenant from the ... day of ... for the term of ... years paying

(3) REDDENDUM
Rent

during the term hereby granted the yearly rent £... (without any deductions except only such as the tenant may be by law entitled to make notwithstanding any contract to the contrary) by equal quarterly payments to be made on the usual quarter days [or state days of payment, if not the usual quarter days] the first payment to be made on ... [or, if the term commences during the currency of a quarter, the first payment of £... being a proportionate part of the quarterly payment to be made on ...] and the last quarterly payment to be made in advance on the quarter day [or day for payment] immediately preceding the expiration or sooner determination of the term together with the quarterly payment falling due on that day;

(4) COVENANTS
Tenant's covenants:
To pay rent

To pay rates and taxes.

2. The tenant covenants with the landlord as follows:

(1) To pay the reserved rents on the days and in manner aforesaid.

(2) To pay all existing and future rates taxes assessments and outgoings [whether parliamentary local or otherwise] now or hereafter imposed or charged upon the owner or occupier of the demised premises except only such as the owner is by law bound to pay notwithstanding any contract to the contrary.

149

To maintain in repair and yield up.	(3)	To [repair and] keep the demised premises including the drains and sanitary and water [electrical gas and central heating] apparatus and all fixtures and additions thereto in good tenantable repair and condition [damage by accidental fire or by tempest or other inevitable accident excepted] throughout the term and to yield up the same in such repair and condition at the determination of the tenancy. [Add, where the lease is for less than seven years PROVIDED nevertheless that this covenant shall not impose upon the tenant any liability which by sections 11 and 12 of the Landlord and Tenant Act 1985 is cast upon the landlord notwithstanding any agreement to the contrary.]
To keep premises in present state.	(4)	Not to make any alterations or additions to the demised premises or erect any new buildings thereon without the previous written consent of the landlord nor to cut maim or injure any of the walls or timbers thereof except for the purpose of carrying out needful repairs nor to permit any of the aforesaid things to be done.
To paint outside and inside.	(5)	To paint with two coats of good oil paint [or paint of suitable quality] in a workmanlike manner all the wood iron and other parts of the demised premises heretofore or usually painted as to the external work in every [third] year and as to the internal work in every [seventh] year the time in each case being computed from the date hereof [and in each case the painting to be done in the last year of the tenancy as well] and on the occasion of every internal painting to (grain varnish french polish] distemper wash stop whiten and colour all such parts as have previously been dealt with and to repaper the parts usually papered with suitable paper of as good quality as that in use at the commencement of the tenancy. [or, where the lease is for less than seven years in the last year of the term to paint with two coats of good quality paint in a workmanlike manner all the internal wood and iron work and other internal parts usually painted and to [grain varnish french polish] distemper wash stop whiten and colour all such parts as have previously been so dealt with and to repaper the parts usually papered with suitable paper of as good quality as that in use at the commencement of the tenancy.]
To pay proportion of construction and repairs of party walls etc.	(6)	To pay a fair proportion [to be determined by the surveyor for the time being of the landlord whose determination shall be binding upon the tenant] of the expenses payable in respect of constructing repairing rebuilding and cleansing all party walls fences sewers drains gutters pipes roads pavements and other things the use of which is common to the demised premises and to other premises. [Add, where the lease is for less than seven years PROVIDED nevertheless that this covenant shall not impose upon the tenant any liability which by sections 11 and 12 of the Landlord and Tenant Act 1985 is cast upon the landlord notwithstanding any agreement to the contrary.]
To permit landlord to enter and view condition of premises and to repair on notice.	(7)	To permit the landlord and his duly authorised surveyor or agent with or without workmen and others upon giving [one week's] previous notice in writing twice a year at reasonable times to enter upon and examine the condition of the demised premises and thereupon the landlord may serve upon the tenant a notice in writing specifying any repairs necessary to be done and require the tenant forthwith to execute the same and if the tenant shall not within ten days after service of such notice proceed diligently with the execution of such repairs then to permit the landlord and his surveyor and agent to enter upon the demised premises and execute

such repairs and the cost thereof shall be a debt due from the tenant to the landlord and be forthwith recoverable by action.

To permit landlord to enter to repair adjoining premises.

(8) To permit the landlord and his duly authorised surveyor or agent with all necessary workmen upon giving [one week's] previous notice in writing at all reasonable times to enter upon the demised premises to execute repairs and alterations on any adjoining premises now or hereafter belonging to the landlord who shall make good all damage occasioned to the tenant by such entry.

To keep insured.

(9) To keep the demised premises insured at all times throughout the tenancy in the joint names of the landlord and the tenant from loss or damage by fire, flood and other risks and special perils normally insured under a householder's comprehensive policy [or a comprehensive policy on property of the same nature as the demised premises] in some insurance office or with underwriters to be named by the landlord [or approved by the landlord which approval shall not be unreasonably withheld] in the sum of £... at least [or a sum equal to the full insurable value thereof from time to time throughout the term] together with architects' and surveyors' professional fees and two years' rent and to make all payments necessary for the above purposes within seven days after the same shall respectively become due and to produce to the landlord or his agent on demand the policy or policies of such insurance and the receipt for each such payment and to cause all monies received by virtue of any such insurance (other than monies received in respect of loss of rent) to be forthwith laid out in rebuilding and reinstating the demised premises or any part thereof in respect of which such monies shall have become payable or been received [in accordance with the original plans elevations and details thereof with such variations (if any) as may be agreed by the landlord or may be necessary having regard to the then existing statutory provisions bye-laws and regulations affecting the same and any necessary planning approval (which it shall be the tenant's obligation to obtain) and] to the satisfaction in all respects of the surveyor for the time being of the landlord and to make up any deficiency out of his own monies PROVIDED ALWAYS (i) that if the rebuilding or reinstatement of the buildings or any part thereof shall be frustrated all such insurance monies (other than as aforesaid) relating to the building or parts in respect of which the frustration occurs shall be apportioned equally [or as may be otherwise agreed] between the landlord and the tenant and (ii) that if the tenant shall at any time fail to keep the demised premises insured as aforesaid the landlord may do all things necessary to effect and maintain such insurance and any monies expended by him for that purpose shall be repayable by the tenant on demand and be recoverable forthwith by action.

Not to assign or underlet.

(10) Not to assign underlet or part with the possession of the demised premises or any part thereof [without the written consent of the landlord] [such consent however not to be unreasonably withheld in the case of a respectable and responsible person].

Notes specifying breach.

(11) To pay all expenses (including solicitor's costs and surveyor's fees) incurred by the landlord incidental to the preparation and service of a notice under section 146 of the Law of Property Act 1925 notwithstanding forfeiture is avoided otherwise than by relief granted by the court.

Private residence.

(12) To use the demised premises for the purpose of a private residence in single occupation only.

Inventory of fixtures.	(13)	To permit the landlord or his duly authorised surveyor or agent upon giving [one week's] previous notice in writing at any time or times during the [last seven years of the] term to enter during the daytime upon the demised premises and make an inventory of all fixtures therein.
To comply with and deliver notices of competent authorities.	(14)	Upon receipt of any notice order direction or other thing from a competent authority affecting or likely to affect the demised premises whether the same shall be served directly on the tenant or the original or a copy thereof be received from any underlessee or other person whatsoever the tenant will so far as such notice order direction or other thing or the Act regulations or other instrument under and by virtue of which it is issued or the provisions hereof require him to do so comply therewith at his own expense and will forthwith deliver to the landlord a copy of such notice order direction or other thing.
To permit landlord to affix notice for reletting.	(15)	To permit the landlord during the three months immediately preceding the determination of the tenancy to affix and retain without interference upon any part of the demised premises a notice reletting the same and during the three months to permit persons with written authority from the landlord or his agent at reasonable times of the day [upon appointment made] to view the demised premises.
Landlord's covenants:	3.	The landlord hereby covenants with the tenant as follows:
For quiet enjoyment.	(1)	That the tenant paying the rent hereby reserved and performing and observing the several covenants on his part herein contained shall peaceably hold and enjoy the demised premises during the term without any interruption by the landlord or any person rightfully claiming under or in trust for him.
Option to renew.	[(2)	That the landlord will on the written request of the tenant served on the landlord not less than ... and not more than ... months before expiration of the term hereby created and if there shall not at the time of service of such request be any existing breach or non-observance of any of the covenants on the part of the tenant hereinbefore contained at the expense of the tenant grant to him a lease of the demised premises for the further term of ... years from the expiration of the term at a rent equal to the total of the rents which may be payable under clause 1 hereof at the expiration of the term with the like provision for the payment of additional rent as is contained in clause 1 (ii) hereof [or the yearly rent of £... or a rent to be determined in manner provided by the third part of the schedule hereto] and containing the like covenants and provisos as are herein contained with the exception of the present covenant for
Options became void unless protected by registration.		renewal the tenant on the execution of such renewed lease to execute a counterpart thereof [and to pay to the landlord the sum of £... by way of premium.] PROVIDED always that this covenant shall become null and void if the option hereby given to the tenant shall not be registered as a land charge at the Land Charges Registry or protected by registration of a notice, caution or other prescribed entry under the Land Registration Act 1925 or any statutory modification or re-enactment thereof for the time being in force within a period of three months from the date of this lease].
Option to purchase.	[(3)	That if the tenant shall desire to purchase the reversion in fee simple in the demised premises and shall within ... years from the commencement of the term hereby created give to the landlord [three] months' notice in writing of such desire then the landlord will upon the expiration of such notice and on payment of the sum of

£... together with all arrears of rent up to the expiration of the notice and of interest on the sum of £... at the rate of £... per cent per annum from the expiration of the notice until payment thereof convey the demised premises to the tenant in fee simple free from incumbrances but until the sum of £... with interest as aforesaid and the arrears of rent shall have actually been paid this lease shall continue in full force and the tenant shall not be released from any of his obligations thereunder. The landlord shall within [one month] from the giving of the notice deliver to the tenant an abstract of his title to the demised premises commencing with a deed dated ... and made between [parties] (being a [conveyance on sale] to the landlord) and within [fourteen days] after delivery of the abstract the tenant shall furnish to the landlord or his solicitor any requisitions and objections which he may desire to make in respect of the landlord's title (time being of the essence of the contract) and if the tenant shall insist on any requisition or objection which the landlord shall be unable or unwilling to comply with the landlord shall be entitled to give notice in writing to annul the contract of sale arising under this clause and the tenant's notice and if within [ten days] of such notice being given by the landlord the objection or requisition which gave rise to it shall not be withdrawn the said contract shall be annulled accordingly [or. The tenant shall accept without objection the title of the landlord but shall have delivered to him at his own expense such abstract of title as he shall require and the landlord shall be able to furnish].

(5) PROVISOS: 4. Provided always and it is hereby agreed as follows:

Power of re-entry.
  (1) If the rents hereby reserved or any part thereof shall be unpaid for twenty-one days after becoming payable (whether formally demanded or not) or if any covenant on the tenant's part herein contained shall not be performed or observed or if the tenant or other person in whom for the time being the term hereby created shall be vested shall become bankrupt or enter into any composition with his creditors or suffer any distress or execution to be levied on his goods then and in any of the said cases it shall be lawful for the landlord at any time thereafter to re-enter upon the demised premises or any part thereof in the name of the whole and thereupon this demise shall absolutely determine but without prejudice to the right of action of the landlord in respect of any breach of the tenant's covenants herein contained.

Option to determine.
  [(2) If the tenant [or the landlord or either party] shall desire to determine the term hereby granted at the expiration of the first ... or ... years thereof and shall give to the landlord [or tenant or other party] ... month's previous notice in writing of such his desire [in case of determination by tenant add and shall up to the time of such determination pay the rent and [reasonably] perform and observe the covenants on his part hereinbefore reserved and contained] then immediately on the expiration of such ... or ... years as the case may be the present demise and everything herein contained shall cease and be void but without prejudice to the rights and remedies of either party against the other in respect of any antecedent claim or breach of covenant.]

Service of notices.
  (3) Any notice under this lease shall be in writing and may be served on the person upon whom it is to be served either personally or by leaving it for him at the demised premises (if he is the tenant) or at his last known place of abode, or by sending it by registered post or the recorded delivery service to such premises or place; and in the case of a notice to be served on the landlord it may be served in like

153

manner upon any agent for the landlord duly authorised in that behalf.

or

(3)   The provisions of section 196 of the Law of Property Act 1925 as amended by the Recorded Delivery Service Act 1962 shall apply to all notices given under this Lease

---

SCHEDULE

PART I
Parcels

Parcels.

All that dwelling-house with the outbuildings yard and garden thereto belonging commonly called ["The Laurels", being No 99, New Road in the borough of Nonesuch in the county of .... which premises are delineated and coloured pink on the plan annexed hereto together with full right and liberty in common with the landlord and all other persons having the like right at all times and for all purposes to pass and repass over and along the road coloured brown on the said plan with or without animals and vehicles the tenant paying a proper proportion (to be determined by the land-lord's surveyor) of the costs of keeping the road in repair [together with the right in common with all other persons entitled to the like privilege to use the ornamental garden called..... Garden subject to such rules and regulations as may from time to time be prescribed by the landlord the tenant paying a proper proportion to be deter-mined as aforesaid of the costs of keeping the said garden and the fences thereof in good order].

(6) EXCEPTIONS &
RESERVATIONS

PART II
Exceptions and Reservations

Right
passage of
water, soil, etc.
Right to
light and air.

(1)   Reserving unto the landlord at any time hereafter and from time to time full right and liberty to execute works and erections upon [or to alter or rebuild any of the buildings erected on] his adjoining and neighbouring lands and to use his adjoining and neighbouring lands and buildings in such manner as he may think fit notwith-standing that the access of light and air to the demised premises [on the northeast side thereof] may thereby be interfered with. Except and reserving the right of passage and running of water, soil gas and electricity as heretofore used and enjoyed from the other buildings and land of the landlord [and by other tenants] through the sewers drains channels pipes conduits and cables on in or under the demised premises [the approximate lines and positions whereof are shown by dotted [red] lines on the plan annexed hereto] [the tenant or tenants of such other buildings and land (or other persons using such sewers drains channels pipes conduits or cables) on request paying his or their share of the cost of cleansing and repairing the same as need shall require such share to be determined by the landlord's surveyor for the time being whose determination shall be binding on all persons using the same.]

PART III
Rent Revision

Agreement or
determination
of new rent.

1.   The rent for the further term (hereinafter called the new rent) shall be such annual sum as shall be agreed between the landlord and the tenant or determined as hereinafter provided to be the current market rental value of the demised premises at the time of such

agreement or determination and shall be paid without any deduction by equal quarterly instalments on the usual quarter days (hereinafter called rent days) the first of such quarterly instalments to be paid on [date].

Agreement. 2. Any agreement between the landlord and the tenant as to the new rent shall be in writing signed by the parties.

Determination by surveyor 3. If such agreement has not been made six months before the date on which the further term is due to commence either party hereto may require an independent surveyor (hereinafter called the surveyor) to determine the new rent.

Appointment of surveyor. 4. The surveyor may be nominated by agreement between the landlord and the tenant or appointed by the President for the time being of the Royal Institution of Chartered Surveyors on the application of either party hereto.

Substitute appointer 5. If the said President shall for any reason not be available or be unable to make such appointment at the time of application thereof the appointment may be made by the Vice President or next senior officer of the Institution then available and able to make such appointment or if no such officer of the Institution shall be so available and able by such officer of such professional body of surveyors as the landlord shall designate.

Notice of surveyor's appointment. 6. Notice in writing of his appointment shall be given by the surveyor to the landlord and the tenant inviting each to submit within a specified period (which shall not exceed four weeks) a valuation accompanied if desired by a statement of reasons.

Surveyor to act as expert. 7. The surveyor shall act as an expert and not as an arbitrator. He shall consider any valuation and reasons submitted to him within the period but shall not in any way be limited or fettered thereby and shall determine the new rent in accordance with his own judgment and opinion as to the true current market rental value of the demised premises.

Notice of surveyor's decision. 8. The surveyor shall give notice in writing of his decision to the lessor and the lessee within [two] months of his appointment or within such extended period as the landlord may agree.

New rent not to be less than current rent. 9. If the surveyor comes to the conclusion that the current market rental value of the demised premises is less than the current rent the new rent shall nevertheless be the same as the current rent and the decision of the surveyor shall so state.

Effect of default, etc by surveyor. 10. If the surveyor shall fail to determine the new rent and give notice thereof within the time and in the manner hereinbefore provided or if he shall relinquish his appointment or die or if it shall become apparent that for any reason he will be unable to complete his duties hereunder the landlord or the tenant may apply to the President or other person as hereinbefore provided for a substitute to be appointed in his place which procedure may be repeated as many times as necessary.

Surveyor's decision final 11. The decision of the surveyor shall be final on all matters hereby referred to him.

Time when rent due at new rate.	12.	Rent shall not be due at the rate of the new rent notwithstanding that the said further term may already have commenced until after the tenant has been given such notice thereof as is hereby provided and if the said further term shall have commenced before the tenant has been given such notice the rent shall for the time being and until such notice is given be at the rate of the current rent but on the first rent day after the giving of such notice to the tenant there shall fall due in addition to the appropriate instalment of the new rent a sum by way of additional rent equal to the difference between the new rent and the current rent for the period since the commencement of the further term.
Surveyor's fees.	13.	The fees of the surveyor shall be shared equally between the landlord and tenant.
NOTE:		Formerly this precedent continued with 14 below; but we strongly recommend **against** making time 'of the essence'.
Time of essence	14.	As respects all periods of time referred to in this schedule time shall be deemed to be of the essence of the contract.
(Attestation Clauses)		In witness whereof the Landlord hath caused its common seal to be hereunto affixed and the Tenant has hereunto set his hand the day and year first above written.

(On the Counterpart) (Executed by the tenant, and delivered to and retained by the landlord. Stamped 50p)

SIGNED AND DELIVERED

by the above-named   [Tenant]

in the presence of   [Witness]

(On the Lease Itself) (Executed by the Landlord, and delivered to and retained by the tenant. Stamped *ad valorem* on rent.)

THE COMMON SEAL OF [The Landlord]

was hereunto affixed in the presence

of

.... Director

.... Secretary

TWENTY SIX

EMERGENCY APPLICATION FOR AN INJUNCTION

In your first few years in civil practice you will frequently be asked to appear at court at very short notice to seek an injunction without notice to the other side. These injunctions, formerly known as *ex parte* injunctions, are permitted under CPR, Part 23. Probably only domestic violence gives rise more frequently to such applications than do problems concerning residential tenancies.

26.1   Immediate Action

Typically you will not receive any papers beyond a backsheet which will either be faxed to your chambers or typed by your clerk. Try to discuss the matter on the telephone with your instructing solicitor before you reach court. That will enable you to find out roughly what the case is about and to arm yourself with any books you think may be helpful; generally, though, one of the major works on civil procedure such as *Blackstones*, *Jordans*, the 'Green Book' or the 'White Book' will be sufficient.

26.2   Action at Court

Once at court you should make contact with your client. If your solicitors are not already there you should let the court staff know that you have arrived, ensure that they are expecting the case to be dealt with that day and request sufficient time to prepare yourself fully. There is no need to wait for the solicitor to arrive before taking instructions from the client.

26.2.1   ISSUING CLAIMS

The court staff will be very keen for claims to be issued before allowing you in front of a judge. It is usually inappropriate for counsel to do this as a fee has to be paid. Do not ever agree to pay this yourself, however much you believe the solicitor's promise to reimburse you immediately. Doing so could amount to handling clients' money and hence constitute professional misconduct.

Judges are aware of the dilemma barristers can be placed in if solicitors do not attend. Usually they will agree to hear you so long as you give an undertaking on the solicitor's behalf that a claim will be issued by the end of the following working day. You, of course, need to obtain specific instructions from the solicitors before offering such an undertaking.

26.3   Documents Required

You will need to prepare a witness statement unless your solicitors have indicated to you that this has already been done by them. The witness statement should set out in ordinary language the facts of the case and contain a statement of truth signed by the witness. It should exhibit any relevant document, such as a tenancy agreement. With experience you will learn what to include and what to leave out. If in doubt you should put it in. The witness statement you prepare at court will of necessity be in manuscript. Judges appreciate that this is unavoidable, but it goes without saying that you must ensure that it is legible — avoiding joining your letters may make your writing much easier to read. It will be necessary to make at least one photocopy. If you are rushed into court before having a chance to complete the statement the judge will rely on it as if it were signed and completed but ask for an undertaking that it will be completed and a copy filed with the court by the end of the next working day.

You should obtain a Form N244 from the court office and specify on it the relief you are seeking in precise terms. The judge will almost inevitably alter what you have written, frequently to the extent that it is unrecognisable, but completing the form in the first place is a courtesy that will be appreciated.

Sometimes the judge will require an undertaking from your client that he or she will pay damages if it is subsequently decided that the injunction should not have been awarded and the landlord has suffered loss as a result. Modern practice tends to be not asking for that undertaking where the person seeking the injunction is in receipt of public funding. However, it is right that you should explain the possibility to your client before going into court anyway.

The judge will approach the case on the basis of balance of convenience and on the degree of urgency. In, for instance, a case for wrongful eviction he or she will not attempt to decide a complex question of whether there is a tenancy or a licence. The main considerations will be who will suffer more if the injunction is not granted and whether the landlord should be given an opportunity to appear before an order is made. If you are for an allegedly wrongfully evicted tenant who has nowhere else to stay you will probably not find it difficult to persuade the judge on these points. In drafting your statement put greater emphasis on points that are relevant to the balance of convenience and urgency than the substantive merits, remembering that it is, however, necessary to establish sufficient ground to show an arguable case. If you have authorities that you think are helpful by all means cite them if the judge asks for submissions, but try to avoid referring to *American Cyanamid* as if it were a new case being pointed out to the judge for the first time!

26.4 Court Procedure

Often on an application without notice the judge will read the statement before coming into court and will indicate that he or she has already found in your favour; in that case you need say very little. But sometimes the judge will need persuading or think it appropriate to make counsel work a little before granting the injunction. (Judges often do this out of kindness to junior barristers: it is much more satisfying, and impresses the client, to appear to have overcome some judicial reservation in obtaining the order.) If that happens it may be desirable to call your client to give evidence to supplement what is said in the statement and clear up any difficulties that the judge may see in your case. The judge will indicate the procedure that he or she wishes you to follow.

26.5 Adjournment

Normally, whether the injunction is granted or not, the matter will be adjourned for about a week to give the other side the opportunity to attend. This hearing is sometimes known as the 'return date'. The costs of the application will usually be reserved, to be considered at the adjourned hearing.

TWENTY SEVEN

LANDLORD AND TENANT LITIGATION AND PUBLIC FUNDING

In landlord and tenant cases, like most others, the grant of public funding (which of course used to be called legal aid, a term which continues to be used by many lawyers and judges) to one or both parties has a considerable effect on the way proceedings should be conducted by both.

27.1   Obtaining Public Funding

In residential cases tenants are generally eligible for public funding and landlords are not; the ownership of the property that is the subject-matter of the dispute is likely to mean that the landlord's capital exceeds the prescribed limit. Where a tenant wishes to bring a claim for, say, wrongful eviction or an injunction to prevent harassment, emergency funding can usually be obtained, sometimes over the telephone, if the solicitor's firm does not have a franchise that enables it to grant funding.

Where emergency funding is not available or not applied for a tenant may be able to obtain an adjournment whilst his or her public funding application is considered. In possession proceedings this will normally enable the tenant to remain in the property a little bit longer, even if the proceedings are eventually decided against him or her. While the application is being considered it is important to the landlord that rent is paid; rent that is not paid before trial may prove irrecoverable afterwards if a possession order is granted. If you are against a tenant who (probably in person) is asking for an adjournment for consideration of his or her public funding application, ask the court to make the granting of the adjournment conditional upon the tenant paying off a substantial proportion of the existing arrears and all future instalments. It may be impractical to enforce such an order but its making may coerce the tenant into making payments he or she would not otherwise have made.

27.2   Costs

Once a party has received public funding the courts are generally unable to make a full costs order against him or her even if the other party succeeds. (The relevant legislation, the Legal Aid Act 1988, s. 17, is discussed in the *Civil Litigation Manual*, **Chapter 35**.) Usually the court considers what the costs position would be if that party were not publicly funded and decides for instance to award the claimant costs assessed at £1,000. It will then add the proviso that the costs order is not to be enforced without the permission of the court. This at least leaves open the possibility that the successful party will be able to recover his or her costs if the loser's financial position improves substantially in the future. Sometimes the court may be willing to order the losing party actually to pay a small part of the costs awarded against him or her. It is sometimes suggested that the loser should pay to the other party an amount equivalent to the total he or she had to pay as a contribution to his or her own funding. In practice, unless there is also a substantial money award, it is not usually worth enforcing a costs order.

Where a successful party is unable by reason of s. 17 to enforce a costs award that he or she has obtained, there is provision in the Legal Aid Act 1988, s. 18, for him or her to apply for an order that the Legal Services Commission, which controls public funding, pay his or her costs. This provision will not be of any benefit to a landlord who has successfully brought a possession claim as it only assists parties who have not brought the proceedings, but it would assist, for example, a landlord against whom an unsuccessful claim for wrongful eviction had been made.

27.3   Settlements

When negotiating a settlement both parties should be aware of the effects of public funding on the resulting order. Any property an assisted person recovers or retains will be subject to the Legal Services Commission's charge, equivalent to the actual costs of the claim over and above any contribution made by the assisted person (Legal Aid Act 1988, s. 16). You should, however, bear in mind that you owe just as great a duty to the public fund as you do to your client. The natural tendency to favour your client's interests at the expense of those of the fund should be overcome. However, if your opponent seems unable to overcome this tendency on behalf of his or her client, then it is not improper to take advantage of it.

Suppose it is agreed between counsel that the publicly funded tenant will inevitably be ordered to give up possession to the privately paying landlord. There is, however, a valid 'Part 20' counterclaim by the tenant for harassment, which appears to be worth around £500. The only issue that cannot be resolved is how long the tenant should be allowed to leave the property. He or she wants three months; the landlord would like him or her to go in 14 days. The statutory charge has the effect that there is no practical value to the tenant in enforcing his or her claim for damages — they will be swallowed up by the charge (even though the tenant should recover the costs of his or her counterclaim, the costs relating to the possession claim are probably greater than the £500). Therefore, to avoid his or her client paying the £500 to the tenant, the landlord's barrister might properly suggest that the tenant be allowed to stay for a longer period. The tenant's barrister would probably agree to this on the client's behalf. Whilst theoretically he or she had to consider the effects on both the Legal Services Commission, which would be the recipient of the £500, and the client, the client's interests will inevitably and in this instance properly come first.

TWENTY EIGHT

WORKED EXAMPLE OF HOUSING ACT POSSESSION CLAIM

28.1 Instructions to Advise and Settle Proceedings

Counsel will find enclosed:

(1) copy tenancy agreement

(2) copy rent book

(3) copy notice to quit

(4) copy recent correspondence

1. Instructing Solicitors act for Mrs May Charlesworth who is, and for many years has been, the freehold owner of 3 Falcon Lane, London, W5.

2. Shortly before Christmas 1996 Mrs Charlesworth's elder (and recently bereaved) sister who lived in Australia was diagnosed as having cancer. So Mrs Charlesworth, who had not seen her sister for many years, decided to travel overseas and to look after her for so long as might be necessary.

3. Being of limited means and to ease the financial burden, Mrs Charlesworth apparently agreed with Mrs Florence Oates, a longstanding friend and neighbour, that Mrs Oates would rent the house whilst Mrs Charlesworth was abroad and until her return. This arrangement was mutually beneficial since at the time Mrs Oates had just separated from her husband and was in immediate need of accommodation and was also afforded some time to look elsewhere for more permanent housing. Mrs Charlesworth left all her furniture in the house.

4. Instructing Solicitors understand that no written agreement was entered into but Counsel will see from the accompanying rent book that the tenancy was initially granted for 3 months at a weekly rent of £50. However, in March 1997, at which time Mrs Oates was still looking for premises of her own, a written tenancy agreement (copy enclosed) was signed by both parties for a further 3 months at the same rent.

5. Her sister has now made a good recovery from the cancer and Mrs Charlesworth returned to the UK at the start of May 2001 since when she has been lodging with her son and daughter-in-law and their baby in very cramped conditions. Unfortunately, despite the expiry of her tenancy, Mrs Oates has reneged on their understanding and now refuses to vacate Mrs Charlesworth's house, claiming that she has a right to remain there indefinitely. Counsel will see that the rent has been paid in full.

6. Instructing Solicitors, who are not entirely familiar with landlord and tenant law, are nonetheless aware that, following the Housing Act 1996, all residential tenancies granted on/after 28th February 1997 are shorthold. Thus, Instructing Solicitors consider that possession can be recovered using the accelerated (paper) procedure. Finally, as a precautionary measure, Instructing Solicitors have served a notice to quit (copy enclosed) on Mrs Oates.

7. In the circumstances, Counsel is asked to advise and to settle the necessary proceedings as a matter of urgency.

   Dated this the 4th day of November 2001.
   BLOGGS & CO.

28.2 Analysis

28.2.1 TYPE OF TENANCY: WHICH, IF ANY, REGIME?

Not HA 1985 (secure tenancies) because private sector landlord.

Not RA 1977 (regulated tenancies) since granted 1996/7: HA 1988, s. 34.

LTA 1954, part 1 and LG&HA 1989 only apply to long tenancies (>21 yrs).

This analysis leaves only HA 1988 (assured tenancies).

Tenancy is not excluded from HA 1988 by reason of tenant being a corporate body or the rent level falling outside either the lower/upper thresholds.

CONCLUSION: tenancy is an assured tenancy under HA 1988.

28.2.2 ASSURED OR ASSURED SHORTHOLD UNDER HA 1988?

Here there are two successive tenancies.

Basic rule: 'once assured, always assured': HA 1988, s. 20(3).

Similarly: 'once shorthold, always shorthold': HA 1988, s. 20(4).

Underlying philosophy is that like follows like; former governs latter.

By reason of HA 1988, sch. 2A, para. 7 (inserted by HA 1996, sch. 7) the same concept applies in relation to tenancies granted since 28 February 1997 which would *prima facie* be shorthold automatically by virtue of HA 1988, s. 19A (inserted by HA 1996, s. 96).

With the above in mind, consider the status of the original tenancy here. It was granted pre- 28 February 1997.

Thus to be an assured shorthold it must fulfil the requirements of HA 1988, s. 20.

Those requirements include: six months minimum term and prior notice. Neither satisfied here.

CONCLUSION: original (and hence replacement) tenancy is assured (non-shorthold) tenancy under HA 1988.

28.2.3 ANY GROUNDS FOR POSSESSION UNDER HA 1988?

Having regard to Instructions, peruse HA 1988, sch. 2.

Note: no material to support allegation of tenant default.

In the circumstances, only possible candidate is Ground 1.

28.2.4   DETAILED CONSIDERATION OF GROUND 1

(a)   Mandatory or discretionary? Mandatory: HA 1988, s. 7(3).

(b)   Is it available in principle? Yes, because fixed term of the most recent tenancy has expired: HA 1988, s. 7(6).

(c)   Is it made out here?
Condition of past occupation (Ground 1, para. (a)), seemingly yes;
Alternative condition of future occupation (Ground 1, para. (b)), likewise;
Condition, in either case, of service of prior written notice — no!

(d)   Might discretion to dispense with such notice be exercised here?
Reference to authorities cited in textbooks and on CD-rom, etc.
Ascertainment of the guiding principles.
Application of principles to the facts in this case.

ASSESSMENT: likelihood that discretion be exercised in the landlord's favour.

CONCLUSION: good case under HA 1988, sch. 2, Ground 1.

28.2.5   MISCELLANEOUS POINTS

Need to serve preliminary notice under HA 1988, s. 8.

Length of such notice: HA 1988, s. 8(4A).

Irrelevance of notice to quit: HA 1988, s. 5(1).

28.3   Advice

IN A PROPOSED CLAIM

IN THE . . . COUNTY COURT

BETWEEN:

MAY CHARLESWORTH	<u>Proposed Claimant</u>
and	
FLORENCE OATES	<u>Proposed Defendant</u>

_____

ADVICE
_____

1.   INTRODUCTION
I am instructed on behalf of Mrs May Charlesworth, the owner of 3 Falcon Lane, London, W5. I am asked to advise as to whether my client can recover possession of her house which is currently occupied by the proposed defendant.

2.   CONCLUSIONS
I conclude that:

(1)   Mrs Oates is an assured tenant;

(2)   she is not an assured shorthold tenant;

    (3)   nonetheless, Mrs Charlesworth has reasonable prospects of recovering possession under Housing Act 1988, sch. 2, Ground 1 (although the court would have to be persuaded that it is just and equitable to dispense with the requisite written notice under Ground 1); and

    (4)   before any proceedings are commenced a notice under Housing Act 1988, s. 8 must be served on Mrs Oates.

My reasons follow.

3.   BACKGROUND
The salient background to this matter is well known to my client and is fully set out in my Instructions (to which reference should be made). In sum, in December 1996 Mrs Charlesworth let her house to Mrs Oates for 3 months at a rent of £50 per week. At that time Mrs Charlesworth was about to depart for Australia to care for her sister and she let the house to help finance the trip. Mrs Oates was a neighbour and an old friend of my client whose marriage had recently broken down. It seems that she was happy to rent the house on an interim basis (whilst Mrs Charlesworth was abroad) because this would give her an opportunity to search for a new place of her own. A new tenancy agreement, again for 3 months but on this occasion in writing, was granted in March 1997. Mrs Charlesworth has since returned to the UK and naturally wishes to resume occupation of her house. However, Mrs Oates, who has paid all the rent due, refuses to leave.

4.   STATUS OF TENANCY
In general terms, since 15th January 1989 every tenancy of residential premises granted by a private sector landlord to an individual (not corporate) tenant has been an assured tenancy within the meaning of the Housing Act 1988, s. 1. Whilst exceptions include tenancies at low or very high rents: HA 1988, s. 1(2) and sch. 1, a rent of £50 per week is not within any such exception.

5.   Assured tenancies afford the tenant security of tenure and can be terminated by court order only if the landlord can establish one or more of the mandatory/ discretionary grounds for possession set out in HA 1988, sch. 2. The majority of the grounds centre on default by the tenant in paying the rent or complying with the terms of the tenancy agreement. No such considerations arise in this case.

6.   An assured shorthold tenancy is a species of assured tenancy which retains all the usual characteristics of an assured tenancy but in addition enables the landlord to recover possession at or after the expiry of the fixed term, subject only to the landlord having served on the tenant a notice requiring possession of requisite duration: HA 1988, s. 21. However, until recently (see below) there were special rules applicable to the creation of an assured shorthold: HA 1988, s. 20. The main requirements were, in brief, that the tenancy in question had to be for a fixed term of not less than 6 months and that before it was granted the landlord had to serve the tenant with a written notice in the prescribed form stating that the tenancy was to be an assured shorthold: ibid.

7.   My Instructing Solicitors refer to the impact of the provisions of the Housing Act 1996 on residential tenancies. In this context, it is correct to say that HA 1996, s. 96(1), inserting a new s. 19A into HA 1988, provides (*inter alia*) that an assured tenancy which is entered into on or after the day on which that section comes into force is an assured shorthold tenancy. In other words, the special rules for creation of assured shorthold tenancies have been abrogated in relation to all new tenancies. The relevant provisions were brought into force on 28th February 1997. *Prima facie*, therefore, the most recent tenancy granted by Mrs Charlesworth in March 1997 was an assured shorthold.

8.   However, it is crucial to note that the original tenancy granted by my client was not an assured shorthold because (i) it predated the coming into force of HA 1996, s. 96 and (ii) it did not satisfy the requirements of HA 1988, s. 20 (since it was for

only 3 months and, further, it seems that no prior notice was served in respect thereof).

9. The foregoing is significant because HA 1996, s. 96 and sch. 7, inserting a new sch. 2A into HA 1988, provide a list of exceptions to the general rule that tenancies granted after 28th February 1997 will automatically be assured shorthold. For present purposes, I draw my Instructing Solicitors' attention to HA 1988, sch. 2A, para. 7 which in essence states that a replacement tenancy which is granted by the same landlord to an existing tenant whose former tenancy was a non-shorthold will itself be an assured non-shorthold tenancy (unless, as is not the case here, the tenant serves notice to the contrary prior to the grant). In practice therefore, the rule is 'once (fully) assured, always (fully) assured': the status of the new tenancy is governed by the status of the old tenancy. Indeed, a similar, though not identical, provision in relation to pre-HA 1996 tenancies is to be found in HA 1988, s. 20(3).

10. Therefore I conclude that, contrary to the views held by my Instructing Solicitors, Mrs Oates holds the premises under an assured tenancy *simpliciter*, i.e. not an assured shorthold tenancy. Consequently, I regret to advise that possession cannot be sought by Mrs Charlesworth under the accelerated procedure provided by CPR, Part 55, rr. 55.11 and 55.12.

11. POSSIBLE GROUND FOR POSSESSION?
However, all is not necessarily lost because, albeit on the limited information available to me, I advise that my client has, in my view, reasonable prospects of recovering possession of her house under HA 1988, sch. 2, Ground 1. In brief, this (mandatory) ground for possession applies where: (a) prior to the tenancy the landlord seeking possession occupied the property as his or her only or principal home; or (b) the landlord seeking possession requires the house as his or her only or principal home. It seems to me that on the facts of this case Mrs Charlesworth's situation (as owner-occupier) would almost certainly fall within not just one but indeed both of the above limbs!

12. But there is one further hurdle to surmount: HA 1988, sch. 2, Ground 1 also stipulates that prior to the commencement of the proceedings in question the landlord must have given to the tenant written notice that possession might be recovered under Ground 1. Regrettably, though entirely understandably, it does not appear that Mrs Charlesworth served such a notice.

13. Fortunately, the statute expressly provides that the court may dispense with the requirement of such written notice if it would be 'just and equitable' so to do. In this context, the following propositions may be drawn from the authorities (some of which were based on an identically framed provision within the Rent Act 1977, sch. 15, Case 11): (i) the court may look at all the circumstances of the case in determining whether it would be just and equitable to dispense with the require-ment of written notice: *Bradshaw v Baldwin-Wiseman* (1985) 49 P & CR 382, CA; (ii) oral notice, if given, may be an important factor favouring dispensation: *Fernandes v Parvardin* (1982) 5 HLR 33, CA; (iii) nonetheless, oral notice is not a prerequisite of such dispensation: *Boyle v Verrall* [1997] 1 EGLR 25, CA; (iv) taken in conjunction with all other relevant matters, dispensation may be appropriate where discussion concerning the landlord's intention to resume occupation at some later stage occurred prior to the grant of the tenancy: *Boyle v Verrall*; and (v) even a failure to indicate to the prospective tenant that the prospective landlord might subsequently require the premises back for his or her own occupation, whilst an important factor, is not conclusive against the landlord: *Mustafa v Ruddock* [1997] EGCS 87, CA.

14. Turning to the present case, I stress that I would probably be greatly assisted by the sight of a statement from Mrs Charlesworth detailing the circumstances in which she granted the original tenancy to Mrs Oates. However, nonetheless, I advise that, in my opinion, my client can advance a powerful case for dispensation

with the Ground 1 notice. My belief is founded upon the following facts and assumptions: (i) being longstanding friends and neighbours, Mrs Oates must surely have known that 3 Falcon Lane constituted Mrs Charlesworth's home; (ii) moreover, it seems that she was probably well aware of the special reason which caused my client to move out; (iii) there appears to have been at least some discussion between the parties on this subject and that my client, having nowhere else to go, would inevitably wish to resume occupation upon her return to this country; (iv) indicative of the last point is the fact that Mrs Charlesworth left her furniture in the subject premises; (v) overall, the surrounding circumstances indicate the arrangement was envisaged by both parties to be of a transient, rather than a permanent, nature, with advantages to each; and (vi) the present circumstances of my client further militate in support of her regaining possession of the house. Of course, it must be recognised that Mrs Oates may have a different recollection of the material events!

15. As requested, I have duly settled draft possession proceedings; my Instructing Solicitors should fill in the blanks by supplying the appropriate information. The Particulars of Claim should accompany a claim form for possession (N5).

16. SECTION 8 NOTICE
Finally, I advise that, prior to the issue of proceedings, my Instructing Solicitors will have to serve on Mrs Oates a notice of proceedings for possession under HA 1988, s. 8. Unfortunately, the date to be specified therein (as the date before which proceedings will not be commenced) will have to be not less than 2 months from the date of service of the s. 8 notice: HA 1988, s. 8(4A) as inserted by HA 1996, s. 151(4). Whilst service of the notice will undoubtedly delay matters, it would not, in my view, be sensible deliberately to bring a claim without having served such a notice, seeking merely to rely upon the court's power (under HA 1988, s. 8(1)(b)) to dispense with the notice; such a course would, I believe, add unnecessary difficulty to this case. For the sake of completeness, I add that service of a notice to quit by a landlord under an assured tenancy is of no effect: HA 1988, s. 5(1).

If I can be of any further assistance my Instructing Solicitors should not hesitate to telephone me in Chambers.

A COUNSEL

10th November 2001

28.4　Draft Particulars of Claim

IN THE . . . COUNTY COURT

Claim No.

BETWEEN:

MAY CHARLESWORTH　　　　Claimant

and

FLORENCE OATES　　　　Defendant

PARTICULARS OF CLAIM

1. The Claimant is, and at all material times has been, the freehold owner of the dwelling-house situate at and known as 3 Falcon Lane, London, W5 ('the Property').

2. By an oral tenancy agreement made on or about [insert date] December 1996 ('the original tenancy'), partly evidenced by the terms of a rent book dated [insert], the Claimant demised the Property to the Defendant for a term of 3 months from [insert date] at a weekly rent of £50.

3. Subsequently, by a written tenancy agreement dated [insert] March 1997 ('the replacement tenancy'), the Claimant demised the Property to the Defendant for a term of 3 months from [insert] March 1997. A copy of the replacement tenancy is attached to the Particulars of Claim.

4. In the premises, the Defendant is, and has at all material times been, an assured tenant of the Property within the meaning of the Housing Act 1988, s. 1 and is, and has been since the expiry by effluxion of time (on [insert] June 1997) of the term granted by the replacement tenancy, a statutory periodic tenant of the Premises by virtue of s. 5 of the said Act.

5. For the reasons set out below, the Claimant seeks possession of the Property under the Housing Act 1988, s. 7(3) and sch. 2, Ground 1.

6. Prior to the commencement of the original tenancy the Claimant had occupied the Property as her only or principal home continuously from about [insert date] to [insert] December 1996.

7. Further or alternatively, the Claimant now requires the Property as her only or principal home and she did not acquire the reversion on either the original or the replacement tenancy for money or money's worth.

8. Further, the Claimant avers that in all the circumstances it is just and equitable for the Court to dispense with the requirement of written notice under Ground 1. Without prejudice to the generality of the foregoing, the Claimant will rely upon the following facts and matters.

PARTICULARS

(i)   Prior to the grant of the original tenancy the Defendant, being a longstanding friend and neighbour of the Claimant, was well aware that the Property constituted the Claimant's home;

(ii)   On or about [insert] December 1996 the Claimant left the Property in order to visit and look after her (recently bereaved) elder sister in Australia who at the time was ill with cancer;

(iii) Prior to the grant of the original tenancy the Defendant was fully aware of the Claimant's sole reason for leaving her home and travelling abroad;

(iv)   For her part, the Claimant was aware that the Defendant had very recently separated from her husband and that she was at the time in need of accommodation and had yet to locate suitable permanent housing;

(v)   The Claimant, being of limited means, recognised that the income to be derived from letting the Property would be necessary to assist the financing of her stay in Australia;

(vi)   The Claimant, not having any letting experience, also perceived a desirability in having as a tenant for the Property a longstanding friend such as the Defendant whose conduct would be likely to prove satisfactory;

(vii) By reason of various conversations between the parties prior to the grant of the original tenancy the Defendant was aware both that the Claimant would desire to resume occupation of the Property upon her return from Australia and also that upon such return the Claimant would have no alternative accommodation in which to live;

(viii) Consequently, in entering the original tenancy agreement the parties jointly viewed the same as a mutually beneficial, albeit temporary, arrangement, the Defendant clearly understanding that the Claimant would desire to resume occupation of the Property at some point in the future and both parties envisaging that the Defendant would seek to secure alternative housing of her own whilst the Claimant was abroad;

(ix) The replacement tenancy was granted because at that time the Claimant was still engaged in caring for her sister in Australia and the Defendant had not by then obtained premises elsewhere;

(x) On [insert] May 2001, the Claimant returned to the UK, her sister having recovered from the cancer;

(xi) Since her return the Claimant has had to lodge with her son and daughter-in-law and their [insert age] child in [describe extent of their accommodation and the conditions experienced by Mrs Charlesworth]; and

(xii) The Claimant is not presently in a position to afford accommodation of her own and, further, she does not currently have the use of her own furniture (all of which she left in the Property, expecting to return to the same).

9. On [insert date] a notice in accordance with the Housing Act 1988, s. 8 dated [insert] (a copy of which is attached) was served on the Defendant by or on behalf of the Claimant.

10. A reasonable rent for the Property would be £[insert] per day.

11. To the best of the Claimant's knowledge only the Defendant is in possession of the property.

12. Further, the Claimant claims interest pursuant to the County Courts Act 1984, s. 69 on all sums recovered in this claim, at such rate and for such period as the Court thinks fit.

AND the Claimant claims:

(1) Possession of the Property;

(2) Damages for use and occupation at the daily rate of £[insert] from the date on which possession is ordered herein until the date on which the Defendant delivers up vacant possession of the Property to the Claimant; and

(3) The above interest, to be assessed.

STATEMENT OF TRUTH

Dated, etc.

COUNSEL

TWENTY NINE

LANDLORD AND TENANT PRECEDENTS

29.1 Part 8 Application for Declaration that Consent to Subletting and Change of Use Unreasonably Withheld and Damages Under LTA 1988

IN THE NONESUCH COUNTY COURT   Claim No.

BETWEEN:

BLAIR LIMITED   Claimants

and

HAGUE LIMITED   Defendants

DETAILS OF CLAIM

The claimant seeks the following remedies:

(1) A Declaration that the Defendants' refusal or withholding of consent to the proposed subletting by the Claimants of the [rear two rooms on the first floor] of 10 Downing Street London W1 2PB to Ashdown & Company Limited is unreasonable.

(2) A Declaration that notwithstanding the Defendants' refusal or withholding of consent the Claimants are entitled to sublet the two rooms to Ashdown & Company Limited aforesaid.

(3) A Declaration that the Defendants' refusal or withholding of consent to the change of use of the two rooms to use as [chiropodist's] is unreasonable.

(4) A Declaration that notwithstanding the Defendants' refusal or withholding of consent to such change of use the Claimants are entitled to permit the use to be changed (or to change the use) of the two rooms to use as [a chiropodist's surgery].

(5) Damages to be assessed under paragraph 9 hereof.

(6) Interest pursuant to County Courts Act 1984, section 69 upon the damages at such rates and for such periods as the Court thinks just.

The grounds for the claim are:

1. By a lease made the 1st April 1998 between Tom Snooks ('the original landlord') and the Claimants as tenants, the original landlord demised the premises known as No. 10, Downing Street, London W1 2PB to the Claimants for a term of twelve years from the 25th March 1998 (subject to a proviso for determination for redevelopment) at an annual rent of £20,000.

2. By clauses 2(14) and 2(7) of the lease the Claimants covenanted:

   (a) not to assign underlet or share possession of the demised premises or any part thereof without the consent of the landlord first obtained; and

   (b) not without the landlord's consent first obtained (which consent shall not unreasonably be withheld) to use the premises or any part thereof save for the heating of air and dissemination of hot air.

3. At all material times the reversion immediately expectant upon the lease has been vested in the Defendants and the term created by the lease remains vested in the Claimants.

4.   By letter dated the 8th January 2002 addressed to the Defendants' Solicitors (Messrs Law & Law) the Claimants by their solicitors requested the Defendants' consent to the Claimants' proposed sub-underletting of the rear two rooms on the first floor of the demised premises to Ashdown and Company Limited and for the change of use of the rooms to use as a chiropodist's surgery.

5.   Ashdown & Company Limited is a respectable and responsible Company and references showing it so to be were sent by the Claimants to the Defendants' solicitors on the 8th January 2002.

6.   By virtue of the Landlord and Tenant Act 1988, section 1 the Defendants owed the Claimants a duty, among others, within a reasonable time to give consent to the application insofar as it related to the proposed sub-underletting, unless it was reasonable not to give consent.

7.   Unreasonably the Defendants now refuse or withhold their consent both to the proposed sub-underletting and to the proposed change of use.

8.   The refusal to the proposed sub-underletting is in breach of the Defendants duty under the Act.

9.   By reason of the breach of duty the Claimants have suffered and continue to suffer damage.

PARTICULARS

(a)   The Claimants had contracted to create the proposed sub-underlease in favour of Ashdown and Company Limited for £50,000.

(b)   Had the Defendants consented to the sub-underletting within a reasonable time, which the Claimants contend should have been by 8th February 2002, the Claimants could have completed the said transaction by 13th February 2002.

(c)   The Claimants accordingly claim interest upon the sum of £50,000 from 13th February 2002 until the date of the actual sub-underlease, to be assessed.

STATEMENT OF TRUTH

Dated etc.

29.2   Acknowledgement of Service to Part 8 Originating Application in 29.1

IN THE NONESUCH COUNTY COURT   Claim No.

BETWEEN:

BLAIR LIMITED   Claimants

and

HAGUE LIMITED   Defendants

GROUNDS FOR CONTESTING THE CLAIM

1.   The Defendants admit the matters set out in paragraphs 1 to 6 inclusive of the Part 8 Application.

2. It is the avowed intention of Ashdown & Company Limited

   (a) to use the two rooms as a chiropodist's surgery and

   (b) to create as great an impediment to the redevelopment of the premises by the Defendants (for which an application for planning approval is now pending) as possible.

3. It would be contrary to good estate management to permit the two rooms to be used for a chiropodist's surgery since (i) the letting value of the adjoining prestige offices would thereby be diminished (ii) the proposed use would introduce pedestrian and vehicular traffic into Downing Street and thereby disturb the Defendants' other tenants in adjacent premises. In that the tenants' leases fall in in the near future, the Defendants are likely to be prejudiced in their negotiations for the renewal thereof or for re-letting of the premises to other tenants if the rooms in Number 10 Downing Street are used in the manner proposed by the Claimants.

4. Accordingly the Defendants aver that they are entitled to withhold their consent both to the proposed change of use and to the proposed sub-letting and paragraph 8 of the Part 8 Application is denied.

5. The Defendants make no admission as to the damages alleged in paragraph 9 of the Part 8 Application.

STATEMENT OF TRUTH

Dated the 29th April 2002

29.3 Instructions to Draft Defence and Counterclaim: Landlord's Repairing Covenant

Instructing Solicitors act for the Alma Court Tenants' Association.

Alma Court is a purpose-built block of six flats each formerly of a rateable value of £1,000. Each flat has been let by the landlord (Alma Limited) upon a standard form of lease, so that the terms of each lease are identical save only for the term and rent. The tenant's covenants in the leases include:

(a) a full repairing covenant;

(b) a covenant that the tenant will 'keep in repair and proper working order the drains, gutters, external pipes attached to the demised premises and all installations for the supply of water, gas and electricity within the demised premises';

(c) a covenant that the tenant will contribute 1/6th of the cost to the landlord of fulfilling the landlord's repairing obligations under the lease (The landlord covenants 'to keep the roofs and common parts of the entire building in which the demised premises are situate in tenantable repair'. Neither the roofs nor the common parts are included in any of the six leases);

(d) a proviso permitting the landlord to enter and carry out any repairs which the tenant, in breach of the tenant's repairing obligations under the lease, had failed to carry out, and permitting the landlord to recover the cost of carrying out such repairs from the tenant.

The leases were granted upon the dates and at the rents and for the terms shown below. All the six tenants belong to the Association.

Flat	Tenant	Date of Lease	Term	Rent
1	A. Brown	1st April 2001	3 years from 25th March 2001	£3,000
2	B. White	28th March 1998	7 years from 25th March 1998	£3,000
3	C. Gray	20th June 1986	7 years from 24th June 1986 (Mr Gray has held over).	£2,600
4	D. Green	10th May 1994	7 years from 25th March 1994	£2,950
5	E. Mauve	4th August 1995	9 years from 24th June 1993	£2,825
6	F. Black	31st December 1961	6 years from 25th December 1961 (Mr Black has held over).	£2,550

A gale in January 2002 blew a number of tiles off the roof and falling tiles broke some of the guttering around the eaves blocking some of the down pipes on the outside walls of flats 1, 3 and 6, which flats have consequently suffered severely from dampness. The landlord served Schedules of Dilapidations upon the tenants, and as nothing had been done by the tenants, in April 2002 the landlord carried out the necessary remedial works to the guttering and down pipes and to the roof over flats 1, 3 and 6 and claimed the cost from the tenants of flats 1, 3 and 6. A copy of the Landlord's Particulars of Claim accompanies these Instructions. The remainder of the roof remains in a state of appalling disrepair, requiring new tiling completely over flats 2, 4 and 5.

Counsel is asked to settle a Defence for the three tenants who have been sued.

It is hoped by the Association that Counsel will legitimately feel able to raise the question of the unrepaired roof in the proceedings, whether by Counterclaim or otherwise. If Counsel so advises, Messrs White, Green and Mauve are willing to be joined in these proceedings.

Enclosure: Landlord's Particulars of Claim.

IN THE . . . COUNTY COURT   Claim No.

BETWEEN

ALMA COURT LIMITED   Claimant

and

ARTHUR BROWN
CHARLES GRAY
FRANK BLACK   Defendants

PARTICULARS OF CLAIM

1. By the leases referred to in the Particulars below, the Claimant demised to the Defendants the flats respectively indicated in the Particulars for the terms of years indicated. Each Defendant covenanted with the Claimant in the lease to which the respective Defendant was a party that he would keep the premises demised to him

in good and tenantable repair and would keep in repair and working order the drains, gutters and external pipes of and attached to the demised premises and further covenanted to pay a proportion of the cost to the landlord of fulfilling the landlord's repairing obligations under the said lease.

PARTICULARS

Flat	Tenant	Date of Lease	Term
1	First Defendant	1st April 2001	3 years from 25th March 2001
3	Second Defendant	20th June 1986	7 years from 24th June 1986 (holding over)
6	Third Defendant	31st December 1961	6 years from 25th December 1961 (holding over)

2. In breach of the covenants the Defendants and each of them (a) have failed to carry out the repairs specified below and the landlord has entered and carried out the works and claims the cost thereof and (b) have refused to pay their due proportion of the cost to the landlord of the repair of the roof which is situate immediately above the defendants' flats.

PARTICULARS

A.	Of Defendants' failure to repair		Cost
	Flat 1	(First Defendant): failure to repair guttering and unblock downpipes from gutters	£400
	Flat 3	(Second Defendant): ditto	£450
	Flat 6	(Third Defendant): ditto	£500

B. Of Claimant's expenditure on roof

Cost of repairing roof above defendants' flats:	£7,200
Proportion due from each defendant therefore:	£2,400

AND the Claimant claims:

Against the First Defendant:	£2,800
Against the Second Defendant:	£2,850
Against the Third Defendant:	£2,900

STATEMENT OF TRUTH

Dated etc.

JANE BRIGGS

Advise and settle defence as requested.

174

29.4   Draft Defence and Counterclaim to 29.3

IN THE . . . COUNTY COURT   Claim No.

BETWEEN

ALMA COURT LIMITED   Claimant/Part 20 Defendant

and

ARTHUR BROWN
CHARLES GRAY
FRANK BLACK   Defendants/Part 20 Claimant

DEFENCE AND COUNTERCLAIM

DEFENCE

1. The Defendants admit the leases of the flats demised to them respectively as alleged in paragraph 1 of the Particulars of Claim.

2. Section 11 of the Landlord and Tenant Act 1985 applies to the leases of the First and the Third Defendants and it is denied that the covenant by the First and the Third Defendants to repair the premises demised to them is of any effect insofar as it requires the First and the Third Defendants to repair the drains, gutters and external pipes of and attached to the demised premises.

3. The second Defendant admits that he covenanted to repair the premises demised to him as alleged in paragraph 1 of the Particulars of Claim and further that he has not carried out the repairs specified in the Particulars under paragraph 2A of the Particulars of Claim but requires the Claimant to prove that this amounts to the breach of the covenant alleged in paragraph 2(a) of the Particulars of Claim.

4. It is admitted that the First and the Third Defendants have not carried out the repairs specified in the Particulars under paragraph 2A of the Particulars of Claim but for the reasons stated in paragraph 2 hereof it is denied that the First and Third Defendants thereby acted in breach of covenant.

5. The Claimant is required to prove the cost of the works described in paragraph 2A of the Particulars of Claim. The Defendants will seek to set off in diminution or extinction of any sums found to be due from the Defendants to the Claimant such sums as are adjudged to be due to the Defendants from the Claimant under the Counterclaim.

6. It is admitted that the Defendants covenanted to contribute 1/6 of the cost to the landlord of fulfilling the landlord's repairing obligations under their respective leases and that the Defendants have not paid any money to the Claimant in respect of the cost of repairing the roof over the Defendant's flats.

7. It is denied that the Defendants are liable to contribute to the cost in the proportions set out in paragraph 2B of the Particulars of Claim and the Claimant is required to prove the cost of the said repairs. The Defendants will seek to set off in diminution or extinction of such sums found to be due from the Defendants to the Claimant hereunder such sums as are adjudged to be due to the Defendants from the Claimant under the Counterclaim hereinafter pleaded.

COUNTERCLAIM

8. The Defendants repeat paragraphs 1 to 7 inclusive of the Defence.

175

9. By virtue of section 11 of the Landlord and Tenant Act 1985 the Claimant covenanted with the First and with the Third Defendant to keep in repair and proper working order the drains, gutters and external pipes of and attached to the premises demised to each of them.

10. By clause . . . . of each of the leases the Claimant covenanted with each of the Defendants to keep the roofs and common parts of the entire building in tenantable repair.

11. In breach of the covenant with the First and with the Third Defendant set out in paragraph 9 hereof the Claimant failed to keep in repair and proper working order the drains, gutters and external pipes of and attached to the premises demised to each of them.

PARTICULARS OF BREACH

[Failure to repair guttering and unblock downpipes]

12. By reason of the said breach the First and the Third Defendants have each suffered loss and damage.

PARTICULARS OF DAMAGE

[Dampness]

13. In breach of the covenant set out in paragraph 10 hereof the Claimant failed to keep in tenantable repair the roof of the entire building.

PARTICULARS OF BREACH

[Claimant's failure to repair roof over Flats 2, 4 and 5]

14. The Defendants claim interest on any damages awarded to them under paragraph 12 above or paragraph 3 below pursuant to Section 69 of the County Courts Act 1984 at such rate and for such period as the Court thinks fit.

AND the First and Third Defendants counterclaim

1. £x damages under paragraph 12.

All the Defendants counterclaim

2. an order that the Claimant do forthwith reinstate the part of the roof over Flats 2, 4 and 5 in the form in which it existed prior to January 1999 [carry out the following works to the roof over Flats 2, 4 and 5 — namely:—].

3. damages for breach of covenant in lieu of or in addition to the relief claimed in paragraph 2.

4. Interest under paragraph 14 of the Counterclaim pursuant to Section 69 of the County Courts Act 1984 to be assessed.

STATEMENT OF TRUTH   JOE BLOGGS

Dated etc.

29.5 Instructions: Particulars of Claim: Damages for Breach of Tenant's Repairing Covenant: 1938 Act not Applying

By a lease dated 31 March 1992 Adam Smith, the freehold owner of a shop known as 14 The High Street Woking, Surrey, demised the shop to Victor Coldstream for a term of ten years from 25 March 1992 at a rent of £9,600 a year. Victor covenanted, *inter alia*, as follows:

To repair and keep the demised premises and all fixtures, fittings and additions thereto in good tenantable repair and condition throughout the term and in such condition to yield up the same at the determination of the tenancy.

When Victor left the premises on 25 March 2002 they were in a state of disrepair. The cost of executing repairs was £12,200. The repairs took a month to effect.

Counsel is asked to settle appropriate proceedings for recovery of damages for breach of covenant.

IN THE   COUNTY COURT   Claim No.

BETWEEN

ADAM SMITH   Claimant

and

VICTOR COLDSTREAM   Defendant

_____

PARTICULARS OF CLAIM

_____

1. By a lease dated 31 March 1992 the Claimant demised to the Defendant the premises known as 14 High Street, Woking Surrey for a term of 10 years from 25 March 1992 at a rent of £9,600 per year.

2. By clause . . . of the lease the Defendant covenanted to repair and keep the premises and all fixtures fittings and additions thereto in good tenantable repair and condition throughout the term.

3. In breach of the covenant in paragraph 2 above the Defendant has failed to repair and keep the premises and all fixtures fittings and additions thereto in the condition required by the covenant.

PARTICULARS OF BREACH

. . .

4. By reason of the breaches of covenant the Claimant has suffered loss and damage and the value of his reversion in the premises has been diminished by an amount equal to
(i) the cost of repairing and redecorating the demised premises and restoring the same to a condition in accordance with the covenant plus
(ii) the loss of rent during the execution of the necessary works of repair and redecorating.

PARTICULARS OF SPECIAL DAMAGE

Cost of repairs £12,200
Loss of rent: one month £800

5. The Claimant claims interest on all sums due pursuant to County Courts Act 1984 section 69 at the rate of . . . per cent per year.

AND the Claimant claims

1. £13,000 damages

2. £ . . . interest to the date of issue of the Summons and then at the rate of £ . . . per day.

<u>STATEMENT OF TRUTH</u>

Dated etc.

JOSEPH COTTON

29.6 Instructions: Particulars of Claim: Forfeiture and Damages: 1938 Act Applying

Facts as in **29.5** except term is 14 years, the lease contains a proviso for re-entry in respect of any breach of covenant, and Victor is still in possession.

Counsel is asked to settle appropriate proceedings for recovery of possession of the demised premises and damages for breach of covenant. He/she is advised that the current value of the premises is £280,000 but that their value would be £300,000 if they had been maintained in accordance with the tenant's repairing covenants.

<u>IN THE . . . COUNTY COURT</u>   Claim No.

BETWEEN

ADAM SMITH   <u>Claimant</u>

and

VICTOR COLDSTREAM   <u>Defendant</u>

_____

<u>PARTICULARS OF CLAIM</u>

_____

1. By a lease dated 31 March 1992 the Claimant demised to the Defendant the premises known as 14 High Street, Woking Surrey for a term of 14 years from 25 March 1992 at a rent of £9,600 per year.

2. By clause ... of the lease the Defendant covenanted to repair and keep the premises and all fixtures fittings and additions thereto in good tenantable repair and condition throughout the term.

3. By clause ... of the lease the Claimant reserved a right of re-entry in respect of the breach of any of the covenants in the lease.

4. In breach of the covenant in paragraph 2 above the Defendant has failed to repair and keep the premises and all fixtures fittings and additions thereto in the condition required by the covenant. Full particulars of the breaches were set out in a schedule of dilapidations annexed to the notice referred to in paragraph 5 below.

5. On ...... 2002 the Claimant caused a notice in accordance with the provisions of the Law of Property Act 1925 section 146 and the Leasehold Property (Repairs) Act 1938 to be served on the Defendant specifying the breaches and requiring the Defendant to remedy them but the Defendant has failed to remedy the breaches or any of them within a reasonable time or at all.

6. The Defendant served on the Claimant a counter-notice under the Act of 1938 and on .... 2002 the court gave permission to the Claimant to commence this claim.

7. By reason of the facts set out above the Claimant has suffered damage and the value of the reversion expectant on the expiry of the lease has been diminished.

PARTICULARS OF DAMAGE

The value of the Claimant's reversion has been diminished by the amount of £20,000, being the difference in value between the premises in their present state, namely £280,000, and their value if maintained in accordance with the Defendant's covenant, namely £300,000.

8. As a result of the matters set out above the lease has become liable to be forfeited and by the service of the claim form the Claimant forfeits the lease.

9. At all material times a reasonable rent for the premises would have been and would now be £.... per year.

10. The premises do not comprise or include a dwelling-house.

11. The Claimant claims interest on all sums due pursuant to County Courts Act 1984 section 69 at the rate of ... per cent per year.

AND the Claimant claims

1. Possession

2. £20,000 damages

3. ... interest to the date of issue of the Summons and thereafter at the rate of £... per day.

4. Rent from date of issue of the claim form to date of service and mesne profits at the rate of [the value of the land stated in paragraph 9 above] from the date of service of the Summons until the date when the Defendant gives up possession.

STATEMENT OF TRUTH   MELANIE SMITH

Dated etc.

29.7   Section 146 Notice: 1938 Act not Applying

SECTION 146 Notice: Tenancy agreement, 1938 Act not
                         applying: costs stipulation.

To Andrew Brown or other the tenant of the premises known as 99 Gray's Inn Place, comprised in a tenancy agreement dated 1st April 1988 and made between Charles Dickens of the one part as 'landlord' and Edward French of the other part as 'tenant' and to all others whom it may concern.

We, Fumble & Co., of 1 High Street, Bumbledon, Solicitors and Agents for the above-named Charles Dickens [or Snooks Limited in whom the reversion immediately expectant upon the tenancy created by the agreement is now vested] hereby give you notice as follows:—

1. By the tenancy agreement your predecesssor in title the above Edward French agreed as follows:

[Quote relevant stipulations]

2. The above-mentioned terms of your tenancy have been broken and the particular breaches of contract which are complained of are as follows:

[Set out particulars]

3. We require you to remedy all the aforesaid breaches in so far as the same are capable of remedy and to make compensation in money to the landlord for such breaches.

4. (a) By the tenancy agreement your aforesaid predecessor in title further agreed to pay all expenses including solicitors' costs and surveyors' fees incurred by the landlord incidental to the preparation or service of a notice under Section 146 of the Law of Property Act 1925 notwithstanding that forfeiture be avoided otherwise than by relief granted by the Court.

    (b) By reason of the matters referred to above in this notice your landlord has incurred £182.75 costs in respect of the preparation and service of this notice and you are required to repay the sum to your landlord.

5. On your failure to comply with this notice within a reasonable time it is the intention of Charles Dickens [or Snooks Limited] aforesaid to re-enter upon the premises by action or otherwise and to forfeit the tenancy agreement in respect of the premises and to claim damages for the breaches of contract.

Dated .... day of .... 19....

(Signed) Fumble & Co.

Solicitor and Agent for the
above-named Charles Dickens
[or Snooks Limited]

29.8 Section 146 Notice: 1938 Act Applying

SECTION 146 Notice: Lease to which 1938 Act applies

To Andrew Brown or other the lessee of Number 99 Gray's Inn Place, comprised in a lease dated 1st April 1988 and made between Charles Dickens of the one part as 'lessor' and Edward French of the other part as 'lessee' and to all others whom it may concern.

We, Fumble & Co., of 1 High Street, Bumbledon, Solicitors and Agents for the above-named Charles Dickens [or Snooks Limited in whom the reversion immediately expectant upon the term created by the lease is now vested] hereby give you notice as follows:

1. By the lease your predecessor in title the above Edward French covenanted as follows:

[Quote relevant covenants]

2. The above-mentioned covenants have been broken and the particular breaches which are complained of are committing or allowing the dilapidations described in the Schedule annexed to this notice.

3. We require you to remedy all the aforesaid breaches and to make compensation in money to the lessor for such breaches.

4. (a) Your predecessor in title the above Edward French further covenanted by the said lease to pay all expenses including Solicitors' costs and Surveyors' fees incurred by the lessor incidental to the preparation or service of a notice under Section 146 of the Law of Property Act 1925 notwithstanding that forfeiture be avoided otherwise than by relief granted by the Court.

    (b) By reason of the matters referred to above in this notice the lessor has incurred £257.00 costs in respect of the preparation and service of this notice, and you are required to repay them the above sum.

5. On your failure to comply with this notice within a reasonable time it is the intention of Charles Dickens [or Snooks Limited aforesaid] to re-enter upon the premises by action or otherwise and to forfeit the lease in respect of the premises and to claim damages for the breaches of covenant.

6. The lessee is entitled under the Leasehold Property (Repairs) Act 1938 to serve on the lessor a counter-notice claiming the benefit of the Act.

7. Such counter-notice may be served within twenty-eight days from the service upon the lessee of this notice.

8. Such counter-notice must be in writing and may be served upon the lessor by handing the same to them personally. Such counter-notice shall also be sufficiently served if it is left at the last-known place of abode or business of the lessor in the United Kingdom. Such counter-notice shall also be sufficiently served if it is sent by post in a registered letter addressed to the lessor by name at the aforesaid place of abode or business and if that letter is not returned through the post undelivered; and that service shall be deemed to be made at the time at which the registered letter would in the ordinary course be delivered.

9. The name and address for service of the lessor is:

> Charles Dickens [or Snooks Limited]
> c/o Fumble & Co.
> Solicitors
> 1 High Street
> Bumbledon
> Surrey

Dated the..... day of.......... 19..........

> (Signed) Fumble & Co.
>
> Solicitors and Agents for the
> above-named Charles Dickens
> [or Snooks Limited]

[Annexe Schedule of Dilapidations]

29.9 Particulars of Claim: Possession: Notice to Quit: Claim outside HA 1988

IN THE . . . COUNTY COURT	Claim No.

BETWEEN

ADAM ADAMS	Claimant
and	
(1) BERNARD EVE	Defendants
(2) EVE EVE	

PARTICULARS OF CLAIM

---

1. This claim relates to residential premises.

2. The Claimant is the owner of and claims possession of the dwelling-house known as Biddulph Manor, Temple Lane, Peacehaven in the County of Sussex ('the House').

3. By a tenancy agreement made on 30th September 1995 between the Claimant as landlord and the first-named Defendant as tenant the Claimant demised the House to the first defendant for a term of three years from the 10th September 1995 at a rent of £1,600 per week. A copy of the tenancy agreement is attached to the Particulars of Claim.

4. At the expiration of the term created by the said agreement on 9th September 1998 the first-named defendant held over and became the weekly tenant of the Claimant of the House at a rent of £1,600 per week.

5. By a notice to quit served on and dated 1st January 2002 the Claimant duly determined the first Defendant's tenancy upon the 8th March 2002 or on whatever day, 4 weeks after the service of the notice, a complete week [period] of the first Defendant's tenancy came to an end. A copy of the notice to quit is attached to the Particulars of Claim.

6. The rateable value of the House on 31st March 1990 was £900 and thus exceeded the rateable value limit in the Housing Act 1988, sch. 1, part 1, para. 2A. Accordingly the first-named Defendant did not become the statutory periodic tenant of the Claimant under the Housing Act 1988, s. 5 when he held over as aforesaid and the Housing Act 1988 does not protect the occupation of either Defendant.

7. The second Defendant is the former wife of the first Defendant and until the expiration as aforesaid of the first Defendant's tenancy of the House the first Defendant permitted the second-named Defendant to reside in the House at first as his wife and (after the dissolution of the marriage of the Defendants on 1st December 1999) as his licensee.

8. To the best of the Claimant's knowledge only the first and second Defendants are in possession of the House.

9. The Claimant claims interest upon all sums due pursuant to section 69 County Courts Act 1984 at .... per cent per year.

10. At all material times a reasonable rent for the House would have been and would now be £ .... per week.

And the Claimant claims:
Against both Defendants:
(1) Possession
Against the first-named Defendant:
(2) £.... mesne profits from
the 8th March 2002 until
the return date of the summons
herein, continuing until possession
be given up at the rate of £....
per week and £..... interest thereon
pursuant to s. 69 County Courts Act 1984
to date of issue of the summons
herein and thereafter at the rate of
£.... per day.

STATEMENT OF TRUTH

Dated etc.

J. BLOGGS

29.10 Particulars of Claim in Form N119: Possession: Forfeiture: Arrears of Rent: Claim under RA 1977, Case I

Continuation Sheet of Particulars of Claim in

BLAKE LETTINGS LIMITED

v

JANE DRUMMOND

Paragraph 3a
By a lease dated 20th March 1988 the Claimant demised to the Defendant the premises known as 10 Gray's Inn Place, London WC2 for a term of 18 years from 25th March 1988.

The lease contained a proviso for re-entry if (inter alia) the rent thereby reserved or any part of it should be in arrears and unpaid for 21 days whether the same should have been formally demanded or not.

Paragraph 4
[The arrears of tent must be set out in schedule form showing:

— dates when arrears arose
— all amounts of rent due
— dates and amounts of all payments made
— running total of arrears]

Paragraph 10
The Claimant also claims interest pursuant to County Courts Act 1984, s. 69 on the arrears of rent/mesne profits at such rate and for such period as the court thinks fit.

Particulars of claim
for possession _N119_
(rented residential premises)

In the _West London Count Court_   Claim No.

Blake Lettings Limited   Claimant

Jane Drummond   Defendant

1.   The claimant has a right to possession of: _10 Gray's Inn Place, London, W8_

2.   To the best of the claimant's knowledge the following persons are in possession of the property: _Jane Drummond_

About the tenancy

3.   (a)   The premises are let to the defendant(s) under a(n) _protected_ tenancy which began on _25th March 1988 (see attached sheet for details)_

     (b)   The current rent is £4000.00 _per year_ and is payable each ~~(week) (fortnight)~~ (month). (_other_   )

     (c)   Any unpaid rent or charge for use and occupation should be calculated at £10.95 per day.

4.   The reason the claimant is asking for possession is:

     (a)   because the defendant has not paid the rent due under the terms of the tenancy agreement.
     ~~(Details are set out below)~~ (Details are shown on the attached rent statement)

     ~~(b)   because the defendant has failed to comply with other terms of the tenancy. Details are set out below~~

     ~~(c)   because: (including any (other) statutory grounds)~~

5.   The following steps have already been taken to recover any arrears:

     Letters from the claimant's solicitors dated 23rd February 2002 and 30th March 2002 claimed arrears of rent and warned that forfeiture proceedings would be commenced unless payment was made within 14 days.

6.   The appropriate (notice to quit) (notice of breach of lease) (notice seeking possession) (_other_ _____) was served on the defendant on   20

     Because of the arrears of rent, the claimant is entitled to forfeit the lease and does so by the service of these proceedings.

About the defendant

7.   The following information is known about the defendant's circumstances:

     No Housing Benefit or arrears are paid direct to the claimant.
     The claimant has no other information about the defendant's circumstances.

About the claimant

8. The claimant is asking the court to take the following financial or other information into account when making its decision whether or not to grant an order for possession:

Forfeiture

9. (a) There is no underlessee or mortgagee entitled to claim relief against forfeiture.

or (b) _____ of

is entitled to claim relief against forfeiture as underlessee or mortgagee.

What the court is being asked to do:

10. The claimant asks the court to order that the defendant(s):

(a) give the claimant possession of the premises;

(b) pay the unpaid rent and any charge for use and occupation up to the date an order is made;

(c) pay rent and any charge for use and occupation from the date of the order until the claimant recovers possession of the property;

(d) pay the claimant's costs of making this claim.

Statement of Truth

*(I believe) (The claimant believes) that the facts stated in these particulars of claim are true.
*I am duly authorised by the claimant to sign this statement.

signed _____ date _____
*(Claimant) (Litigation friend (*where claimant is a child or a patient*)) (Claimant's solicitor)
delete as appropriate

Full name _____

Name of claimant's solicitor's firm _____

position or office held _____
(*if signing on behalf of firm or company*

29.11   Working Draft: Forfeiture: Breach of Covenant: Claim outside RA 1977

NOTE: this is a 'working draft' and **not** a precedent.

[IN THE   COUNTY COURT]   [Claim No.]

BETWEEN

COMPANY LIMITED   <u>Claimant</u>

and

COMPANY LIMITED   <u>Defendants</u>

PARTICULARS OF CLAIM

---

1. By a lease dated the
    demised to
    ('the original tenant') premises known as Number   ('the demised premises') for
    a term of ... years from the ... at a rent of £ ... per year payable quarterly in advance
    on the usual quarter days.

2. By the lease the original tenant covenanted inter alia in the following terms:—

3. The term created by the lease at all material times has been and is now vested in
    the Defendants. The reversion immediately expectant upon the expiration of the
    term is and at all material times has been vested in the Claimants.

4. The lease contained a proviso for re-entry by the lessor if (inter alia) there should
    be any breach or non-observance on the part of the tenant of the covenants on the
    part of the tenant contained in the lease.

5. In breach of the covenants the Defendants have permitted the demised premises
    to become in a state of want of repair and decoration. Full particulars of the
    breaches of covenant complained of exceed 3 folios and were contained in a
    document entitled 'Schedule of Dilapidation' and delivered to the Defendants on or
    about .... together with a notice pursuant to s. 146, Law of Property Act 1925
    requiring the Defendants to remedy the breaches. The Defendant failed to remedy
    the breaches or any of them within a reasonable time or at all.

6. By reason of the breaches of covenant of the Defendants the Claimants have
    suffered damage and the value of their reversion in the demised premises has been
    diminished by an amount equal to (i) the cost of repairing and redecorating the
    demised premises and restoring the same to a condition in accordance with the
    covenants plus (ii) the loss of rent during the execution of the necessary works of
    repair and redecoration.

PARTICULARS OF SPECIAL DAMAGE

Cost of repairs: £
Loss of rent ... weeks at £   per year: £
                                                   _____
                                                        £
                                                   _____

7. By reason of the matters set out above the Claimants are entitled to forfeit the lease and by the issue and service of the claim form herein the Claimants do forfeit the lease.

8. At all material times a reasonable rent for the demised premises would have been and would now be £ ... per year.

[9. The premises of which possession is claimed do not comprise a dwelling-house.] or

[9. The premises of which possession is claimed comprise a dwelling-house the rateable value whereof exceeded the sum specified by section 4 of the Rent Act, 1977 on every date therein specified.] or

[9. The premises of which possession is claimed comprise a dwelling house the annual rent of which under the lease exceeds £25,000.]

10. The following persons may be entitled to claim relief against forfeiture:.........

11. To the best of the Claimant's knowledge the following persons are in possession of the property . . .

12. The Claimant attaches to these Particulars of Claim:

   (a) a copy of the lease dated

   (b) a copy of the Schedule of Dilapidations prepared by . . . and delivered to the Defendant on or about . . .

   (c) a copy of the notice pursuant to section 146 Law of Property Act 1925 requiring the Defendant to remedy the breaches

   (d) a copy of the expert report of . . . dealing with the diminution of value of the reversion/cost of repair.

13. The Claimants claim interest upon all sums due pursuant to section 35A Supreme Court Act 1981 [or section 69 County Courts Act 1984] at the rate of......... per cent per year.

And the Claimants claim:

   (1) Possession

   (2) £.... rent

   (3) Rent or alternatively mesne profits from the date of issue of the claim form to the date of service of the claim form

   (4) Mesne profits at the rate of £... per year from the date of service until delivery of possession

   (5) £.... damages

   (6) £.... interest to the date of the issue of the claim form and then at the rate of £..... per day.

Note: Any of the versions of paragraph 9 will satisfy the court that the tenancy is not protected by RA 1977.

29.12 Particulars of Claim in Form N119: Possession: Notice Seeking Possession: Arrears of Rent: HA 1988, Grounds 8, 10, 11

Continuation Sheet of Particulars of Claim in

OAK PROPERTIES LIMITED

v

JOHN YOUNG

Paragraph 3a
By a written tenancy agreement dated 1 May 1994 the Claimant let to the Defendant the premises known as 4 Bradford Road, London, NW1 on a monthly assured tenancy commencing on 1 May 1994. A copy of the agreement is attached to the Particulars of Claim.

Paragraph 4(a)
   (a)   [The arrears of rent must be set out in schedule form showing:

       — dates when arrears arose
       — all amounts of rent due
       — dates and amounts of all payments made
       — running total of arrears]

   (c)   Housing Act 1988, sch. 2.

Ground 8   Both at the date of the service of the notice under HA 1988, s. 8 seeking possession and at the date of the hearing at least two months' rent is unpaid.

Ground 10   Rent lawfully due from the tenant was unpaid on the date when proceedings for possession were begun and was in arrears at the date of service of the notice under HA 1988, s. 8 seeking possession.

Ground 11   The tenant has persistently delayed paying rent which has become lawfully due.

Paragraph 10
The Claimant also claims interest pursuant to County Courts Act 1984, s. 69 on the arrears of rent/mesne profits at such rate and for such period as the court thinks fit.

Particulars of claim   In the *West London Count Court*   Claim No.
for possession *N119*
(rented residential premises)

Oak Properties Limited   Claimant

John Young   Defendant

1.   The claimant has a right to possession of: *4 Bradford Road, London W11*

2.   To the best of the claimant's knowledge the following persons are in possession of the property: *John Young*

About the tenancy

3.   (a) The premises are let to the defendant(s) under a(n) *periodic assured* tenancy which began on *1st May 1994*

     (b) The current rent is *£290 per month* and is payable each (week) (fortnight) (month) in advance.
     (*other   *)

     (c) Any unpaid rent or charge for use and occupation should be calculated at *£9.05* per day.

4.   The reason the claimant is asking for possession is:

     (a) because the defendant has not paid the rent due under the terms of the tenancy agreement.
     (*Details are set out below*) *(Details are shown on the attached rent statement)*

     (b) because the defendant has failed to comply with other terms of the tenancy. Details are set out below

     (c) because: (including any (other) statutory grounds)
     see attached sheet

5.   The following steps have already been taken to recover any arrears:

     Letters from the claimant to the defendant dated 23.10.2001, 10.11.2001 and letters from the claimant's solicitors to the defendant dated 9.2.2002 and 10.3.2002 claimed rent arrears and warned of court proceedings if the rent was not paid.

6.   The appropriate (notice to quit) (notice of breach of lease) (notice seeking possession) (*other* _____) was served on the defendant on *1st February 2002*.

     A copy of the notice seeking possession is attached to the Particulars of Claim.

About the defendant

7.   The following information is known about the defendant's circumstances:

     No Housing Benefit or arrears are paid direct to the claimant.
     The claimant has no other information about the defendant's circumstances.

About the claimant

8. The claimant is asking the court to take the following financial or other information into account when making its decision whether or not to grant an order for possession:

Forfeiture

9. (a)   There is no underlessee or mortgagee entitled to claim relief against forfeiture.

~~or (b)~~ _____ ~~of~~

~~is entitled to claim relief against forfeiture as underlessee or mortgagee.~~

What the court is being asked to do:

10. The claimant asks the court to order that the defendant(s):

    (a)   give the claimant possession of the premises;

    (b)   pay the unpaid rent and any charge for use and occupation up to the date an order is made;

    (c)   pay rent and any charge for use and occupation from the date of the order until the claimant recovers possession of the property;

    (d)   pay the claimant's costs of making this claim.

Statement of Truth

*(I believe) (The claimant believes) that the facts stated in these particulars of claim are true.
*I am duly authorised by the claimant to sign this statement.

signed _____ date _____
*(Claimant) (Litigation friend (*where claimant is a child or a patient*)) (Claimant's solicitor)
*delete as appropriate

Full name _____

Name of claimant's solicitor's firm _____

position or office held _____
                                    (*if signing on behalf of firm or company*

29.13 Particulars of Claim: Possession: Notice Seeking Possession: Breach of Terms: Claim under HA 1988, Grounds 12, 14, 15

IN THE . . . COUNTY COURT   Claim No.

BETWEEN

NADIA ROLLS   Claimant

and

GARY WILLIS   Defendant

PARTICULARS OF CLAIM

---

1. By a tenancy agreement ('the Agreement') dated 28th May 1995 the Claimant let the premises comprising a dwelling house known as Flat 2, 14 Cobb Road, London E14 ('the Flat') to the Defendant on a monthly furnished tenancy from 1st June 1995 at a monthly rent of £350 payable in advance on the first day of each month. A copy of the tenancy agreement is attached to the Particulars of Claim.

2. The tenancy created by the Agreement is an assured tenancy within the meaning of the Housing Act 1988.

3. By Clause 3(b) of the Agreement the Defendant agreed inter alia to keep in good and substantial repair and condition the Landlord's furniture, carpets and curtains in the Flat at all times during the tenancy.

4. By Clause 3(g) of the Agreement the Defendant agreed not to do or suffer to be done in the Flat anything which might be or become a nuisance or annoyance to the Landlord or to the tenants or occupiers of any adjoining premises.

5. In breach of the term in Clause 3(b) the Defendant has failed to keep in good and substantial repair and condition the Landlord's furniture, carpets and curtains.

PARTICULARS OF BREACH

Curtains, carpets and furniture covers have been badly torn, stained and holes have been burned in them.

6. As a result of the breach stated in paragraph 5 the Claimant has suffered loss and damage.

PARTICULARS OF LOSS

Cost of replacing curtains, carpets and furniture covers damaged beyond repair £4,500.

7. In breach of the term in Clause 3(g) the Defendant has done or suffered to be done in the Flat matters which have become a nuisance and annoyance to the Landlord and to the tenant of adjoining premises.

PARTICULARS OF BREACH

Since February 2002 the Defendant with other persons has played loud and objectionable music on electrically amplified musical instruments in the Flat on one or two

191

evenings every week continuing until one or two o'clock in the morning in disregard of many requests to desist by the Claimant who lives in Flat 1 at the same address and the tenant of Flat 3 at the same address, both of whom were disturbed and prevented from sleeping by the noises described above.

8. On 14th March 2002 the Defendant was convicted at Southwark Crown Court of handling stolen goods contrary to s. 22(1) of the Theft Act 1968.

9. Accordingly the Claimant claims possession of the Flat pursuant to the Housing Act 1988, Schedule 2, Ground 12 by reason of the matters stated in paragraphs 5–7 above, pursuant to Ground 14 by reason of the matters stated in paragraphs 7 and 8 above and pursuant to Ground 15 by reason of the matters stated in paragraphs 5 and 6 above.

10. By notice in the prescribed form (a copy of which is attached) dated . . . April 2002 the Claimant informed the Defendant that he intended to commence proceedings against the Defendant not earlier than . . . and not later than 12 months from the date of service of the notice, under Ground 12 — that obligations of the tenancy had been broken or not performed, Ground 14 — that the tenant had been guilty of conduct which was a nuisance or annoyance to persons residing in the locality and that the tenant had been convicted of using the Flat for illegal purposes and Ground 15 — that the condition of furniture provided for use under the tenancy had deteriorated owing to ill-treatment by the tenant, and the Claimant gave particulars of all those grounds.

11. To the best of the Claimant's knowledge only the defendant is in possession of the Flat.

12. The Claimant claims interest on the damages claimed under paragraph 6 and upon all other sums due pursuant to County Courts Act 1984, section 69 at such rate and for such period as the Court shall think fit.

AND the Claimant claims

(1) possession of the Flat

(2) damages under paragraph 6

(3) rent at the rate of £350 per month until the date of the hearing

(4) rent or mesne profits at the rate of £350 per month from the date of the hearing until possession is given up

(5) interest under County Courts Act 1984, s. 69 on the sums due as stated.

STATEMENT OF TRUTH

DATED etc.

JANE BRIGGS

Some of the precedents were originally drafted by His Honour Judge Colyer QC who has kindly permitted their reproduction here. They have been updated and altered in minor respects for the purpose of this Manual.

INDEX